Lewis Patriarchs
of
Early Virginia
and Maryland

Third Edition

Robert J. C. K. Lewis

HERITAGE BOOKS
2007

HERITAGE BOOKS
AN IMPRINT OF HERITAGE BOOKS, INC.

Books, CDs, and more—Worldwide

For our listing of thousands of titles see our website
at
www.HeritageBooks.com

Published 2007 by
HERITAGE BOOKS, INC.
Publishing Division
65 East Main Street
Westminster, Maryland 21157-5026

International Standard Book Number: 978-0-7884-0906-6

This edition is dedicated to the memory of Mrs. Grace McLean Moses,
author of *The Welsh Lineage of John Lewis (1592-1657)*.
She was both a distant cousin and a close friend.

TABLE OF CONTENTS

INTRODUCTION

In this, the third revision of my attempt to give as many records as possible of the early (pre-1700) Lewis families in Virginia and Maryland, and to give some information about the Lewis families in England and Wales that they may descend from, I have reorganized the book into three sections:

First: a list of as many Lewis families that came from a place specifically named and used a coat of arms that could be of use in identifying their descendants. Then a pedigree of more detailed information on those families known to have had branches in Virginia and Maryland, or claimed as ancestors by the descendants of the immigrants.

Second: information on the various Lewis families of Virginia, grouped geographically.

Third: Information on the various Lewis families of Maryland, grouped geographically.

One of the worst errors of my earlier work was to accept the Lewis History of Gustav Anjou as reliable. Apparently he published a long list of works on various families using the technique of mixing genuine records with false ones that he made up. Still he was useful in pointing the way to the genuine material, but nothing in his works should be trusted without being independently verified. See *The Genealogical Journal*, published by the Utah Genealogical Association, Vol. 19, Numbers 1 & 2, 1991; pp. 47-58: "We Wuz Robbed! The modus operandi of Gustave Anjou," by Robert Charles Anderson, CG, FASG.

On the positive side, the great number of county records published since the last edition, particularly by Ruth and Sam Sparcio of the Antient Press in McLean, Va., has allowed me to correct many errors and add vital new information to many families. I have also added many families in trying to make this Lewis information as complete as possible. I want to remind everyone using this work that because of time and money considerations, I have been forced to rely on secondary sources. Anyone wishing to make sure their information is accurate and find additional clues, such as how the individual signed their name, should get as close to the original documents as possible, or hire one of the many outstanding professional genealogists now available to do the research for them.

I would especially like to thank David Moulton, Library Director of Strayer University in Washington, D.C., for his assistance with the bibliography.

Robert J.C.K. Lewis
Easter, 1998

PART 1

SOME LEWIS FAMILIES

OF

ENGLAND AND WALES

I. A LIST OF 39 LEWIS FAMILIES, THEIR LOCATIONS AND COATS OF ARMS

Note: From their arms, most of these families originated in Wales, many probably moved to England when the Tudors came into power.

*1. Lewis of Abernant Bychan, Cardiganshire. Arms: Gules, three snakes nowed in a triangle, argent. (Ednowain ap Bradwyn.) Ref.: *Arch. Camb.*, 1851, p. 79.

2. Lewis of Bodior and Henllys, Anglesey. Arms: Argent, a chev. sable betw. three Cornish choughs ppr., in the beak of each an ermine spot. (Llowarch ap Bran.) Ref.: Burke, *Gen. Arm.*, p. 606.

3. Lewis of Burton Hall, Morton, Denbighshire. Arms: Vert, seme of broomslips, a lion rampant or. (Sandde Hardd.) Ref.: P. Bartrum, *Wel. Gen. 300-1400*, pp. 821,3,7; P. Bartrum, *Wel. Gen. 1400-1500*, Ref.: Sandde Hardd, 7 C.

4. Lewis of Cil, Oswestry, Shropshire. Arms: Argent, a cross patoneé betw. four Cornish choughs ppr., on a chief azure a boar's head couped argent. (Idnerth Benfras.) Ref.: *Arch. Camb.*, 1873, pp. 308-9.

5. Lewis of Clenfiew, Pembrokshire. Arms: Gules, three serpents nowed in a triangle argent, within a bordre engr. or. (Ednowain ap Bradwyn varient.) Ref.: Burke, *Gen. Arm.*, p. 605.

6. Lewis of Festinog, Merionethshire. Arms: Ermine a saltire gules. (Osborne Fitzgerald [Osburn Wyddel].) Ref.: Burke, *Gen. Arm.*, p. 606.

7. Lewis of Ffrwdgrech, Brecknockshire. Arms: Sable a chevron betw. three bloody spearheads Argent. Ref.: Burke, *Ext. and Dor. Baronetcies*, p. 313. See Lewis of Llangorse, #23 of this list.

8. Lewis of Galthorpe, Denbighshire. Arms: Ermine, a lion rampant azure. (Elidir ap Rhys Sais.) Ref.: *Arch. Camb.*, 1851, p. 77.

9. Lewis of Gilfach, Carmarthenshire. Arms: Azure a stag armed and crowned or. (Owain Gethin.) Ref. Burke, *Gen. Arm.*, p. 605; *Arch. Camb.*, 1851, p. 79.

*10. Lewis (Lewys) of Gladestry, Radnorshire. Arms: Sable, an eagle displayed argent. (Llewelyn Crugeryr.) Ref.: *Arch. Camb.*, 1864, p. 20, 24; 1880, pp. 148-50.

11. Lewis of Glan yr Arfon (Glanarfon), Llanferis Parish, Yale. Arms: Gules, a chevron ermine betw. three Englishmen's heads ppr. (Ednyfed Vychan.) Ref.: *Arch. Camb.*, 1851, p. 73; 1875, p. 42.

*12. Lewis of Gwersyllt Uchaf, Denbighshire. Arms: Ermine a lion rampant azure, (Elidir ap Rhys Sais.) Ref.: See Lewis of Galthorpe, #8 of this list.

13. Lewis of Gwinfe, Carmarthenshire. Arms: Gules, a griffin segreant or. (Llowden of Cardigan.) Quartered Sable three horses' heads erased argent. (Brochwel Ysgythrog.) Ref.: Burke, *Gen. Arm.*, p. 605.

*14. Lewis of Harpton Court, Radnorshire. Arms: Quarterly: 1st and 4th, Argent an eagle displayed gules. (Llewelyn Crugeryr var.) 2nd and 3rd, Argent a lion ramp. sable, ducally crowned or. (Rhys Grug.) Ref. Burke, *Dor. and Ext Peerages*, p. 335-6. Burke, *Gen. Arm.*, p. 605. See Lewis of Gladestry, #10 of this list.

15. Lewis of Hendrebiffa, Flintshire. Arms: Gules, on a bend arg. a lion passant sable. (Cynwrig Efell [Kynrick Evell]) Ref.: *Arch. Camb.*, 1851, p. 71.

*16. Lewis of Henllan, Narbeth, Pembrokshire. Pedigree from Gwynfardd, via Gwrwared whose arms were: Azure, a lion ramp. in an orle of eight cinq-foils, or. Includes Lewis of Lampeter Velfrey. Pemb. Their arms were: Azure, a chevron ermine betw. three garbs (wheat sheaves.) Ref.: Burke, *Gen. Arm.*, p. 608.

17. Lewis (Lewys) of Ledstone Hall and Marr, Yorkshire. Arms: Sable, a chevron betw. three trefoils or. See Lewis of Thorndon Hall, #37 of this list. Ref.: Burke, *Ext. and Dorm. Baronetcies*, p. 313. Burke, *Gen. Arm.*, p. 606.

18. Lewis of Llanarchayron (Llanayron), Cardiganshire. Arms: Gules, on a mount in fess vert three towers triple-towered argent betw. three scaling ladders or. (Cadifor ap Dinawl varient.) Ref.: Burke, *Gen Arm.*, p. 605.

*19. Lewis of Llandewi Rhydderch, Monmouthshire. Arms: Chequy or. and sable, on a fess gules three leopards' heads jesant de-lis or. (Descended from Sir Wm. de Valence via Sir Robert Wallis.) Ref.: Burke, *Gen. Arm.*, p. 605; Bradney, *Hist. of Mon.*, Vol. I, pp. 285, 301-2; Vol. IV, pp. 134-5. Note: In Jamaica these arms are on the tomb of the dau. of Samuel Lewis of Llandewi. In Va. and Md. they were used by the descendants of Mr. Joseph Lewis of Bristol and Richmond Co., Va. Ref.: Vermont, *America Heraldica*, p. 26.

20. Lewis of Llanelidan, Dyffryn Clwyd, Denbighshire. Arms: Azure a lion salient (or rampant) or. (Eunedd ap Gwerngey, also given as Efnedd [Evnedd] ap Morien.) Sometimes quartered with: Azure, a fesse or betw. three horses' heads erased argent. (Rhys ap Marchen.) Ref.: *Arch. Camb.*, 1877, pp. 29-31.

21. Lewis of Llaneyrgain (Northop) Flintshire. Arms: Ermine, a lion ramp. azure. (Elidir ap Rhys Sais) Ref.: Dwnn, *Heraldic Visitations of Wales*, Vol. II, pp. 307, 325.

* 22. Lewis of Llangatock, Crickhowell, Brecknockshire. Arms: Argent, a dragon head and neck erased vert, holding in its mouth a bloody hand. Ref.: Burke, *Gen. Arm.*, p. 605; Bradney, *Hist. of Mon.*, Vol. I, pp. 338-9. Note: In America, these arms are on the tombstones of the Lewis family of Poropotanck Cr. and the silver of the Lewis family of Warner Hall. Ref.: Bolton, *An American Armory*, p. 102; *Va. Mag. of Hist. and Biog.* Vol. 56, p. 197; V. 62, p. 481.

23. Lewis of Llangorse, Brecknockshire. Arms: Sable, a chevron erm. betw. three spearheads argent. (Bleddin ap Maenarch varient.) Ref.: Burke, *Gen Arm.*, p. 605; Morant, Gen. Armory Two, p. 101; Burke, *Ext. and Dor. Baronetcies*, p. 313.

24. Lewis of Llanllyr and Gernos, Cardiganshire. Arms: Gules, three snakes nowed in a triangle argent. (Ednowain ap Bradwen.) Ref.: *Arch. Camb.*, 1860, p. 175.

25. Lewis of Llwyn Gwren, Machynlleth, Montgomeryshire. Arms: Or. a griffin segreant gules. (Griffith/Gruffydd Goch) Note: Griffith Goch, Lord of Rhos and Rhyoniog, was a descendant paternally of Marchudd ap Cynan. Ref.: Burke, *Gen. Arm.*, p. 430.

26. Lewis (Lewes) of Llysnewed, Cardiganshire. Arms: Gules, three snakes nowed in a triangle argent. (Ednowain ap Bradwyn.) Ref.: Burke, *Gen. Arm.*, p. 605.

27. Lewis of Malvern Hall, Warwickshire. Arms: Gules, three snakes nowed in a triangle argent, within a bordure engrailed or. (Ednowain ap Bradwyn varient.) Ref.: Burke, *Gen. Arm.*, p. 606. (Note: Same as Lewis of Clenfiew.)

28. Lewis of Pengwerne, Merionethshire. Arms: Ermine a saltire gules. (Osbern Wyddel.) Ref.: Burke, *Gen. Arm.*, p. 605.

*29. Lewis of Plas Gwyn, Pentreath, Anglesey. Arms: Gules, a chevron betw. three roses argent. (Einion ap Geraint.) Note: These arms are the same as those assigned to Rhodri Mawr, King of Wales. Ref.: Dwnn, *Heraldic Visitations of Wales*, Vol. II, p. 265.

30. Lewis of Presadfedd and Cemlyn, Anglesey. Arms: Gules, a chev. betw. three lions rampant or. (Hwfa ap Cynddelw.) Ref.: Burke, *Peerage and Baronteage*, 18th ed. 1856, pp. 1122-3.

31. Lewis of Rossenden in Bleane, Kent. Arms: Argent, a chev. gules betw. three beaver tails ppr. (Not a Welsh coat.) Ref.: Burke, *Gen. Arm.*, p. 605. Harl. Soc., *Grantees of Arms to the End of the XVII Century*, p. 155. Note: In America these arms are used by the descendants of George Lewis of Scituate and Barnstable, Mass. (D. 1663.) See Burke, *Distinguished Families of America*, p. 2787.

32. Lewis of Shrewsbury, Shropshire. Arms: Ermine, a lion ramp. within a bordure azure. (Elidir ap Rhys Sais varient.) Note: In America, these were the arms of Thomas Lewis of Saco, Maine (D. 1639/40.) He, however, left no known male issue. He did have a land grant of 4x8 miles. Ref.: W.G. Davis, *NEHGR*, Jan. 1947, pp. 3-23.

33. Lewis of St. Pierre, Monmouthshire. Arms: Or., a lion ramp. sable guardant. (Gwaithfoed of Cardiganshire varient.) Ref.: Burke, *Gen. Arm.*, p. 605.

34. Lewis of Stanford, Nottinghamshire. Arms: Argent on a fesse azure three boars' heads couped argent, in chief a lion pass. gules. (Howell ap Gruffydd of Cefn-hir, Mochnant, Montgomeryshire.) Ref.: Burke, *Gen. Arm.*, p. 606.

35. Lewis of Stocke (Stoke), Dorset and Somersetshire. Arms: Ermine, on a fesse azure three boars' heads couped argent. (Howell ap Gruffydd varient.) Ref.: Burke, *Gen. Arm.*, p. 605. Note: Grant was to Barnaby Lewis of Stock, Dorset, gent. out of Montgomery, Conf. 16 Feb. 1694-5 by W. Dethick, Garter. Ref.: Harl. Soc., *Grantees of Arms to the end of the XVII Century*, pt. 1, p. 155.

36. Lewis of Sutton Magna, Shropshire, Arms: Gules, a griffin segreant or. (Llowden of Cardigan.) Ref.: Burke, *Gen. Arm.*, p. 605. Harl. Soc. Vol. 29, pt. II: *The Visit. of Shropshire*, pp. 325-6.

*37. Lewis of Thorndon Hall, Essex; also of Hertfordshire and York. Arms: Sable, a chevron betw. three trefoils argent. (Einion ap Collwyn varient?) Ref.: Burke, *Gen. Arm.*, p. 605. Note: In New England, these arms are on the tomb of Jonathan Clark Lewis (D. 1781) of Groton, Mass., a descendant of William Lewis of Cambridge and Farmington, Mass. (D. 1683), who came in the *Lion* in 1632. Ref.: Boulton, *An American Armory*, p. 102.

*38. Lewis of Van, Glamorganshire. Arms: Sable, a lion rampant argent. (Cydrich ap Gwaithfoed.) Ref.: Burke, *Gen. Arm.*, p. 605. Note: There were branches of this family at Carnllwyd, Llanishen, New House, and Penmark, Glamorganshire.

*39. Lewis of Wrexham, Denbighshire. Arms: Vert, a lion rampant or. (Sandde Hardd.) Ref.: Burke, *Gen. Arm.,* p. 606-Lists arms only, no location. Note: This family is descended paternally from Elidir ap Rhys Sais through Lewis of Gwersyllt, but changed to those of Sandde Hardd after marrying an heiress of that line. Ref.: *Cae Cyriog Ms*. Note: Wm. Lewis of Wrexham married Dorothy, dau. of Rev. Thos. Brereton. See Harl. Soc. Vol. 29, Pt. I: *The Visit. of Shropshire*, p. 67.

* This indicates that an illustration of the arms and/or the pedigree showing the origin of the family follows after this list.

Note: Further information on these coats of arms and their families can be found in my book: *Welsh Family Coats of Arms*, Heritage Books, Inc., Bowie, Md. 1995.

II. SOME LEWIS FAMILIES THOUGHT TO BE

OR CLAIMED AS THE ORIGIN OF

VIRGINIA AND MARYLAND LEWISES

GALL-FEL-Y-SEIRFF-A-DINIWED
FEL-Y-COLOMENNOD

LEWIS OF ABERNANT BYCHAN

Arms: Gules, three serpents nowed in triangle argent within a
          bordure or

Crest: A horse's head couped, bridled proper

Motto: (Old Welsh translates) = "As wise as Serpents, as
          harmless as Doves"

PEDIGREE OF LEWIS OF ABERNANT BYCHAN, ISCOED,
CARDIGANSHIRE, WALES, I

Coel Hen (Coelius - Dux Brittanarum, ca. 400 A.D.)
Ceneu
Maeswig Gloff/Mar
Arthwys
Cynfelyn
Cynwyd Cynwydion
Cadrod Calchfynydd (Ancestor in traditional pedigrees, but too late to have been Yspwys father)
(?) (According to tradition Yspwys came from "Spain" with Aurelius Ambrosius and uther pendragon,
     (King Arthur's father) ca. 466 A.D.)
Yspwys of Moel Ysbiddon (the stranger's mount)
Yspwys Mwyntyrch

Unhwch Unarchen   Mynan
Maeldaf Hynaf of Moel Esgidton (= Ysbiddon)
Heuan   Mor
Kynvan
Morgynhor   Marchudd
Rynn   (founder of 8th Noble Tribe - some
Kedyvor (Cadivor)   pedigrees trace Ednywain AP Bradwen
Kynerth (Cynarth)   back through Marchudd.)
Kyndelu
Morud   A Quo the Tudors   Bleudud (Bleddyn)
Bleydud (Bleddyn)
Mael
Bradwen (Bratwen)
Ednywain AP Bradwen (Head of one of the 15 noble tribes) Arms: Gules, 3 snakes enowed, Argent.
Peredur
Gwen
Tudor
Llywelyn = Elen, dau. of Gronwy
Llywelyn Fychan
Llywelyn Dalrain
Dafydd Llwyd
Maredudd
Dafydd (David)
Lewis AP David = Siwan, Heiress of Rhys ap Sion, a descendant of Gronwy Goch, Gronwy the Red,
                 Arms: Argent, a horses head, bridled, gules. (Used as crest by Lewis of Abernant)

(NOTE:
For the time & origin
of Yspwys see:
P. Bartum "Maelda
Mynar and Ednywain
AP Bradwen" in
Bulletin of the
Board of Celtic
Studies, Vol. 20
(1960) pp. 236-239)
and P. Bartum
"Late Additions to
'Bonedd Ysaint'"
in Cym. Trans. 1959
p. 93 (Sec. 47)

(Males Only)

James Lewis   Huw Lewis Lewis (D.S.P.)   David Lewis   Rhys Lewis Nicholas (D.S.P.)   John Lewis, Esq.   Wm. (D.S.P.)

1 = Elsbeth 2 = Ann   ┌Richard*   George   James David Hercules
James Sir John ┬Jason   John
Thomas. John   ├Nicholas   Thomas Geo. Ludwig John
James   ├Huw   David Thomas
                 └George   (b. 1609-1613)

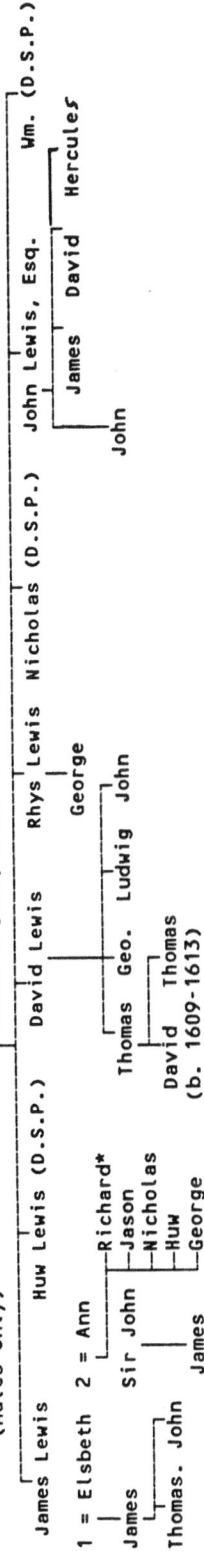

Sources: P. Bartrum, Welsh Genealogies 300-1400; V. I, pp. 8, 10 28; V. II, pp. 255-258.
          P. Bartrum, Welsh Genealogies 1400-1500; V. III, p. 496.
          P. Bartrum, Ped. of the Patriarches; Nat. Lib. of Wales J. 1963, p. 110
          Lewis Dwnn, Vol. I, pp. 39-40.
* Richard is mentioned in the pedigree as 'a great gamester' (Gambler?)

LEWIS OF GLADESTRY

LEWIS, OF HARPTON COURT.

PEDIGREE OF LEWIS OF GLADESTRY AND HARPTON COURT, RADNORSHIRE, WALES

Coel Hen (Coelius) - Dux Britanniarum ca. 400 A.D.
Ceneu
Gurwst Ledlum
Meirchion Gul
Elidir Lydanwyn = Gwawr, Dau. of Brychan
Llywarch Hen
Dwg
Gwair
Tegid
Alcwn
Sandde = Celeinion, dau. of Tudwal
Elidir
Gwriad = Nest, dau. of Cadell
Merfyn Frych (D. 844) King of Isle of Man
 = Esyllt, dau. of Cynan
Rhodri Mawr (Roderick the Great) King of Wales (D. 848)
Cadell (d. 910) Prince of Deheubarth (South Wales)
Howell DDA (Howell the Good) King of Wales (D. 948)
Owen AP Howell (D. 984)
Cadell AP Einion = Elinor, dau. of Gwerstan)
Tewder Mawr (Theodore the Great) Prince of South Wales)
Rhys AP Tewder (D. 1093) Prince of South Wales
Gruffudd AP Rhys (1090 - 1136) = Gwenllian, dau. of Gruffudd ap Cynan
Rhys AP Gruffudd (The Lord Rhys) Ruler of S. Wales
Rhys Gryg (Rhys the Hoarse) (D. 1233) Lord of Ystrad Twyi
 = Gwenllian, dau. of Madog ap Meredydd, Pr. of Powys
Rhys Mechyll (D. 1244) = Matilda/Maud, dau. of Wm. de Braose (D. 1230) Baron of Brecon,
 She = (2) Roger Mortimer of Wigmore (D. 1282) in 1247.

Philip - Elen, dau of Llewelyn ap David of Cemmis.

Llewelyn AP Philip (Llewelyn Crugeryr) Lord of Crugeryr = the Eagle's Barrow. Granted new arms, Sable, an eagle displayed, argent. (Lev. 1371.)

Dafydd AP Llewelyn Crugeryr = Maud, dau of Rhys Huby of Badland, Radnorshire.
Steven AP David = Elsbeth, dau. of Hywel ap Gruffudd Ddw
Lewis AP Steven = Malt, dau. of John ap Ievan; Ddyddgu
David Lewis = Lleuou, dau. of Gruffudd ap Llewelyn of Gladestry, Radnorshire.
Jenkin Lewis (Of Gladestry, M.P. 1558) = Annes, dau. of Wm. Holl

NOTE:
Several other
pedigrees for
this section:
see Lewis Dwnn
V. II, p. 253
P. Bartrum Wel.
Gen. 300-1400
pp. 787-9.

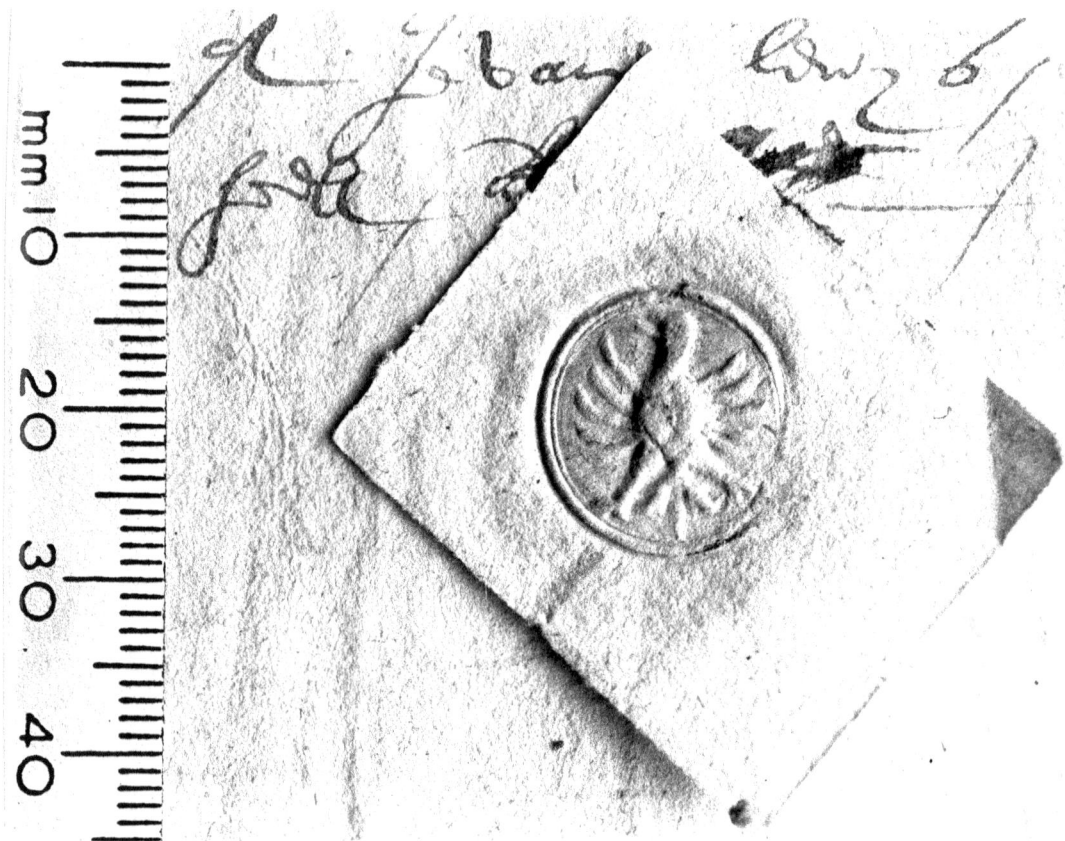

Photo of seal on will of John Lewis (d. 1597)
(National Library of Wales Photo)

LEWIS OF GLADESTRY

The paternal line comes down through Rhodri Mawr, King of Wales, Howell the Good, King of Wales, to Rhys ap Tewder, Prince of South Wales. His grandson, Rhys ap Gruffudd, gave up the Title of Prince and was known as the Lord Rhys (D. 1197.) One of his sons, Rhys Grug (the Hoarse) (D. 1233) Lord of Ystrad Twi, had, as his second wife, a member of the De Clare family. It was his son, Rhys Mechyll (D. 1244) who married Maud/Matilda De Braose. The next person on the pedigree who is undisputed is Llewelyn Crugeryr[*] (Llewelyn of the Eagle's mound/barrow.) He was living in 1371, and his father is given as Philip who married Elen, dau. of Llewelyn ap David of Cemmis (Kemmys.) Llewelyn appears to have been granted a new coat of Arms: Sable, an eagle displayed, argent. Probably circa 1350-55, the same time that the attainder against the Mortimer family was repealed.

From Llewelyn Crugery down through Iaun, eldest son of Jenkin Lewis of Gladestry,[**] and his children, the pedigree is given in Lewis Dwnn, Vol. 2, pp. 252-3 etc. The fact that John Lewis of Llanishen (D. 1597) used these arms on the seal on his will; and the fact that he was also known as John ap Jenkin, make it very probable that he was a younger son of Jenkin Lewis of Gladestry.

---

[*] Note on Castle Crugeryr (also known as Castle Crukeri): One of the links in the chain of castles the De Braoses built across Radnorshire. Located in the Parish of Llanvihangle Nant Melin (formerly Llanwenny). Gerald of Wales mentions a crusade being preached here in 1188. It was probably then that the De Braoses dedicated the tithes of the parish to the knights of St. John of Jerusalem in perpetuity. Wm. De Braose (d. 1230) may have been hung here by Llewelyn the Great: The verse went "He was made 'Crogyn' (hang dog) at Crukein." Later the castle was known as 'Tomen' for the tomb or barrow on which it was built. See: Arch. Camb. 1859, p. 157-8- 1875 pp. 247-81; and pp. 339-41. Jones, Hist. of Brec. (1898 AD) p. 37 note 4. Lloyd, Hist. of Wales, Vol. II p. 670-1. Williams, Hist. of Co. of Radnor, pp. 176-8.

[**] Note on Gladestry (Welsh: Llanfair Lethonow): This estate did not remain in Lewis hands very long. Sir Gelli Meyrick, eldest son of Rowland, Bishop of Bangor married a dau. of Ievan Lewis, eldest son of Jenkin Lewis of Gladestry. He was steward of Robert, Earl of Essex, who knighted him in the square of Cadiz after the victory there. Sir Gelli obtained many other grants, including half of Wigmore. He was executed after the fall of the Earl and his estates became crown property. This included Gladestry, see: Arch. Camb., 1864, pp. 17-31; Williams, Hist. of Co. of Radnor (1905), pp. 173-175.

PEDIGREE OF LEWIS OF GWERSYLT AND WREXHAM

(Sources: P. Bartrum, Wel. Gen. 300-1400, V. 4, pp. 870, 887; P. Bartrum, Wel. Gen. 1400-
         1550, V. 10, p. 1695; Harl. Soc. V. 29, Pt. 1: Visit. of Shrop., p. 67; Cae Cyriog Ms.)
Rhys Sais (desc. fr. Tudor Trefor)
Elidir ap Rhys Sais (liv. 1081)
Madog ap Elidir (6th son)
Llewelyn ap Madog
Madog ap Llewelyn
Morgan ap Madog
David ap Morgan, Lord of Sutton
David ap David, Lord of Sutton (Liv. 1361)
Gruffydd ap David, Lord of Sutton

                                        = Gwerfyl, dau. of Gruffydd ap Bleddin,
                                            Lord of Morton, desc. fr. Sandde Hardd

Robert ap David, (Sr. Line) (Liv. 1492)   Thomas ap David, (Jr. Line)
    = Elen, dau. of David ap Gruffud   (Liv. 1515)
                                                    = Mali, dau. of Ieun Deca

Lewys ap Robert (Vicar Gen. 1488)   Lewys ap Thomas
    = Angharad, dau. of Wm. ap   = Janet, dau. of Robt. ap Edward
        John, Lord of Boresham
John (ap) Lewis   John (ap) Lewis, of Gwersyllt Uchaf
    = Margaret, dau. of Wm. Allington   = Emma, dau. of John Puleston

                                             John Lewis of Gwesyllt Uchaf

William Lewis of Wrexham   Edward Lewis, sold Gwersyllt Uchaf to
    = Dorothy, dau. of Thos. Brereton,   Bishop Robinson
        Rec., Son of Edw. B., of
        Boresham & Dorothy Hanmer

John Lewis of Gwersyllt
    = Catherine, dau. of David ap Richard.

John Lewis, Atty.   William Lewis   Lancelot Lewis
    (1) = Stacey, dau. of
        Richard Powell of London
    (2) = Elizabeth, dau. of
        David Offley of London
(MANY DESCENDANTS)

PEDIGREE OF LEWIS OF HENLLAN, NARBETH, PEMBROKESHIRE

Note: This family traces back to Gwynfardd, a Lord of Dyfed (Pembrokeshire), whose arms are those of his descendant, Gwrwared: Azure, a lion rampant within an orle of eight cinque-foils, or. A branch of these Lewises at Lampeter Velfrey, Pemb., used the Arms: Azure, a chevron ermine between three garbs. (Burke, Gen. Arm. p. 606.)

From Gwrwared the pedigree descends to Llewelyn of the woods, son of Owen ap Robert, who in 1369 married Nest, and had Philip of Pant-teg (Velfre). His son, Lewis had a son David ap Lewis, whose descendants began to use Lewis as a surname. (P. Bartrum, *Wel. Gen. 300-1400 A.D.,* pp. 496, 500, 501; & *Wel. Gen. 1400-1500,* p. 942. Also in T. Nicholas, *Ann. & Antiq. of the Cos. & Co. Fam. of Wales,* V. II, p. 904-5.) Note: Some of the early Lewis immigrants to Pa. are poss from this family. See the entries for Daniel, Henry and John Lewis, fr. Redstone, Narbeth and Pembrokeshire in T. A. Glenn's *Welsh Founders of Pa.,* pp. 188-189.

The Arms of Lewis of Lampeter Velfrey are on the tomb of Hugh Lewis, Esq., (D. 1785) in Jamaica. Ref.: J. H. Lawrence-Archer, *Monumental Inscriptions of the British West Indies,* pp. 56-57. A note at the bottom of p. 57 says that a Thomas Lewis by will (1701) leaves to his bro. Hugh and sister Gwinn, his estate in the par. of Cwmr Toyddwr (?) Wales, called Nant Lamptir.

HENLLAN : THE SEAT OF J. L. G. POYER LEWIS, ESQ. (*from a photo. by Allen*).

(T. Nicholas, Ann. & Antiq. of Cos. & Co. Fam. Wales Vol. 2, p. 840, 1875.)

HENLLYS: THE SEAT OF J. L. HAMPTON LEWIS, ESQ.

(From T. Nicholas, Annals & Antiq. of the Cos. & Co. Fam. of Wales, 1875, Vol. I, p. 5).

LLANAERON : THE RESIDENCE OF MRS. LEWIS.

(T. Nicholas, Annals & Antiq. of the Cos. & Co. Fam. of Wales, 1875, V. I, p. 133).

```
LEWIS OF LLANDEWI RHYDDERCH
```

Lewis (Wallis/De Valence) of Monmouthshire

From: Sir Robert Wallis/DeValence (living ca 1300)

Arms: Chequy or and Sable on a Fess Gules three Leopards
          Heads Jessant de Lis or.
          In: Bradney, Joseph A., History of Monmouthshire, Vol.
          I, p. 285

Crest: A Leopards Head Jessant de Lis or.

PEDIGREE OF LEWIS (WALLIS/DE VALENCE) FAMILY
OF LLANDEWI RHYDDERCH, MON.

Sources: P. Bartrum, Welsh Genealogies A.D. 1400 - 1500, Vol. 10, p. 1746.
J. A. Bradney, Hist. of Monmouthshire, Vol I, p 285, 301-2; Vol. IV, Pt. 1, pp. 134-5
G. Moses, John Lewis (1592-1657), Supplement.

(Sir William de Valence, Lord of Llanarth, Triley, & Gwern-y-com)

Sir Robert Wallis, Kt., Lord of Llanarth, Triley, & Gwern-y-com

Sir Thomas Wallis, Kt., Lord of Llanarth, Triley, & Gwern-y-com

William Wallis, Lord of Llanarth, Esqr. (Temp. Henry IV)

Robert Wallis = Joan, dau of John Tomlyn

Gwilym (Wm.) Wallis, = Gwentlian, dau of Sir Wm. ap Thos. (Herbert) of Raglan Castle

John ap Gwilym (Wallis) = Mary, dau of Thos. Welsh

Sir Lewis ap John (Wallis) = Lucy, dau. to Llewelyn ap Thos. Lloyd of Bedwellty
(Vicar of Abergavenny)   (also had issue by Morfudd, dau. of Philip ap David of Tyle-Glos.)

Sons:

John Lewis
= Magred, dau of
Lawrence ap John

Dr. David Lewis
(d. 1584) D.C.L.
(s.p.) (See art.
in Dict. of Natl.
Biog.)

William Lewis
of Llandewi Ysgrid, Esqr.
= (1) Mary, dau of James
ap Watkin of Llandewi Rhyd,
= (2) Eliza. dau of Wm.
ap John Proger (Herbert)
of Wern-Ddu

Richard Lewis
= (?)

Richard Lewis, Jr.
Vicar of Llantelio
Portholey (1610-14) Dau. Johane
= John Lewis of Va. (1592-1657)

Thomas Lewis

By (1)
William Lewis = Cecil, dau of Matthew
of Llandewi   Herbert of Coldbrook, Esqr.
Rhydderch, Esq.

By (2)
David Lewis = Eliza. dau of
of Llandewi   Wm. ap. Thos Coes
Ysgrid, Gent.   of Llanmelyn

(Others)

David Lewis
of Llandewi Rhyderch, Esqr.
(Sheriff 1624)
a quo Lewis of Llandewi Rhydderch

William Lewis
of Llanmelyn, Gent.
(Liv. 1665)

Richard Lewis   Thomas Lewis
(No additional information on Richard & Thos.)

LLANARTH COURT.

(J.A. Bradney, *A Hist. of Monmouthshire*, V. I, Pt. II, p. 304, 1906)

TRILEY COURT: THE RESIDENCE OF MRS. FIELDER (*from a pencil sketch*).

(T. Nicholas, *Ibid.*, Vol. II, p. 720.)

LEWIS (WALLIS/DE VALENCE)

FAMILY OF MONMOUTHSHIRE

SUMMARY: This family has a pedigree that, on some lines, can probably be traced back further than any other. It descends from the Lusignans of France, who can be traced back to Hugh I, the Hunter. The wife of Hugh II, the Beloved, has lines that go back to the royal families of Judea and Persia. Putting far aside the question of descent from Jesus Christ and Mary Magdalene, the historical evidence seems to indicate that the rulers of the Kingdom of Septima in Southern France were of mixed Jewish and Persian blood, resulting from a forced marriage of the daughter of the Emperor of Persia to the Prince, or leader of the Babylonian Jews, who was of Davidic descent, to create an heir that would be unacceptable to both, as a matter of Arab policy. The heir, however, was the perfect candidate to govern the Kingdom of Septima, whose Jewish population had been promised one of their own as a ruler by Pepin the Short, in return for their killing the Moslems of the city and opening its gates to his army. This was done, but only after he had converted to Christianity and been baptised with a Christian name. (See the final chapters in *Holy Blood, Holy Grail.*)

In England, the Lusignan, William de Valence, cut a wide swath; as half brother to Henry III, he could do pretty much as he pleased, and created much resentment. As guardian of the De Cantilupe heir to the Lordship of Abergavenny, it was perhaps inevitable that he would exercise his rights and bring into being Sir Robert de Valence/Wallis from whom descends the Lewis (Wallis/De Valence) family of Monmouthshire, whose arrns are based on those of the Cantilupes and use the same crest. During the Elizabethan age, they had, possibly through their marriages with the Baker (Cecil) family, become one of the most prominent families in the county, although no more committed to monogamy than the Herberts, with whom they frequently intermarried.

Pedigree of the House of Lusignan

SOURCE: *The Speculum,* Vol. 32, No. 1, 1957 pp. 27-47.

Hugh I "Venator" (The Hunter)
Huntsman for the Count or the Bishop of Poitou.

Hugh II "Carus" (The Beloved)
Built the Castle of Lusignan ca. 1009. Married Agnes, dau. of Sigisbert VII. (See Pedigree charts in *Holy Blood, Holy Grail.*)

Hugh III "Albus" (The White)
Married (?) Emma, wife of Count Wm. Fierobras taxed St. Maixent and gave Hugh III the proceeds.

Hugh IV "Brunus" (The Brown) (d. 1032)
Founded monastery of Notre Dame de Lusignan 1025. Married Audearde, dau. of Viscount Ralph de Thouars. Sons: Hugh & Rorgo.

Hugh V "The Pious"
Married Almodis, dau. of Bernard I, Count of La Marche. Sons Hugh and Jordan.

Hugh VI "The Devil" (d. 1110)
Married Audearde, dau. of Aimery IV, Viscount of Thouars.

Hugh VII "Brunus" (The Brown)
Founded monastery of Bonnevaux. Married Sarazanne (a saracen), ca. 1151, after his return from the Second Crusade. Misidentified with "Melusine." Sons: Hugh, Wm., Rorgo, Simon and Waleran.

Hugh VIII ca. 1164
Married Burgundia, dau. of Geoffry de Rancon.
Sons: Hugh, Robt., Amalric (Amaury), Geoffrey, Guy, and Peter.

Hugh (Not counted when numbers assigned to the Hughs) "Brunus"
Wife unknown. Two sons: Hugh and Ralph, who became Count of Hastings. At this Hugh's death his brother Geoffry became head of the house of Lusignan.

Hugh IX "Brunus" (The Brown) of age 1180 (d. 1219)
Became Count of La Marche ca. 1200 by holding Queen Eleanor of England, (Eleanor of Aquitaine) hostage until he was granted the title.

Hugh X (d. 1249)
Married Queen Isabella de Angouleme, widow of King John of England.

William de Valence (d. 1296)

Married in 1247, Joan, dau. of Warin de Munchesy, Lord of Swancombe and his wife, Joanna, dau. of Wm. Marshal Earl of Pembroke, and one of his heirs. Eva, the sister of Joanna, married Wm. de Braose. (Wm was hung by Llewelyn the Great in 1229.)

Sons by Joan:
    John de Valence (d. 1276/7)
    Wm. de Valence (d. 1282)
    Aymer de Valence (d. 1324)
    Earl of Pembroke (No legit. male issue)
Son by (?) (A de Cantilupe):
    Robert de Valence, also known as Sir Robert Wallis.

LEWIS OF LLANGATOCK, CRICKHOWELL
Lewis (Rhys Goch) of Brecon and Monmouthshire

From: John Lewis, Gent. of Monmouthshire and Poropotanck Creek, Va. (d. 1657)

Arms: Quarterly: 1st, Argent a dragon's head erased vert holding in its mouth a hand Gules (Rhys Goch of Ystrad Yw); 2nd, Gules three castles triple-towered Argent (Prince, later Sir Howell of Caerleon, Glam.) 3rd, Gules three Chevronells Argent (Jestin ap Gwergan) 4th, Azure three Plates (Sir Walter de Trevely of Llandewi Rhydderch, Mon.)

Note: Their cousins, the Moreans of Llanelly Crick Howell used the same arms, except for repeating Rhys Goch in the 4th quarter.

Crest: A dragon's head erased vert holding in its mouth a hand gules.

In: Harris, Malcom, "John Lewis 1594 - 1657". Va. Mag. of Hist. & Biog. Vol. 56 (1948) pp. 195-205. Vol. 62 p. 481. Tombstones of John Lewis and his son Edward Lewis Arms.

Pedigree of Lewis of Llangatock, Crickhowell, Breconshire (Chart I)

Tacitus (Tegid) Roman Praefect in Votadini area ca. 350 AD

Paternus (Padarn Beisrod) (of the red cloak)

Aeternus (Edern) See: Morris, J.: The Age of Arthur, pp. 17, 66, 68.

Cunedda Wledig Conquered N.W. Wales ca. 400 AD Estab. Royal Line

Einion Yrth

Llyr Marini (some pedigrees give ap Mercion ap Gwrwst ap Ceneu ap Coel)

Caradoc Freichfras (Strong arm) Ruled between the Wye & Severn ca. 500 AD

Cawrdaf Ruled area later known as Breconshire.

Caw

Glou

Hoyw

Cynfarch (Ca 680 AD)

Cyndeg

Teithwalch

Tegyd

Tangwydd

Gwngy (Last of this dynasty to rule all the area.)

Einion

Rhys Goch (Red Rhys) Ruler of Ystrad Yw in Breconshire. ca. 1100. Some pedigrees: ap Maenarch ap Dryffin ap Ky ap Gwngy. Arms used by his descendants: Argent, a dragon's head erased vert, holding in its mouth a hand gules. Symbol of Descent fr Caradoc Freichfras- see legend in Bulfinch's Age of Chivalry.

Genillin = Janet, dau. of Prince, later Sir Howell of Caerleon:[*]

    Arms: Gules, three towers triple-towered, argent. (P. Bartrum gives wife as dau. of Cumelyn Foel.) But this is only a varient of Genillyn (Kenellyn Foel) ("The Bald")

Idris = Ann, dau. of Moriddig Warwyn

Ieuan = Gwladus, dau. of Gruffud ap Madog, great grandson of Jestyn ap Gwrgan, last king of Glamorgan.
    Arms: Gules, 3 Chevronels, argent.

Ieuan Fych an = Jane, dau. of Hywel ap Iowerth of Llanffwyst.

David Mwnton = Janet, dau. of Llewelyn ap Rhys of Merthyr Tudful.

Hywel Hir = Annes, dau. of Jenkin Hafard

David = Nest, dau. of Richard Gunter

Gwilym = a dau. of Jenkin Llewelyn

John = Joan, dau. of John Gwlym Fychan

Thomas = Margery, dau. of John ap John of Ewas

Lewis = Maud, dau. of Lewis (See Tuberville Chart 4 (A) in Bartrum: Welsh Genealogies 1400 AD - 1500 AD.

Richard Lewis, of Llangatock Crickhowell, Brec., Gent. d. 1628

    = Nest, dau. of Thomas ap Gwlym ap Llewelyn of Llanelli, Breconshire.

SOURCES: P. Bartrum: *Welsh Geneal. AD 300-1400*, Vol. I, pp. 3,7,9; Vol. 4, p. 806-7.

P. Bartrum: *Ped. of the Patriarchs*, Natl. Lib. of Wales Journ, Vol. 13 pp. 106, 130.

T. Jones: *Hist of Breck*, Chapt. 4.

G. Moses: *Gen. of John Lewis (1592-1657)*, pp 9. fol.

J. A. Bradney: *Hist. of Mon.* Vol. I, pp. 338-9;

M. H. Harris: *John Lewis (1594-1657)*, Va. Mag. of Hist & Biog., Vol. 56 (1948) pp. 195-205.

---

[*] Pedigree of Prince Howell - ap Iorworth ap Owen Wan ap Caradawg ap Gruffudd ap Rhydderch ap Jestin ap Owen ap Howell Dda, King of Wales (See Lewis of Gladestry Pedigree), Bradney, Hist. of Mon. Vol. 3, p. 190.

CHART II OF LEWIS OF LLANGATOCK CRICKHOWELL

Richard Lewis, Gent. (d. 1627)
(Of Llangatock Crickhowell, Brecknockshire.)

= Nest, dau of Thomas Phillip Llewelyn, of Llanelly, Brec.

William Lewis
B.C.L. Oxford
= Jane

—Richard Lewis of Dan y Parc
—Marie
—Elizabeth
—Dorite (Dorothy)

Edward Prichard
= Gwenllian James
| (Had Issue)

Maudelen Lewis

Thomas Prichard
= (?)
|—Wm. Thomas
|—John Thomas

Thomas Lewis

(1) Gwenllian
b. 5 Feb 1611
St. Telios

(1) Lettus
(Lettitia = Lydia)
b. 1 Mar 1615
St. Telios

(1) Watkin
b. 1 Jan 1621
St. Telios

Lewis Prichard
(Ap Richard=Rycketts)

= Catherine

John Lewis (1592 - 1657)
1610 = (1) Johane, dau of
Richard Lewis, Clerk
of Llantelio Pertholey

(Lewis of Llandewi
Rhydderch family)

1630 = (2) Catherine Philip
| (dau. of John of Dyffryn Tudwell(?)
(2) **John Lewis Jr.**
b. 15 Dec 1633 St. Telios
d. ca 1682 Va.

= Isabella, dau of
James Miller,
b. 24 Aug 1640
d. 9 Feb 1703/4

John Lewis III, of Warner Hall
b. 30 Nov 1669
= Elizabeth, dau of Augustine Warner II

a quo Lewis Family of Warner Hall

Edward Lewis
b. 5 Sep 1667
d. 11 Feb 1713
= Susanna

John   William   Ann = Rev. John Skaife
D.S.P.   D.S.P.

Mary = Beverly Whiting

LLYSNEWYDD : THE SEAT OF COL. WILLIAM PRICE LEWES.

(T. Nicholas, Annals & Antiq. of the Cos. & Co. Fam. of Wales, V. I, p. 223).

Lewis (Einion ap Geraint) of Anglesey, Wales
(PLAS GWYN, PENTREATH)

Arms: Gules a Chevron between three Roses Argent.
(also attributed to Rhodri Mawr (d. 878) King of Wales)

Pedigree of Rhodri Mawr & His Family
I: Paternal Pedigree of Rhodri Mawr

SOURCE: P. Bartrum, *Welsh Genealogies A.D. 300 - 1440,* Vol. I, pp. 1,8,9.

Coel Hen/Coel Godebog = Ystradwel, dau. of Gadeon ap Eudaf Hen (Hen = old)
Ceneu
Gwrwst Ledlarn
Merchion Gul
Elidir Lydenwyn = Gwawr, dau. of Brychan, p. 27.
Llywarch Hen
Dwg
Gwair
Tegid
Alcwn
Sandde = Celeinion, dau. of Tudwal, p. 19.
Elidir
Gwriad = Nest, dau. of Cadell, p. 14.
Merfyn Frych (d. 844) = Esyllt, dau. of Cynan Dindaethwy, p. 12
Rhodri Mawr, King of Wales (d. 878)

Pedigree of Rhodri Mawr & His Family:
II. Paternal Pedigree of Esyllt, his Mother

SOURCE: P. Bartrum, *Welsh Genealogies A.D. 300 - 1400,* Vol. I, pp. 1,3.

Padern Beissrudd
Edern
Cunedda Wldig = Gwaiol, dau. of Coel Hen
Einion Yrth = Prawst, dau. of Tidlet/Tithlyn, King of the Picts of Powys.
Cadwallon Lawhir = Meddyf, dau. of Maeldaf Ap Dylan Draws, of Nanconwy.
Maelgwn Gwynedd (d. 547)
Rhun Hir = Perwyr, dau. of Rhun Ryfeddfawr, p. 10.
Beli
Iago (d. 616)
Cadfan = Tandry ddu, dau. of Cynan Garwin, p. 14.
Caddwallon (d. 634) = dau. of Pybba, sister of Penda, King of Mercia (626-655)
Cadwaladr Fendigad (d. 664)
Idwal Iwrch
Rhodri Molwynog (d. 754)
Cynan Dindaethwy, Lord of Dindaethwy, King of North Wales.
Esyllt = Merfyn Frych, Father of Rhodri Mawr, p. 12 (Bartrum, *ibid.*)

Pedigree of Lewis of Plas Gwyn, Pentreath, Anglesea

Enedwy of the same generation and possibly a younger brother ofRhodri Mawr (d. 878 A.D.)
The same arms were used by his descendants as those the Heralds assigned to Rhodri
Mawr: Gu., a chevron between three roses, argent. Cynan or Conan, the grandfather of
Rhodri was known as Cynan Dindaethwy the same land ruled by the descendants of
Enedwy.

Rhufawn

Kathus

Dissaeth

Kadawg

Kadwr

Idnerth

Nynyaw

Madawg

Kynfawr

Tegwaret

Geraint

Einion, ap Geraint, Lord of Pentreath, Dindaethwy, Mon, (Anglesey), Arms: Gules, a
Chevron between three roses, argent.

Gronwy Trefgoed, Lord of Trefgoed, Dindaethwy

Gruffudd

Hywal (Howel)

Iorwerth

Dafyd

Rhys

Llywelyn

Gruffudd (ap Llywelyn ap Rhys ap David ap Ioreth) listed under Plas Gwyn, Pentreath by
Lewys Dwnn in his Heraldic Visitations of Wales, 1588. His three sons are: 1. Lewis,
2. Howel, 3. David. (L.D. II, p. 265.) Ancestry of Geraint given in P. Bartrum, Early
Welsh genealogical Tracts, p. 116, section 6a.

Lewis of Thorndon Hall, Essex

From: Sir Lewis John of Wales and Thorndon Hall, West Horndon, Essex.

Arms: Sable a Chevron between three Fleurs de Lis Argent (Einion ap Collwyn) differenced to: Sable a Chevron betwen three Trefoils Argent by the English Heralds.

Crest: Out of a ducal coronet a plume of (four or five) ostrich feathers.

In: Fairbairn's Crest for Lewis of Essex, Herts and Yorks. Also Lewys.

LEWIS FAMILY OF THORNDON HALL, ESSEX, PEDIGREE

Sources:

Bartrum, P. Wel. Gen.
A.D. 300-1400 Vol. I.
(Coel Hen - Einion Sais)

Bulletin of the Board of
Celtic Studies, Vol. 22
pt. III. Nov. 1967.
(Sir Lewis John & Sons)

Arms assigned to Einion
ap Gollwyn: Sable, a chev.
betw. three fleur de lis
Argent.

Arms of Sir Lewis John:
Sable, a chev. betw.
three trefoils, Arg.

(Knighted 15 May 1439,
by Henry VI. -Shaw:
The Knights of Eng.
Vol. II, p. 12.)

(Arms prob. differenced from
Einion ap Collwyn by the Eng. Heralds.)

Coel Hen - Dux Brittania
Gorst Letlwm
Merchawn
Kynvarch (Cynfarch)
Urien Rheged
Pasgen
Llyminod Angel
Llew
Kadvael
Tangno
Gollwyn (Collwyn) (Head of 5th Noble Tribe)
Einion "Sais" or "Fradwr" (Brought the Normans into Wales to
= Nesta, dau of   fight for Jestin, after he reneged
  Jestyn ap   on his promise of giving Einion his
  Gwergant, last   dau to marry, Eionion asked the Normans
  Welsh king of   for aid. They conquered Glam. & Einion
  Glamorgan.   married the daughter.

(from them descended many families of
S. Wales, including; Apparently) Sir Lewis John, Kt. (d. 1442)

1413 = (1) Alice, dau of Aubrey de Vere, Earl of Oxford.
             All issue prob. hers.
1433 = (2) Ann, dau of John Montague, Earl of Salisbury.

Sir Lewis Fitz Lewis*   Philip   Edmond   Sir John Lewis*   Sir Henry Lewis
(Lewis ap Lewis)   Kt. 10 Jul 1460.

*Attainted during the reign of Edw. IV. Prob. executed along with the Earl of Oxford and others for upholding the Lancasters, 1461.
Sir Richard Lewis, son of Sir Lewis FitzLewis, Kt. Knighted 17 June 1497. (Shaw, Vol II. p. 29.) Family estates restored to him. He had a son John FitzLewis, who inherited them, and had a dau and heiress who married a Mordaunt, and the estate passed into that family.
(Many Lewis families bearing Sir Lewis John's arms or varients are listed in Burke, Gen. Armory, p. 605-6 in Herts, Essex, Norfolk & York.)

THORNDON HALL, ESSEX

Two Views of Thorndon Hall
(T. Wright, Hist. & Topog. of the Co. of Essex... V. II, 1835, pp. 555-6).

Drawn by W. Bartlett.

Engraved by H. Adlard.

THORNDON HALL, ESSEX,
FROM THE NORTH.

LEWIS (EINION AP GOLLWYN) OF ESSEX AND HERTS
(also known as Lewis, or Fitzlewis, of Thorndon Hall)

SUMMARY: The discovery of the true pedigree of this family as revealed in the article, "Sir Lewis John, a Medieval London Welshman" should be of great interest, not only to those families able to trace a line of descent back to him, but also to those students of genealogy interested in the construction of false pedigrees. The pedigree of the family as given in Morant's *Hist. of Essex* shows how it is possible to transform an honest and noble Welshman into the illegitimate son of a French King and push him back a few hundred years at the same time. There are also several New England Lewis families that also descend (apparently) from branches of the family in Norfolk and Suffolk, but, because of the providencial fact that a Lewis of Van family member had the right name at the right time, they have been made members of that much put upon gens. The pedigree from Coel Hen down through Einion is very straightforward. Einion himself has received a very bad reputation because he had been at the English Court and brought the Normans into Wales where they did what Normans always did when the opportunity presented itself. Forgotten is the fact that Einion brought them only because his future father-in-law asked him to – Jestyn wanted them as allies in his war with the Prince of North Wales, and it was only after he reneged on his promise to give Einion his daughter in marriage that Einion asked the Normans to make Jestyn keep his promise. The fact that Jestyn lost his kingdom in the process is only incidental to the course of true love – which it must have been, considering the large number of offspring that traced their descent back to them.

Career of Sir Lewis John (d. 1442)
(of Thorndon Hall Essex)
(Founder of Lewis Families of Herts; Norfolk: York; etc.)

Arms: Sable, a Chevron between three trefoils, argent.
> (Prob. based on those of Einion ap Collwyn: Sable, a chevron between three fleurs de lis, argent.)

Source: "Sir Lewis John, a Medieval London Welshman" by A.D. Carr. 1968. Bulletin of the Board of Celtic Studies, Vol. 22, Pt. 3, pp. 260-270.

1402: Lewis John appointed deputy in London to the King's Chief Butler, Thomas Chaucer (son of Geoffry Chaucer, prob. a relative of Lewis John.)

1404: Lewis John and Thos. Wotton appointed Collectors of Customs in London. (Reappointed through 1413.)

1406: Lewis John appointed Admin. of the goods of Stephen John, citizen and Vintner of London, who died intestate.

1408/9: Lewis John, King's servant granted the daily sum of 12p out of the issues of Oxfordshire.

1412: Lewis John, Goldsmith, in list of main pernors [*sic*].

1413: Lewis John and Thos. Chaucer to be paid £795, 10s for wine for the royal household.

1413: Lewis John (as protoge of Thos. Chaucer-cousin of the Beauforts and four time Speaker of Commons in Parliament) elected Burgess of Tauton and Wallingford.

1413: Lewis John married Alice, dau. of Aubrey de Vere, Earl of Oxford, and widow of Sir Francis Court.

1414: Lewis John petitioned Parliament for exemption from the prohibition forbidding Welshmen from owning land in England.

1414: July - Lewis John licensed to enclose and empark 300 acs. in West Horndon, Essex, to build a lodge there and crenellate it.

1414: Sept. - Lewis John given custody of the Court Manors in Hampshire of Tytherley and Lockerley and was M.P. for Hamp.

1415: Lewis John was at seige of Harfleur and was invalided home. His contingent of two men at arms and six bowmen fought at Agincourt.

1416: Lewis John served as Sheriff of Hants and Essex.

1417: Lewis John one of the pledges for the ransom of Louis, Count of Vendome.

1418: Lewis John granted the Lordship of Blainvill in Rouen by John Vittore. (Granted to Henry Court by Lewis FitzLewis in 1447.)

1418: Lewis John and Roger Salvayn granted control of foreign exchange for two years.

1420: Lewis John Sheriff of and M.P. for Essex.

1423: Lewis John appointed Receiver General of the Duchy of Cornwall and Steward of the Duchy lands in Devon.

1424: Lewis John, to counter slander that he was not of free birth obtained certificates from West Wales officials, testifying that he was of free birth: May 4, Lewis ap Ieuan Fychan, reeve of Kidwelly. May 5, John Bernard, Mayor of Carmarthan, stated: Lewis John, "a Gentleman of our country" was not only free-born, but was "of the best family in this part of Wales from the conquest to the present day."

1428: The Abbot of Whitland stated that Lewis John was descended from the ancient Lords of Wales.

1433: His first wife having died, Lewis John married Anne, dau. of John Montague, Earl of Salisbury.

1435: Lewis John appointed a member of the Commission of Peace for Essex.

1436: Lewis John appointed a member of an embassy to the King of Scots.

1437: Lewis John M.P. for Essex.

1438: Lewis John and Sir John Popham deputed to take instructions to the Earl of Warwick and inspect the garrisons in France.

1440: Sir Lewis John Knighted May 15, by Henry VI. (Lewis John had been present at the coronation of Henry VI as King of France at Notre Dame in 1431.)

1441: Sir Lewis John and Walter Colles in charge of delivery of money to the Duke of York in France.

1443: Death of Sir Lewis John by Oct. His will names his sons: Lewis, Edmond, Philip, John and Henry. Daus: Margaret (I), Elizabeth, Alice, and Margaret (II.) He is to be buried in the Abbey of St. Mary Graces, London.

Epilogue: His widow married (3) John Holland, Duke of Exeter. In 1526 the dau. and heiress of the FitzLewis family married John, 2d Lord Mordaunt and the Essex estates passed to him. In 1572-76 the Mordaunts sold them to Sir Wm. Petre of Ingatestone and his son John, who made Thorndon Hall the family seat.

Sir Lewis John's arms are still extant on the memorial of his dau., Margaret Wake, in Ingrave church, Essex. (Note: Not found there in 1988.)

Lewis Family of Thorndon Hall Records:

In: Index of Persons Named in Early Chancery Proceedings:
Richard II - Edward IV. (1385 - 1467) Preserved in the Public Record Office, London. (Pub. by Harlean Soc. Vols 78 & 79) (1928 & 1929, ed. by Claude A. Walmisley.)

Vol. 78, p. 116:Lewis John; page 93, Suite #258.
Sir Lewis John, Kt. page 122, Suite #35.

Vol. 79, p. 11:Lewis Fit Lewis page 122, Suite #35
Sir John Lewis, Kt., page 122, Suite #35
Sir Henry Lewis, Kt., page 357, Suite #359

Death of the Earl of Oxford and his son and followers for treason:
In: Three 15th Cent. Chronicles, ed by John Gairdner, printed for the Camden Soc. 1880; Reprint. by the Royal Historical Society 1965. p. 78: (Spelling modernized)

First year of Edward IV (1461):
This year was imagined and wrought great treason against the King by the men of the Earl of Oxford and his son Aubry, with other knights and the King's rebels, traitors and adversairie without the land, which treason God sent the King himself knowledge and anon they were taken and judged to death. First the Lord Aubry was drawn the 20th day of Feb. through London to Tower Hill, and there he was beheaded; and the 23rd day of Feb. was Sir Thos. Tudnam, Kt. and Sir Wm. Tyrrell and John Montgomery, Squire, drawn from Westminster through London to Tower Hill and there beheaded upon a scaffold. And the 26 day of the same month was John Vere, the Earl of Oxford led through London to the Tower Hill and there was beheaded on the same scaffold. And the first day of March was Sir Wm. Kennedy, Kt. led from Westminister through London to the Tower Hill and eleven other men with him and there beheaded on the same scaffold.

Early Lewis Records in Hertfordshire Parish Reg.
(Poss. Descendants of Lewis of Thorndon Hall)

Abbotts Langley: John Lewys = Adice Cogdell 1542
Robert, son of John Lewis chr. 18 Oct. 1543
John, son of John Lewis, chr. 31 Aug. 1546

Thos, son of John Lewis, chr. 6 Apr. 1546

Harpenden: Philip Lewis = Ann Dary 14 Oct. 1571
            Eliza. dau. of Philip Lewis, chr. 18 July 1572
            Joan, dau. of Philip Lewis, chr. 1 Nov. 1573
            John Lewis, son of Philip, chr. 4 Sep 1575
            Thos., son of Philip Lewis, chr. 31 Jan. 1577
            Philip, son of Philip Lewis, chr. 24 Dec. 1579
            Grace, dau. of Philip Lewis, chr. 14 Mar. 1584

Great Arnwel: Harry Lewis, chr. 13 July 1572
            Edward Lewis, chr. 17 Feb. 1593

Cheshunt: Tedder (Tudor/Theodore) Lewis = Ellen Herring 23 July 1570
            Abraham, son of Tedder Lewis chr. 15 Jan. 1580
            Edward Lewis, son of Tedder, chr. 1584

St. Albans: John Lewis, son of Lewis Lewis chr. 3 May 1571
            Henry Lewis = Margaret Watt 6 July 1595

Therfield: John, son of George Lewis, chr. 28 May 1553
            Robert Lewis = Francia Wood 13 Apr. 1556

Welwyn: George Lewis = Lucy Bristowe 6 Oct. 1594
            George, son of George Lewis chr. 15 Apr. 1604

    Note on Sir George Lewis, Rector of Welwyn 1575-1606, died 28 Mar. 1606, age 55.
    Coat of Arms: A Chevron between three fleurs de Lis (Brass) Will in p. C.C. 25
    Stafforde. (See: East Herts. Archeological Soc. Trans. Vol. 7, Pt. 1, pp. 73 + 1923/24)

Some Lewis Entries from Herts Session Rolls 1581-1698:

Vol I, p. 91, 23 July 1627:
    Nicholas Kilby of Harding, Weaver, with his wife, son, and 2 daus broke into the
    house of Philip Lewys and assaulted Ann, his wife, with a hatchet Note: James Lewis,
    son of Edmond Lewis (d. 1662) of Lanc. Co., Va., married a Kilby (Kilbee.)

Vol I, p. 133, 10 July 1630: George Lewis of Wethamstead, Grocer, on the high way there
    violently assaulted John King, Gent. Note: An Edward Lewis, Grocer, was one of the
    investors in the Va. Co.

Vol 4, p. 200, 1 July 1669/70: Edward Lewis of Chesthunt, Gent. converted an outhouse into
    a cottage without assigning to it four acs. of land.

Lewis of Van, Bedwas, Glamorganshire, Wales

From: Edward Lewis of Van, Esq. (living 1559)

Arms: Quarterly: 1st, Sable, a lion rampant, argent; 2nd, Sable, a chevron between three fleurs de lis, argent (Einion ap Collwyn); 3rd, Gules three chevronells argent (Jestin ap Gwergan); 4th, Sable, a chevron between three spearheads argent (Bleddin ap Maenarch.)

Crest: A Lion rampant, Argent

(Tomb of Sir Edward Lewis of Van and Edington, Wilts. (d. 1630) Edington church. In: Clark, Geo. T. Limbus Patrum Morganiae et Glamorganiae, p. 49.)

Note: The drawing of the Coat of Arms and the Van were done by George Robert Lewis and are used with his permission. He also took and gave permission to use the photos of the tomb in Edington, Wilts. Church of All Saints.

The Arms of Sir Edw. Lewis of Van, Impaled with
those of his wife, Lady Anne Beauchamp.

The Van, Bedwas, Glamorganshire, as drawn by G. R. Lewis.

Plaque on the tomb listing the children of Sir Edw. Lewis of Van.

Tomb sculptures of the children of Sir Edw. Lewis of Van in 1630.

Tomb effigy of Sir Edw. Lewis of Van (D. 1630)

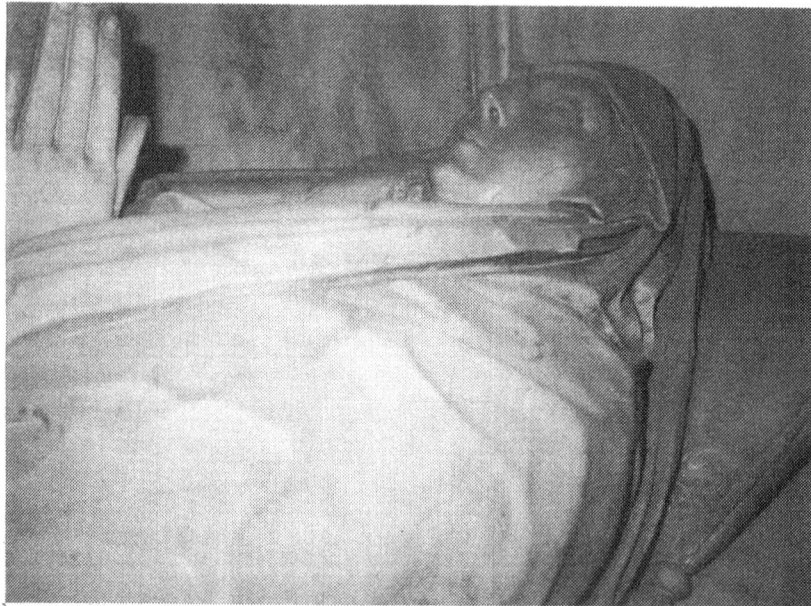

Tomb effigy of his wife, Lady Anne Beauchamp

Statue of Robert Lewis, 4th son of Sir Edward,
approx.. 2 years old in 1630, followed by his sister, Anne.

Photo of the Van, taken in 1992, as it was undergoing restoration.

LEWIS OF VAN, GLAMORGANSHIRE

SUMMARY: This has always been an interesting family, and its prominence has made it a happy hunting ground for the professional genealogist looking for a Lewis family for their client to descend from. A Robert Lewis of this family was put forward as the ancestor of the Warner Hall Lewises in spite of the fact that their coat of arms is different (although one of the quarters is the same.) In addition, a close reading of the Lewis of Van Pedigree in <u>Limbus Patrus</u> by Clark[*] would have revealed that this Robert had an older brother, Richard, who was born in 1626, meaning that poor Robert would have been only eight years old or less when he was torn from the bosom of his family and sent to Virginia in 1635 to found a dynasty.

Another problem has been that the family has a traditional pedigree in which they descend from Gwaethfoed, who has been shown to be a composite of no less than four or five Gwaethfoeds. See P. Bartrum's "Pedigrees of the Patriarchs." All this could have been avoided if their ancestor, Ivor Bach, had not killed one of the leading bards of the day. They seem to have taken their revenge by mucking up his pedigree and making him the son of Meurig ap Cadivor, instead of Meurig Fychan. This Meurig Fychan is mentioned in several historical references as being Ivor's father. In addition Ivor's mother was the dau. of Edwin, King of Upper Gwent, who had made a peace treaty with Meurig, King of Glamorgan, who thus becomes the most likely candidate to be the father of Meurig Fychan (Jr..) Unfortunately, Meurig Sr. broke his treaty and blinded and imprisoned Edwyn, who then died. The whole sad story is recorded in one of the charters in the Book of Llandaff. For this reason I have amended the pedigree to show the descent through the Kings of Glamorgan and their ancestors in Brittany who go back to Vortimer, son of Vortigern. who died fighting Saxons in France, and whose battles were later added to King Arthur's saga by Geoffry of Monmouth.

---

[*] Clark, Geo. Thos. *Limbus Patrum Morganiae et Glamorganiae* pp. 49-50, 52 London, 1886.

Lewis of Van Family - Amended Pedgree

Sources:

Bartrum, P.: *Welsh Genealogies A D. 300-1400*; Vol. I, pp. 5, 13, 16, 17, 25, 43, Vol. II Cydrich 1-5.

Morris, J.: *The Age of Arthur*. 1973. pp. 131, 228-230.

Archaeologia Cambrensis. 1850. pp. 205 - 212.

Vortigern, High King of Britain ca. 425 A D. = Severa, dau. of Magnus Maximus (Emperor d. 388.)

Vortimer - Riothamus, High King of Britain ca. 460 A.D. (Killed in France fighting Saxons.)

Daniel Dremrud, Ruled the Alamanii in Burgundy.

Budic I, Emperor of Armorica (Brittany). Killed by Clovis 509 A. D. Family fled to Wales.

Howell - Riwal pardoned by Childebert, Count of Brittany, 513, on return from Wales. Assassinated 524.

Cybyddon, Killed by brother Cano, who was killed by Clotaire I.

Budic II, King of Cornualle in Brittany, fled to Wales ca. 545 570. Married Anrlawfed, sister of St. Telio. Regained throne with help of a Visgoth, Theodoric.

Theodoric, King of Cornouialle. Fled to Wales. Married Enynny, sister of Urien Rheged. Killed fighting Saxons 586 A.D.

Meurig, Installed as King of Glywysig (later Glamorgan) by St. Cadoc. Married Onbrawst, dau. of Gwrgan Mawr, King of Ergyng. (530 - 610.)

Athrwys, King of Glewysig. (560 - 600.)

Morgan, King of Glewysig. (585 - 665.)

Ithel, King of Glewysig. (620 - 680.)

Rhys, b. 665.

Brochwel, b. 700.

Gwriad, b. 740. = Ciengar, Dau. of Maredudd.

Arthfael b. 775. = Brawstudd, dau. of Gloud.

Rhys, b. 800.

Hywel, (830 - 886.) King of Glywysig. = Lleucu.

Owain - d. ca. 930. = Nest, dau. of Rhodri Mawr, King of Wales (d. 878.)

Morgan Mawr - d. 974. King of Morgannwg (incl. Glywysig)

Owain- King of Morgannwg.

Hywel - d. 1043. King of Morgannwg.

Meurig - King of Morgannwg. Killed Edwyn, (Addon), King of Upper Gwent.

Meurig Fychan (Same as Meurig ap Cadivor in Traditional Lewis of Van Pedigree, but listed as Meurig Fychan in: ABT 16; see Bartrum, P. , Early Welsh Gen. Tracts, p. 105.) = Gwladys, dau. of Edwyn, King of Upper Gwent. See Bradney, J. A. Hist. of Mon. Vol. I, p. 335.

Ivor Bach, Lord of Senghenyd. = Nest, dau. of Gruffudd ap Rhys, (Lord of South Wales) See Lewis of Gladestry Pedigree.

Gruffud, Lord of Senghenyd. = dau. of Wm. Earl of Gloster, (whom his father had taken hostage.)

Hywel Felyn = Sara, dau. of Sir Mayo Le Sore of St. Fagan's.

Madog = Iwerydd, dau. of Lewis (fr. Bleddyn ap Maenarch)

Llewelyn = Joan, dau. of Rhys, (fr. Einion ap Collwyn)

Llewelyn Fychan = Gwerful, dau. of Ieuan (fr. Bleddyn ap Maenarch)

Rhys = Margred, dau. of Sir Thos. Basset of St. Hilary.

Llewelyn = Jane, dau. of Gruffud; (fr. Rhys Goch)

Richard Gwyn = Jonet, dau. of Ieuan

Lewys d. 1521/22 = Gwladys, dau. of Ieuan, (fr. Twdwr Fawr)

Edward Lewis of Van (I) = Ann, dau. of Sir Wm. Morgan of Prescoed.

Sons: Thomas Lewis of Van (Eldest); Edward Lewis (A), of Llanishen: William Lewis (A); Edmund Lewis; William Lewis (B), of Glentaff; Lewis Lewis; Edward Lewis (B) of Penarth.

Note: For the chart of the children of Edward Lewis (I) of Van see P. Bartrum, *Welsh Genealogies A.D. 1400-1500,* p. 416 (Cydrich 5E) which indicates which ones were legitimate and which were illegitimate. The pedigrees of the legitimate lines are continued in G.T. Clark: *Limbus Patrum Morganiae et Glamorganiae,* pp. 47-58.

PART 2

EARLY LEWIS FAMILIES

OF

VIRGINIA

I. LEWIS FAMILIES ON THE
SOUTH SIDE
OF THE
JAMES RIVER

ISLE 0F WIGHT CO. LEWIS RECORDS

Note: Of the early Isle of Wight Co. Lewis families, only that of Richard Lewis is listed in the 1704 Quit Rent List, the rest had died out or moved elsewhere.

1. Arthur Lewis (D. 1671) Family:

1671: Arthur Lewis died intestate 1671. Admin. requested by Toby Keeble who had married his widow. (B.A. Chapman, Wills and Administrations of Isle of Wight Co., Va. 1647-1800, pp. 10, 68.) The following John Lewis may have been a son of Arthur:

1700: John Lewis, age 37, d. 1700. Will mentions son Arthur, to live with my cousin John Maynard; daus., Mary and Sarah, to live with brother-in-law John Kingsmichael, their uncle. (Chapman, *ibid.,* p. 42.)

2. Benedict Lewis (D. 1675) Records:

1664: Benedict Lewis on an Isle of Wight Co. jury, Apr. 1664. (J.B. Bodie, 17th Century Isle of Wight, p. 534.)

1669: Benedict Lewis wit. power of atty. of Robert Morgan to wife Elizabeth, Jan. 1669/70. (Bodie, *ibid.,* p. 563.)

1675: Benedict Lewis died intestate. Admin. requested by his relict, Hannah, 9 June 1675. (Chapman *op. cit.,* p. 70.)
Appraisal of estate of Benedict Lewis presented by widow. Taken by John Vicars, Michell Bulgham, and Toby Keeble. (Chapman, *op. cit.,* p. 13.) (Rec. 9 Aug. 1675.)

3. Daniel Lewis (D. 1698) Records:

Note: His wife was poss. a dau. of Richard Bennett, Sr., (D. 1709), a nephew of Gov. Richard Bennett.

1698: Will of Daniel Lewis, dtd. 23 July 1698: Wife, Sarah, son, Daniel, dau. Sarah. (Bodie, *op. cit.,* p. 296; Chapman, Op. Cit.: pp. 39, 50) Note: His dau. Mary, who married (Thos.) Throp, mentioned in R. Bennett will.

4. Richard Lewis (D. 1667) Family Records:

Note: his land pat. was at White Marsh, the same area as the the land of William Lewis (D. 1663.) It is possible that this Richard Lewis is the same as Richard Lewis of

Lancaster/Middlesex Co. who died ca. 1667/8, and whose eldest son was named William (D. 1684.)

1667/8: Pat. of Gov. Wm Berkley to Miles and Richard Lewis, sons of Richard Lewis, dec'd: 400 acs. in Chuckatuck, to Thos. Jordan's trees, adj. Jeremy Rutter. dtd. 29 Jan. 1667/8. (Nugent, C. & P. II, pp. 29, 278, 318; Bodie, *op. cit.,* p. 600.)

1678: On back of pat. to Miles and Richard Lewis for 400 acs, lying in Nasemond Co.: Miles Lewis, son and heir of Richard Lewis, formerly of Chuckatuck, dec'd, assns. to Robert Coleman of Isle of Wight Co. this pat. 12 Sept. 1678. (Bodie, *op. cit.,* p. 580.)

1683/4: Appraisal of estate of John Gardiner by Richard Lewis, et. al. 21 Feb. 1683/4. (Chapman, *op. cit.,* p. 25.)

1687: On back of same pat. of 1667/8: Richard Lewis, now of Lower Norfolk, sells to John Campbell of Nansemond his share of sd. pat. 17 Feb. 1687/8. (Bodie, *op. cit.,* p. 601.)

1691: Will of Richard Lewis of Low. Par.: Wife Sarah, son Richard, plantation where Wm. Duck lives; son Thomas land rented James Cullie, dau. Ann, dau. Eliz., unborn child. Dtd. 13 Dec. 1691, rec. 26 Mar. 1692. (Chapman, *op. cit.,* p. 33.)

1696: Richard Lewis (III) wit. will of Thos. Moore, dtd. 28 Sept. 1696. (Chapman, *op. cit.,* p. 36-7.)

1704: Richard Lewis of Isle of Wight listed with 100 acs. on Quit Rent lists.

1711: Legacy to Elizabeth Lewis, dau. of Richard Lewis by Richard Reynolds of Newport Parish. (Chapman, *op. cit.,* p. 52.)

5. Thomas Lewis (D. 1670) Family Records:

1670: Appr. of estate of Thomas Lewis ordered 2 July 1670: Appr. by Geo. Hardy, John Snellock, Thos. Ward and John Allen. Presented by Mrs. Rebecca Lewis 9 Sept. 1670. (Chapman, *op. cit.,* p. 9.) Note: Rebecca was the dau. of Col. John George.

Admin. of estate of Thomas Lewis, who died intestate req. by relict Rebecca, 9 Aug. 1670. Securities: Lt. Col. John George, Morgan Lewis. Rec. 20 Oct. 1670. (Chapman, *op. cit.,* p. 68.) Note: Thos. Lewis had son John and dau. Joyce.

After Thos. Lewis' death Rebecca married Philip Pardoe.

1692: Will of John Lewis: Leg. to: Philip Brantley and his five children, sister, Joyce Brantley, Philip Pardoe, Eliz. Pardoe, my mother, Rebecca Pardoe to be exec. dtd. 1 Dec. 1692. (Chapman *op. cit.,* p. 34.)

6. Morgan Lewis (D. 1677) Family Records:

1666: Estate of Richard Jeffries appr. by John Snellock, Morgan Lewis, John Newman and Thos. Ward. dtd. 10 Sept. 1666. Chapman, *op. cit.,* p. 6.)

1676: Appr. of est. of Morgan Kanedy ord. 11 May 1676. Morgan Lewis sec. for Henry Goad who married the widow. (Chapman, *op. cit.,* p. 14.)

1676/7: Will of Morgan Lewis: Wife Sarah, dau. Sarah, my 3 daus. John Ingram. Dtd. 26 Jan. 1676/7. Wit. Geo. Hardy, Sr., Philip Pardoe. (Chapman, *op. cit.,* p. 15.)

1677: Appr. of est. of Morgan Lewis by Geo. Hardy, Sr., Richard Hansford and Philip Pardoe. 7 June 1677. Presented by Mrs. Sarah Lewis. Rec. 9 June 1577. (Chapman, *op. cit.,* p. 72.) Note: After the death of Morgan Lewis, Sarah married a Peddington. See will of Col. John George, (Chapman, *op. cit.,* p. 17.)

7. Thomas Lewis (D. 1672) Family Records:

1658: A Thomas Lewis (signed X) a member of a jury 20 July 1658. Other members were Thos. Taberer and Francis England et al. (Bodie *op. cit.,* p. 525-6.)

1672: Thomas Lewis died intestate Admin. req. by relict, Martha, 9 Dec. 1672. Sec. John Britt and Sgt. John Davis. (Chapman, *op. cit.,* p. 69.) Note: Thomas Lewis appears to have had at least one son, Anthony:

1679: Anthony Lewis, an orphan living with Joyce Cripps, mentioned in her will dtd. 18 Apr. 1679. (Chapman, *op. cit.,* p. 20.) Note; She was the wife of George Cripps and widow of Francis England.

1717: Will of Anthony Lewis dtd. 30 Sept. 1717: Wife Eliz., sons Thomas and Anthony - left his land on Blackwater. Execs: my wife and two sons. Rec. 23 July 1739. (Chapman, *op. cit.,* p. 136.)

1738: Est. of John Williams appr. by Anthony Lewis. Chapman, *op. cit.,* p. 133.)

1739: Est. of Anthony Lewis appr. 24 Sept. 1739. (Chapman, *op. cit.,* p. 136)

8: William Lewis Family Records:

1635: A William Lewis, age 26, was a passenger on the *Globe* leaving London for Va.
Note: This may apply to the Wm. Lewis later known as Maj. Wm. Lewis who was a surveyor. Nicholas Jernew, also a passenger with his family, was also a surveyor later.

1639/40: William Lewis appointed a viewer of tobacco in Isle of Wight Co. From Hamstead (Pagan) Pt. to Mr. Robt. Pitts. (Bodie, *op. cit.,* p. 172.)

1645/6: Approx. date of sale of land by Anthony Jones to Robt. Winchell, next to him and Wm. Lewis.(Bodie. *op. cit.,* p. 530.)

1650: John Upton sells John Valentine, planter, 100 acs. formerly held by Thos. Bush. 9 Jan. 1650/1. Wit. by Wm. Lewis. (Bodie, *op. cit.,* p. 519.)

1652: Will of John Valentine dtd. 8 May 1652 appts. John Marshall and Wm. Lewis as Executors. (Bodie, *op. cit.,* p. 518.)

1662/3: Wm. Lewis, late of this colony, appointed John Lewis his Exec. Probated req. 9 Feb. last. Rec. 23 Mar. 1662/3. Security: Mr. Andrews, Mr. Izard. (Chapman, *op. cit.,* p. 63.)

1669: John Lewis of Low. Parish sells to Joseph Bridger of same, 170 acs. in poss. of John Lewis and John Harris pat. 3. June 1635 by John Seward and ass'd to Thomas Huison (*sic* - should be Hinson) who sold to his father, Wm. Lewis, which is 300 acs. for 20,000 lbs. tobo. Land lying at White Marsh. dtd. 16 Nov. 1669. (Signed by John Lewis and Lettice Lewis.) (Bodie, *op. cit.,* pp. 556-7.) Note: Lettice is an unusual name and may have been a dau. of Epaphroditus and Lettice Lawson, who owned land in Up. Norfolk (Nansemond) and Isle of Wight Cos. near Wm. Lewis.

JOHN LEWIS, SON OF WM. LEWIS, RECORDS:
1651: (Approx. date) John Lewis and Thos. Walter wit. will of John Vasser, overseers James Pyland and Thos. Walter. (Bodie, *op. cit.,* p. 518.)

1665: John Lewis and Thos. Walter wit. power of Atty of Wm. Cook. 9 Apr. 1665. (Bodie, *op. cit.,* p. 538.)

1669: Sale of 170 acs. by John and Lettice Lewis to Jos. Bridger. See under Wm. Lewis above.

1676: John Lewis security with Sgt. John Davis for admin. of est. of Wm. Mason, 10 Apr. 1676. (Chapman, *op. cit.,* p. 71)

1677: John Lewis (signs "I"- same as on deed to Jos. Bridger) signs petition asking mercy for Wm. West, who was involved in Bacon's Rebellion. (Bodie, *op. cit.,* p. 163.)

1678: John Lewis, John Dunn, James Hunter and Thos. Poole appr. est. of John Vicars, whose will was wit. by Jos. Bridger and Toby Keeble. Rec. 8 June 1678. (Chapman, *op. cit.,* p. 16.)

1684: The estate of Francis Wrenn appr. by John Carroll, Timothy Fenn, Wm. Hutchins and John Lewis. Dtd. 14 Feb. 1684. (Chapman, *op. cit.,* p. 25.)

1688: The estate of James Hunter appr. by Wm. Pitt, John Lewis, Tobias Keeble. Rec. 6 June 1688. (Chapman, *op. cit.,* p. 29.)

1686: The will of James Hunter appts. Capt Thos. Godwin, Marcy Lewis and John Lewis to be assts. to his wife, Ann. Dtd. 2 Apr. 1686. Rec. 1 May 1688. (Chapman, *op. cit.,* p. 28.)

1689: The will of John Grave, a Quaker, left a legacy to John Lewis. Dtd. 10th day 10th month 1689. (Chapman, *op. cit.,* p. 32.)

1690: The will of John Lewis, dtd. 8 Aug. 1690, leaves legacies to his wife Ann and her three children: Wm. Macon, Mary Hawkins and Ann Surbe. It was aclnowledged in court by John Lewis on 9 Aug. 1690. (Chapman, *op. cit.,* p. 32.) Note: Apparently the filing of this will with the court was a condition of the marriage, but John Lewis seems to have stayed alive for another dozen years.

1702/3: Ann Lewis, wife of John Lewis, dec'd, makes her son, Wm. Mackond, atty to pay all her debts. 1 Feb. 1702/3. (Bodie, *op. cit.,* p. 649.)

1712/13: Appr. of estate of John Lewis by John Davis, John Munger, John Bidgood and John Harrison, dtd. 16 Feb. 1712/13. Ann Lewis, the widow, signed. (Chapman, *op. cit.,* p. 53)

9. William Lewis (D. 1684) Records

Note: Poss. a son of Wm. Lewis (D. 1662/3) He may be the William Lewis who owned land in Kingston Par. ca. 1664-1684 - see his Glouchestor Co. Records.

1671: Thos. and Eliz. Greenwood assn. 150 acs. on Seward's Cr., granted 28 July 1641, to John Jennings, 19 Aug. 1671. Wit. by Thos. Smith and Wm. Lewis. (Bodie, *op. cit.,* p. 562.)

1672: Will of Wm. Warren wit. by Timothy Fenn and Wm. Lewis, dtd. 24 Aug. 1672. (Chapman, *op. cit.,* p. 12.)

Wm. Lewis and Timothy Benn sec. for Admin. of will of Wm. Warren, Mr. Robert Kae his Executor. dtd. 24 Oct. 1672. (Chapman, *op. cit.,* p. 69.)

1674: After John (*sic*) Geenwood's death, his widow married James Pyland. Greenwood gave John (*sic*) Chitty, a relative, 50 acres. Eliz. is now married to John Edwards and they sell John Jennings 100 acs. Wit. by Timothy Fern (Fenn) John Davis and Wm. Lewis. (Re 1671 entry above) (Bodie, *op. cit.,* p. 571) Note: according to the will of Thos. Greenwood, dtd. 19 Mar. 1656, he left Valentine Chitty 50 acs. (Chapman, *op. cit.,* p. 3.)

1675: Appr. of estate of Richard Gross by Peter Banton, John Walton, Wm. Hittchens and Wm. Lewis. dtd. 23 Aug. 1675. (Chapman, *op. cit.,* p. 13.)

1682: John Wakefield and wife Sarah to Robt. Thomas: all rights to pat. of 1050 acs, dtd. 3 Feb. 1682. Wit. by Wm. Lewis and Valentine Chitty. (Bodie, *op. cit.,* p. 594.) Note: This land included 700 acs. pat. by Christopher Lewis - see his records below.

1682: Giles Linscott makes Francis Wren his atty. 9 Dec. 1682. Wit. by John Hole, Thos. Garry, John Shepard and Wm. Lewis. (Bodie, *op. cit.,* p. 594.)

1684: Will of Wm. Lewis dtd. 10 _ 1684: Wife Martha, Eldest dau. Mary, Second dau. Sarah. Robert Thomas Executor, children's guardians: Robt. Thomas and Wm. Evans. Rec. 1 May 1684. (Chapman, *op. cit.,* p. 24.)

1700: Approx. date filed - undated appr. of the est. of Wm. Lewis by James Browne, Thos. Grosse, James Hunter and John Watts. (Chapman, *op. cit.,* p. 42.)

10. Christopher Lewis (D. 1673/4) Records:

Note: Although ChristopherLewis mentioned no issue in his will, his records may be important in identifying some of the early Lewis families origins. He was a headright of John Upton, merchant of London, for land located near that of William Lewis. He was a vintner and may have been a member of the Vintner's Co. of London and appeared in its records. He had land on both sides of the Isle of Wight/ Surry Cos. line. where other Lewises were located. His tombstone, according to his will, should be located in the ruins of the old Southwark parish church in Surry Co. and may reveal additional information if ever excavated.

1635: Christopher Lewis is a headright for a pat. of John Upton for 1650 acs. on Pagan Pt. Cr., Isle of Wight Co. He is also mentioned again in a repat. of same land and another pat. for 1500 acs. adj. Ambrose Bennett's land. (Nugent, C. & P. I, pp. 25, 69, 99)

1649: Christopher Lewis pats. 400 acs. James City (later Surry) Co. at Blackwater on Eastmost Br, pointing up to Chipoakes Cr. bounded S. on land of Francis England.... (Nugent, C. & P. I, p. 183.)

1652: Christopher Lewis pats.750 acs., Isle of Wight Co. 26 July 1652. Abt. a mile to the Swd. of Henry White's plantation at the Blackwater. (Nugent, C. & P. I, p. 261.)

1661: Indenture 1 Mar. 1661/2 Betw. Christopher Lewis of Low. Par. Surry Co. and Bartholomew Owen: 200 acs. on west side of Gray's Cr. named the Great Level, adj. Jno. Watkins, orphan son of John Watkins, dec'd. eastward to land that Thos. Andrews holds of sd. Lewis, and north to Lewis himself, west to Col. Browne's orphans, being part of a division Chrstopher Lewis bought of Christopher Lawson. Wit. Geo. Jordan, Thos. Warren, Ro: Stanton. (Signed) Christopher Lewis, Jane Lewis. (E.T. Davis, Surry Co. Records 1652-1684, p. 39.)

1662: Barth. Owen of Gray's Cr. Southwarke Par. Surry Co. Gent., to Chris. Lewis, winecooper, certain livestock. (Davis, *ibid.,* p. 40.)

1662: Indenture betw. Christopher Lewis and Jane his wife of Southwarke Par. and Wm. Foreman for 60 acs. of land, part of a divident bought of Christopher Lawson, North to Barth. Owen, west to Ann Browne's and south to where Lewis now lives. Wit. John Corker. dtd. 25 Mar. 1662. (Davis, *op. cit.,* p. 40.)

1662: John Hux, planter, sells to Xpher Lewis a mare. 2 June 1662. (Davis, *op. cit.,* p. 40.)

1665/6: Gyles Linscott of Warrencock, Surry Co., shoemaker, sells to Christopher Lewis, winecooper, certain livestock. Wit. Geo. Watkin, Stephen Storeman. dtd. 3 Jan. 1665/6.

1667: Christopher Lewis makes bond with Christopher Lawson for a debt that Thomas Andrews shall have of Anthony Rossey. 31 June 1667.

1668: Roger Williams to pay Christopher Lewis 1730 lbs. tobo. Wit. Will Browns Richard Wilbacke.

1672/3: Power of Atty. fr. James Jones of Charles City to Wm. Sherwood to appear in all suits for him personally or as executor. Dtd. 4 Mar. 1672/3. Rec. 29 Jan. 1675/6.

1673: Will of Christopher Lewis, dtd. 1 Sept. 1673: To the church at Southwarke Parish a silver flagon of two quart measure. To Wm. Thompson, minister, 1500 lbs. tobo. to be paid in 1675. To four godchildren: Solomon Davis in Isle of Wight Co.; Luke Measell; Katherine Owen; Christopher Moring. to Jno. Carr; To Roger Williams his son, young Roger; Christopher; to Mary Jones, dau. of James Jones, cooper; to the orphan of Mr. Thomas Harris, sunken marsh mill, he now living with David Williams at ye mouth of Chipoakes Cr.; to the surgeon (chyrurgian) that hath cured Samuel Maggot's dau. ; To Wm. Thompson, son of Mr. Wm. Thompson; and to (his) sister, Katherine Thompson; to Charles Beckett. Desires to be buried in the chancel &: exers. to lay a tombstone over me.... Exer. James Jones. Prob. 7 Apr. 1674. Wit. Will. Foorman, Jno. Charles, Jno. Corker. (E. T. Davis, Wills and Admins. of Surry Co., Va. 1671 - 1750, pp. 110-111.)

1674: Probate of Christopher Lewis' will, by James Jones, given at James City by Sir Wm. Berkeley, Knt., Governor. dtd. 7 Apr. 1674.

1673: Wm. Thompson, clerk, and Katherine his wife to John Salway, both of Surry Co. for 6000 lbs. tobo sell that parcel of land commonly called Christo. Lewis nigh the church at the head of Gray's Cr. guessed to be about 70 acs., bounded E. by line of marked trees running through Andrew's his old field. S. by swamp which parts sd. land fr. John Whitson's land. W. is bounded by a valley running betwixt Wm. Foreman's and the sd. land. N. with young Luke Mizell's line of marked trees. Dtd. 1 Aug. 1673. Wit. Wm. Corker, Wm. Parker, Geo. Watkins, Mathias Marriott, Thos. Andrews (E. T. Davis, *op. cit.,* p. 85.)

Note: Surry Co., Va. Lewis Records:

There are very few Lewis records in Surry Co. after the death of Christopher Lewis. A Stephen Lewis appears on a list of pardoned rebels dtd. 6 Feb. 1676; Stephen Lewis buys land from John Price 3 July 1677; He sells the 50 acs. of land and a mullato boy to Wm. Edwards in Nov. 1677 along with a horse to John Edwards. (Davis, Surry Co. Records 1652-1684, pp. 102, 104, 105.) In the list of tithables taken June 10, 1674, two Lewises appear: Thomas Lewis, charged with one tith. and Henry Lewis, a tithable of James Redick. Both have vanished from the next list (of 1678) and do not reappear. (Bodie, Colonial Surry, pp. 186 ff.)

Note: Since Bodie did not publish the list for each year, the original record books should be checked. Only two other Lewis wills or estates are listed in Wills and Administrations of Surry Co., Va. 1671 - 1750, by Eliza. Timberlake Davis, p. 111: The Estate admin. of Morgan Lewis filed by Patrick Maygaratery 18 Feb. 1718, and signed by Sam and Jno Judkins and Wm. Thompson. He may have been from an Isle of Wight family. The other is the will of Richard Lewis (Dtd 18 Mar. 1732/3 and Prob. 17 Sep 1735.) He appears to be ident. with the Richard Lewis of Isle of Wight who is not mentioned in those records after 1711. He leaves legacies to Sarah Tyas, dau. of John and Ann ; and to Wm. Simmons and Capt. Thomas Edmonds. In the Isle of Wight and Surry records, however, he appears to have had at least two daus., Elizabeth and Mary; and some of the Lewises who start to appear in the North Carolina records may have been his.

CHARTS OF ISLE OF WIGHT COUNTY, VIRGINIA LEWIS FAMILIES

1. Arthur Lewis (d. 1671)
   = _____
   | She = (2)
   | Toby Keeble
   John (1663-1700)
   = _____
   3 children
   ├── Arthur
   ├── Mary
   └── Sarah

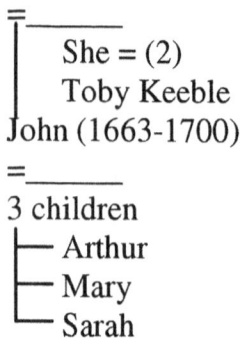

2. Benedict Lewis
   (d. 1675)
   = Hannah
   Estate appr.
   by Toby Keeble et. al.
   (D.S.P.?)

3. Daniel Lewis
   (d. 1698)
   = Sarah, dau. of
   | Richard Benett
   | (Nephew of Gov.)
   └── Daniel

4. Richard Lewis (d.1667)
   = (?) dau of a Miles?
   | of Chuckatuck, Nan. Co.
   | (Adj. White Marsh,
   | Isle of Wight Co.)
   | Issue:
   ├── Miles Lewis - no further records
   └── Richard Lewis - of Lower Norfolk Co. in 1688
        d. 1691
        = Sarah
   ┌──────┬──────┬──────┐
   Richard   Thos.   Eliza   Ann

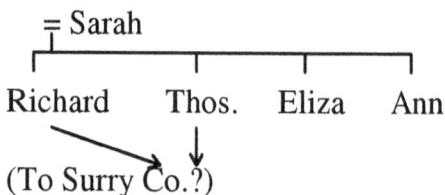

   (To Surry Co.?)

5. Thomas Lewis
   (d. 1670)
   = _____
   | Dau. of
   | Lt. Col.
   | John George
   | She = (2)
   | Philip Pardoe
   ┌────────────┐
   John   Joyce
   (D.S.P.)

6. Morgan Lewis
   (d. 1677)
   = Sarah
   | Dau. of
   | Lt. Col.
   | J. Geo.
   | 3 daus:
   ├─Sarah
   │
   └

7. Thos. Lewis
   (d. 1672)
   = Martha
   |
   └── Anthony
        (will dated 1717
        but filed 1739)
        (mentioned as Orphan
        1679 in will of Joyce
        Cripps, widow of Francis
        England.)
        = Eliza
   ┌──────────┐
   Thomas   Anthony
   (sons left land on Blackwater)

8. William Lewis (d 1662) of Isle of Wight Co., Va.
   = _____
   |
   John (d. ca. 1700) (?)
   = (1) Lettice (Lawson?)
   = (2) Marcy
   = (3) Ann Macon, (widow of Neal)
   Isle of Wight.
   (John Lewis filed his will with
   the court in 1690, but the
   appraisal was not filed until 1712, one week prior to her
   son's and son-in-law's.)

9. William Lewis (Jr.)?
   (d. 1685)
   = Martha
   | Issue:
   └──────────┐
   Mary and Sarah only
   ones mentioned in
   his will.

11. Thomas Lewis, Sr. (D. 1725?) Family Records Of Prince George County, Virginia

1704: Thomas Lewis Sr. owned 200 acs. Pr. Geo. Co. (Note: Pr. George Co. was formed in 1703 from what had been the area of Charles City Co. south of the James River. (des Cognats, Eng. Dupl. of Lost Va. Records, p. 225.) He may be identical with the Thomas Lewis in the 1674 Surry Co. tithable list.

1714: 13 Sept.: Thos Lewis of Bristol Par. Pr. Geo. Co. deeds his son, John Lewis, 100 acs. adj. the Appomatox Riv. pt. now in poss. of sd. John Lewis and pt. in poss. of John Chapman.

1716: Will of Thos. Lewis dtd. 14 Oct. but not probated until 13 July 1725, mentions grandson, Edward Lewis, granddau. Ann Lewis and son John Lewis, leaving the latter the 100 acs, on which he now lives.

1717: 19 July; Thos. Lewis named as owner of land adj. land sold by Wm. Gower to Lewis Green on east side of city Cr. Bristol Parish, Pr. Geo. Co.

1717: 10 Sep.: Thos. Lewis acquited from paying levy for the future.

1718: 11 Aug.: Wm. Mitchel and wife Kath. deed Stith Bolling of Surry Co, 100acs. called "Simmons" S. side Appomatox Riv. adj. Thomas Lewis Sr., et al.

1725: Prob. date of death of Thos, Lewis, Sr, Will probated 13 July.

Thomas Lewis (Jr.) Records:

1714: 13 Sep.: Estate account of Thomas Lewis recorded by Susan Lewis, widow and relict. Children:

    Thomas (D. Feb. 1725/6)

    Edward (D. 1738/9)

    Ann

    Honour: = (Edward)? Woodlief (Jr.) Note: Mr. John Woodlief owned land in Charles City Co. S. side of the James Riv. adj. the pat, of James Mumfort in 1689. (Nugent, C. & P. II, p. 333.)

1725/6: Will of Thomas Lewis (III) dtd. 4 Feb. 1725/6 and prob. 8 Feb. 1725/6 mentions only sister Honour Woodlief and dau. Elizabeth.

John Lewis (D. 1754) Records:

    Children and birthdates fr. the Bristol Parish Register:

        Elizabeth: b. 22 Nov. 1705

        Mary: b. 12 June 1707

        Ann: b. 16 Apr. 1710

        John: b. 26 Sept. 1711

        William: b. 22 Apr. 1718

        Frances: b. 11 Feb. 1715/16

Susan: b. 11 Apr. 1718
Thomas: b. 29 Apr. 1720

1716.   22 Nov.: Survey for John Lewis, 251 acs. N. side of Nottoway Riv. & Upper side of Buckskin Cr.

1718:   14 July: John Lewis pats. 251 acs. N. side Nottoway Riv. and upper side of Buckskin Cr. (Nugent, C. & P. III, p. 208.)

1719:   13 July: John Lewis of Bristol Par., Pr. Geo. Co. deeds Richard Bland of Westover Parish land granted to sd. John Lewis 14 July 1718: 251 acs. N. side of Nottoway Riv. & Upper side of Buckskin Cr., at mouth of Cr. Rec. 14 July 1719.

1724:   28 Jan.: Survey for John Lewis, 100 acs. N. side of Nottoway River.

1728:   3 Feb.: John Lewis pats. 100 acs. (New Land) Pr. Geo. Co. N. side of Nottoway River. (Nugent, C. & P. III, p. 350.)

1754:   4 Nov.: Will of John Lewis mentions grandson, John; daus.: Mary, Ann and Susanna; wife Mary. Prob. 9 Mar. 1758. Note: Wife Mary was probably the dau. of Richard Moore, who mentioned his dau. Mary Lewis in his will of 1727.

Note: The above references which are not cited are from the Pr. George Co. Records quoted in Cook; *Pioneer Lewis Families*, Vol. IV, pp. 61-2, 70-1; and Vol. V, pp. 39-40, 42.

II. LEWIS FAMILIES ON THE
NORTH SIDE
OF THE
JAMES RIVER

1. Records Of John Lewis (1611 - ca. 1673) Of Warwick County, Virginia:

1634: John Lewis, age 23, passenger on the *Merchant Bonaventure* to Va. 2 Jan. 1634. (P. Coldham, Compl. Bk. of Emigration, 1607-1660, pp. 121-22.)

1635 and 1637: John Lewis, headright of Wm. Spenser at Lawne's Ck. (Nugent, C. & P. I, pp. 28 & 81.) (A Francis Spenser was also a fellow passenger to Va.)

1642: John Lewis, headright of Capt. Samuel Mathews, Esqr. for 3,000 acs. 20 Aug. 1642, butting upon Warwick Riv. West, somewhat South. Bounded on North with Potash Quarter Cr., Adj. Christopher Boyce. (Nugent: C. & P. I, p. 133.)

1647: 22 June: Ordered that the suite depending betweene James Merryman and John Lewis concerning the rent of the land and the spoyle of the orchard belonging unto John Radish, whose atty the sd. Merryman is, be dismist, he, the said Lewis to pay all the court charges... (Virginia Genealogist 1957, Vol. I, No. 2, p. 61: [10 pages of Warwick Co. Ct. Orders at Wm. & Mary Lib.])

1647: John Lewis and Richard Wooton pat. 100 acs. Warwick Co. 30 Aug. 1647, next to the head of Deep Cr. upon Shotball Quarter, adj. James Merryman. Due by purchase from said Merryman. Note: Preceding pat. reads: John Williams pats. 150 acs. Warwick Co. 30 Aug. 1647. Next the head of Deep Cr. adj. James Merryman. Part of a pat. granted unto John Rodis (Rode) who assigned same to sd. Merryman. (Nugent, C. & P. I, p. 169.)
Rode's pat. is as follows: John Rode, 1,000 acs. Warwick Co. 27 July 1645: At the head of Deep Cr. adj. Christosher Boyse. Due by purchase of survey and rights fr. Wm. Edwards who first bought the same of sd. Boyce. (Nugent, C. & P. I, p. 156-7.) (Note: a Katherine Lewis was claimed by Boyse in several of his patents as a headright.)

1663: John Lewis pats. 137 acs. Warwick Co. 10 Dec. 1663. Beginning at Cuckold's Quarter, S. on land of Col. Mathews N.E. on Main Br. of Sd. Quarter. E. toward lands of John Hayward and W. on land of Col. (Miles) Cary.

1663 (or 1665) 21 Oct.: John Lewis - his wife this day refusing to take the oath of allegience being tendered her - is committed into the sheriffs custody to remain close prisoner until she takes the oath.

John Lewis - his wife absenting herself from church - is fined fifty lbs. of tobacco. (Va. Genealogist Vol. 18, No. 4, 1974, p. 287: One page of Warwick Co. Orders taken by a Union Soldier, 1862.)

1673: Approx. date of death of John Lewis of Warwick Co., estimated from the bequest of 1,000 lbs. of tobacco to the widow of John Lewis by Maj. Gen. Richard Bennett, former gov. and Quaker convert who left bequests to several Quaker families in his will dtd. 15 Mar. 1674, proved 12 Apr. 1675 in Nansemond Court and copy probated in England 3 Aug. 1676. (In: Bodie, J.B.; Seventeenth Cent. Isle of Wight, pp. 286-8.)

1678: Mr. John Mathews, 2944 acs. Warwick Co., Denbigh Par., 29 Mar. 1678. p. 641. Beg. on NW side of Deepe Cr; by old feild where Jno. Lewis lived; to an old feild called "Shortbolt" adj. Jno. Lewis downe Pouash Cr. to the mouth: downe Warwick River, & c. Granted Samuel Mathews, Esqr. & due said John as being his grandsonn & heir. (Nugent, C. & P. II, p. 183.)

1682: Mr. Miles Cary, 1590 acs., Warwick Co., 20 Nov. 1682, p. 201. Beg. in Farmers Feild, on Back Cr. Run; by Clayborne Neck Damms; on Mr. Hen. Cary, neer Poquoson Mill Path; neer the Orway Sw; neer N. side of Oken Sw; to John Lewis, by main br. of Potash Run; on Capt. John Matthews, to Col. Cole's; to Lahour and Vaine Feild; on land of Thomas Cary, in possession of his mother Mrs. Ann Cary; neer the Dead Cow branch; neer Druit's old feild; to Magpye Sw; to thicket parting Hattlie's old feild from Brown's &c. 750 acs. being part of 1050 acs. granted Zachary Cripps, dec'd., 10 Sept. 1645, & by his son Zachary sold to Col. Miles Carey, dec'd., who bequeuathed to his son, Miles in fee simple. (Nugent C. & P. II, p. 247.)

Note: Neither Warwick Co. nor its records exist today. Its area is included in the city of Newport News.

2. John Lewis Of Henrico Co. (D. 1688) Family Records:

Note: The founder of this family was possibly the William Lewis who is listed as a headright of Rice Hoe (How) for 300 acs. James City Co. 4 June 1639, S. on his own land E. on David Jones. (Nugent, C. & P. I, p. 110.) He is probably the same Wm. Lewis that appears in several headright lists with Lyddy (Lydia) How. (Nugent, C. & P. I, pp. 393, 426, 444, 468.) He was probably the original owner of the land listed as Lewis' in the pat. of Mr. James Haley in 1684: Mr. James Haley pats. 593 acs. James City Co. 26 Apr. 1684, 493 acs. adj. Jones at the lower end of Long Thicket, adj. Ellerbies, Dobyes, Wolfes, LEWIS', and Phillips' lines. 100 acs. by the cow or rowling path along Mr. Philips' line to Mr. Freeman. (Nugent, C. & P. II, p. 281.) The Ellerby pat. is: Edward Ellerby pats. 100 acs. James City Co. 16 Apr. 1683, fr. James River, along Mrs. Nowell's line, granted Wm. Havent 20 Oct. 1661 (Nugent, C. & P. II, p. 258.) Doby's pat. is: John Doby pats. 352 acs. James City Co. 16 Apr. 1683, fr. Ellerbies' line to Drinkards line to Mt. Sinai bridge, pt. of 600 acs. granted Wm. Havent 20 Oct. 1661. (Nugent, C. & P. II, p. 258.) The Mrs. Nowell mentioned in the Ellerbie pat. was Lydia How, who had married Jonathan Nowell (Noell.) On 15 Apr. 1690, Lydia Nowell, widow, pat. 1752 acs. James City Co. sd. land granted to Wm.

Fry viz.: 750 acs. 17 Apr. 1653, 252 acs. 6 Feb. 1655 (part of Rice Hoe pat.) and 750 acs. pat. 29 Apr. 1656. Land escheated for want of heirs of his son, Joseph Fry. (Nugent, C. & P. II, p. 345. William Lewis, son of John Lewis (D. 1688) appears to have sold this Lewis land at about the same time, as he was a burgess for James City Co. by virtue of owning this freehold. See his records.

1662: Jno. Lewis and Thomas Michell pat. 1680 acs. New Kent Co. 15 Jan. 1662. Beg. at Mr. Michells land, N.N.E. by Westover path to Col. Gooch's Cor. tree. (Nugent, C. & P. I, p. 422.) Note: This land appears to have been on the boundary of James City & New Kent Cos. fr. the 1664 pat. of Thos. Michael for 740 acs. James City Co. On Brs. of Chickahominy swp. beg. in line of Gooch and Pullum... (Nugent, C. & P. I, p. 485.) Then the 1665 pat. of Robt. Jarrett (Garrett) along line of Mr. Thos. Michell... betw. Westover path & path leading to Mr. Jonathan Newell's. (Nugent, C. & P. I, p. 475.) (Note: It is possible the John Lewis in this pat. is John Lewis of Poropotanck Ck. & Glost. Co.)

1672: A pat. for Thos. Mitchell, planter, for 2436 acs. dtd. 28 Feb. 1682/3, beg. by Mr. Robert Jarrett... pt. land granted 15 Jan. 1662 and pt. granted John Lewis and sd. Mitchell same day, which sd. Lewis his pt. sold to sd. Mitchell & acknowledged same in the Co. Ct. of New Kent 28 Feb. 1672. (Nugent, C. & P. II, p. 253.)

1673: 7 Nov.: John Rogers & John Lewis pat. 400 acs. Henrico Co. N. side James riv. adj. Wm. Humpphries, E. side Mill Run. (Nugent, C. & P. II, p. 141.)

1678: John Lewis, along with John Pleasants et al. sign a petition to His Majesty's Commissioner for Va. from the inhabitants of Henrico Co. (Cal. of State Papers, Col. 1677 - 1680, America and the West Indies, p. 48.)

1678/9: 24 Feb.: An inventory of the estate of Hugh Mackmyell taken by Wm. Humphries and John Lewis.

1679: 2 June: John Lewis listed with three tithables at a court held at Varina for Henrico Co.

1685: 1 Apr.: Sarah, wife of John Lewis, aged about 40, deposed there was a boar running about their plantation which Thos. Holms laid claim to and so did Henry May. (Henrico Co. Record Bk. I, 1677-1692, p. 314.)

1688: 2 Apr.: Petition of Wm. Lewis for probate of last will & Test. of John Lewis, dec'd. Granted. (Henrico Orders 1678-1693, p. 266.)

1688: 1 Aug.: Samuel Trotman, who married the widow & relict of John Lewis, declared that Wm. Lewis, Execr. would not permit him to make use of his sd. pt. of land, fencing, etc. (*ibid.*, p. 281.)

1689: 2 Dec.: Thos. Cocke and Wm. Randolph divided the personal estate of John Lewis into three parts and delivered one-third unto the widow, one-third unto Wm. Lewis, son &

Execr. and one-third due Sarah, the dau. of sd. dec'd. to Wm. Lewis, her guardian. (Henrico Co. Rec. Bk. 5, 1688-1697, p. 105.)

William Lewis (D. 1706) Records:

1687: 21 Oct.: Mr. Robt. Woodson, Sr.; Mr. John Woodson, Sr.; Wm. Lewis and Thos. Charles pat. 470 acs. Henrico Co., Varina Parish, N. side James Riv....on W. Br. of Deep Run... (Nugent, C. & P. II, p. 314.)

1688: 1 Dec.: Wm. Lewis, Exer. of John Lewis dec'd. petitions for the tuition of Sarah Lewis, his sister, now an orphan of about a dozen or thirteen years. (Henrico Co. Order Bk. & Wills 1678-1693, p. 290.)

1689: 1 Aug.: Wm. Lewis, aged about 28 yrs. gives a deposition concerning a horse race at Malvern Hills. (Henrico Co. record bk. 5, 1688-1697, p. 75.)

1691: 17 Apr.: List of Burgesses: Henry(sic) Bray and Wm. Lewis, Burgesses for James City Co. (Va. Hist. Mag. V. 13, p. 94.) Note: the first name is later corrected to James Bray.

1692: 16 Apr.: List of Burgesses for session begun 1 Apr.: James City Co.: Henry Duke and William Lewis - question was raised as to his eligibility, as since the last session he had sold his freehold in James City Co., but the House voted that he retain his seat. (Va. Hist. Mag. V. 15, pp. 437-8.)

1704: Va. Quit Rent List: Wm. Lewis of Henrico Co. listed with 350 acs. (L. des Cognets, Jr., Engl. Dupl. of Lost Va. Records, p. 218.)

1706: 24 Dec.: Nunc. will of Wm. Lewis: Home plantation- 100 acs. purchased of Wm. Porter, Jr. and 100 acs. on N. side of White Oak Swp to eldest son, John. 200 acs. on three Run & a parcel on White Oak Swp. & Deep Run to be divided betw. them to sons William and Joseph. All residue of estate to wife... Presented by Eliz. Lewis, relict of the deceased Wm. Lewis. Proved by Geo. Payne and Eliz. Johnson to be words spoken by sd. Wm. Lewis the day before he died. Rec. 1 May 1707. (Henrico Co. Deeds & Wills 1706-1709, p. 34.)

CHART OF JOHN LEWIS (D. 1688) FAMILY OF HENRICO CO.

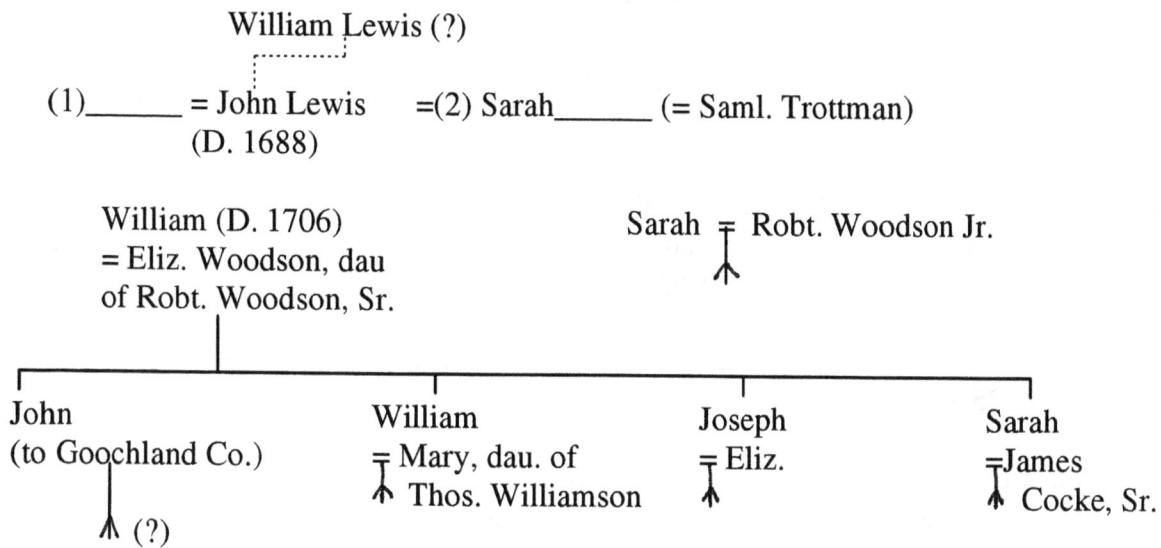

William Lewis (?)

(1)_____ = John Lewis   =(2) Sarah_____ (= Saml. Trottman)
                (D. 1688)

William (D. 1706)   Sarah = Robt. Woodson Jr.
= Eliz. Woodson, dau
of Robt. Woodson, Sr.

John   William   Joseph   Sarah
(to Goochland Co.)   = Mary, dau. of   = Eliz.   =James
                          Thos. Williamson   Cocke, Sr.
          (?)

III. LEWIS FAMILIES ON THE
SOUTH SIDE
OF THE
YORK RIVER

1. Records Of Henry Lewis (D. 1696) Of York And Eliz. City Co., Virginia:

1665: Elizabeth Lewis, Dau. of Henry and Ann, b. 29 July. Chas. Par. York Co., Va. (L.C. Bell, Chas. Par., York Co. Hist. and Reg., p. 125.)

1669: Henry Lewis, son of Henry and Ann, b. 10 Oct. Chas. Par. York Co., Va. (L.C. Bell, *ibid.,* p. 125.)

1671: Thomas Lewis, son of Henry and Ann, bapt. 6 June. Chas. Par. York Co. Va (L.C. Bell, *ibid.*, p. 125.)

1674: Ann Lewis, dau of Henry and Ann, b. 19 Nov. Chas. Par. York Co., Va. (L.C. Bell, *ibid.,* p. 125.)

1677: Ann Lewis, Wife of Henry, Died 28 Oct. Chas. Par. York Co., Va. (L.C. Bell, *ibid.,* p. 125.)

1688: Will of Henry Fason (Vandonerick) dtd. 23 Apr., leaves Henry Lewis the plantation Henry Lewis is seated upon for life. (Will was probated 26 Feb. 1693/4.) York Co., Va. Deeds etc., No. 9, p. 305. (Note: Henry Forson Vandeavoratt pat. 504 acs. York Co., Va. New Poquoson Par. 29 Apr. 1692 - Repat. of land bought 1675 and land pat. 1666. Adj. Owen Davis et al. - Owen Davis land adj. David Lewis - See his records. [Nugent, C. & P. II, pp. 376, 384.])

1688: Estate account of Garden (Gordon) Giggots by Henry Lewis, Recorded 10 Sept. 1692, Eliz. City Co., Va. (R.C. Neal, Eliz. City Co., Va. Deeds, Wills, Court Orders etc., 1634, 1659, 1688-1702, p. 25.)

1691: Henry Lewis sued Mr. James Slater in an action of trespass for marking a bull yearling which belonged to him. 3 witnesses swore it was plt.'s. Bull yearling ruled property of plt. Slater ordered to pay his witness, James Jenkins. Lewis ordered to pay his witnesses: John Sandiford, Gray, and Thos. Wollston. (J. Dorman, York Co., Va. Deeds, Orders, Wills, Etc. No. 9, 1691-1694, Pt. 1, p. 4.)

1692: Judgement granted ag. Henry Lewis for 300 lbs. tobo. to Capt. Campbell for Attorny's fees, sd. Lewis and Wm. Armistead, the same being in lieu of a greater claim payable to Campbell. (R.C. Neal, *ibid.,* p. 85.)

1692: 10 Sep.: Henry Lewis, Exectr. of Gordon Giggotts, dec'd, produced his account of the estate. He has paid to the several creditors 1504 lbs. of tobo. beyond assets. Whereas Lewis having had cattle in his custody and three of them are left, he is willing to allow the tobo. in lieu of the cattle. Ordered that Lewis give bond for payment. (R.C. Neal, *ibid.,* p. 87.)

1693: 29 Sept.: Ordered that Geo. Bland pay 40 lbs. tobo. to Mary Dawson for one day's attendance as evidence for him ag. Henry Lewis. (R.C. Neal, *op. cit.,* p. 105.) George Eland, suing Henry Lewis for assault and battery. A trial by jury was held. Jury finds for the plt. Six pence damage with costs. (R.C. Neal, *ibid.,* p. 108.)

1693: Judgement granted ag. Henry Lewis for 100 lbs. tobo. to John Smith, blacksmith. Due plt. for mending Lewis' gun. Lewis complains that repairs are not proper and plt. is ordered to amend or fix the gun with costs at exon. (R.C. Neal, *ibid.,* p. 119.)

1694: It is ordered that Wm. Waterson serve as Constable in the room of Henry Lewis, and that he repair to the next Magistrate to be sworn. (R.C. Neal, *ibid.,* p. 135.)

1694: 18 Sept.: Orphans Court: Henry Lewis renders an account of the horses and mares of Garden Giggotts, dec'd. Vizt: 1 Mare 4 years old: 1 mare 2 years old; 1 mare 2 years (R.C. Neal, *ibid.,* p. 138.)

1694: Guardianship of the orphan John Giggots and his estate removed from Henry Lewis and given to Francis Rogers. (R.C. Neal, *ibid.,* p. 145.)

1694: Guardianship of the orphan Edward Giggotts and his estate removed from Henry Lewis and given to Abraham Parrish. (R.C. Neal, *ibid.,* p. 145)

1696: Henry Lewis died 12 Dec. Chas. Par. York Co., Va. (L.C. Bell, *op. cit.,* p. 229.)

SOURCES:

L.C. Bell, *Charles Parish, York Co., Va. Hist. & Reg.* 1932. pp. 125, 228-9.

J. F. Dorman, *York Co., Va. Deeds, Etc.* No. 9, pt. 1, 1976. p. 4; pt. 2, 1977, p. 84.

R. C. Neal, *Eliz. City Co., Va. (Hampton) Deeds, Wills, Court Orders, Etc.* 1986, Heritage Books, Inc.

2. Roger Lewis Of York Co. (D. 1657):

(?) 1624/5: Roger Lewis, age 19, Mrs. Mary Maddison's muster, to Va. May 1617 in the *Edwin* at Shirlow (Shirley) Hundred. (In J. Dorman, Adventures of Purse and Person, p. 14.)

1636: Roger Lewis, headright of Issabel Thresher, widow of Robert Thresher, 16 Feb. 1636, for 450 acs. upon the Back Cr. of New Poquoson Riv., N. upon Thos. Brice. (Nugent, C. & P. I, p. 54.)

1657: Will of Roger Lewis dtd. 20 Apr. 1657: Appoints Humphrey Thompkins as guardian of his three minor children. (York Co. Wills Bk. I, p. 112.) (Inventory, dtd. 10 Sep 1658, lists movable goods at a value of 5 lbs: 14s:8p.)

1659: Account of cattle belonging to orphans of Roger Lewis, by Hump. Tomkins: 10 cows, 1 old bull, 3 heifers, 7 calves, (1 pr. to John Parsons and Isaak Embry for bringing one of the above and one of the wild gang.) 2 old cows and 2 calves dead last winter, 2 barrows 2 years old. 10 Sept. 1659. Humph. Tomkins. (B. Weisiger, York Co., Va. Records 1659-1661, p. 8.)

1660: Account of the cattle of the orphans of Roger Lewis brought in by Humphrey Tomkins 10 Sept. 1660. (B. Weisiger, York Co., Va. Records 1659-61, p. 42.)

1661: A grant of 600 acres in Charles River (York) Co., on the south side of New Poquoson bound on one side by Ray's Ck. and on the east by the bay, was originally granted to Wm. Brocas, who assn. to Humphrey Lloyd, Gent. who assn. to Robt. Lucas, who assn. to Capt. Thos. Burbage, who assn. to Crist. Calthorpe. On 13 Jan. 1661/2, Christopher Calthorpe appointed attys. to deliver the pat. of 600 acres, late in the occupation of Roger Lewis, and after his decease in occupation of Humphrey Tomkins, exec. of sd. Lewis, to William Hay, Gent. (York Co., Va. Records 1659 - 1662, B. Weisiger, comp., pp. 120-1.)

Note: this land was known as "Lewis Neck." See pat. of Capt. Wm. Hay for 1695 acs. 16 Dec. 1663. (Nugent, C. & P. I, p. 503.)

Roger Lewis Jr. (d. 16 Mar. 1693 York Co.) (Chas. Par. Reg.)
= (1) Ann (d. York Co. 16 July 1688) (Chas. Par. Reg.)
    Issue: Roger, bapt. 29 Sep 1678; d. 3 May 1689 (Chas. Par. Reg.)
        Charles, bapt. 8 May 1680 (not listed in div. of estate 26 Mar. 1694)
        Ann, bapt. 6 May 1682
        Eliz., bapt. 25 Feb. 1683
        Elinor, bapt. 15 Oct. 1688 (Chas. Par. Reg.)

= (2) Mary
    Issue: Sarah, bapt. 16 Feb. 1691; d. 28 Aug. 1693

1694: Order for a probate of the nuncupative will of Roger Lewis was granted unto Richard Hunt, hee being appoynted trustee per the will which was proved By Wm. Hawthorne, Geo. Holloway and Elliner Morgan. It is further ordered that Capt. Dannll. Taylor, Mr. Armiger Wade and Mr. Willm. Wise on 30 instant devide the estate. (J. Dorman, York Co., Va. Deeds, Orders, Wills, Etc. No. 9. 1691-1694, Pt. Two, p. 88.)

1694: Orphans of Roger Lewis Jr. Division of Estate. Made by order of 26 March 1694: To Ann Lewis; To Elizabeth Lewis: To Elliner Lewis. (Signed) Dannll. Taylor, Armiger Wade, Wm. Wise. Presented in court 24 May 1694. (J. Dorman, York Co., Va. Deeds, Orders, Wills, Etc., No. 9. 1691-1694, Pt. Two, p. 109.)

3. David Lewis (D. 1669) York Co., Va. Records:

1638: David Lewis, headright of Thos. Symonds, 2 Mar. 1638, for 250 acs. Upper Co. of New Norfolk (Nansemond) E. on Nansemond Riv. (Nugent, C. & P. I, p. 103.)

1648: Will of Richard Simons. Dtd. 13 July 1647. Prob. 11 Nov. 1648. Mentions his brother, Thomas Simons, dec'd. Wit: Davy (X) Lewis. (B. Fleet, Va. Col. Abs. Vol. 3., 1988 Ed., p. 115. York Co. 1648-1657.)

1650: David Lewis, son of David, b. 21 Oct. 1650. (L.C. Bell, Charles Parish, York Co., Va. Hist. & Reg. 1648-1789, p. 125.)

1659: David (W) Lewis signed a jury inquest re a maid servant of Anthony Franklin of New Poqoson, Margaret Wynn, who hanged herself. 7 June 1659. (B. Weisiger, York Co., Va. Records, 1659-1661, p. 13.)

1663: John Lewis, son of David by Mary, b. 19 June 1663. (L.C. Bell, *op. cit.*, p. 125.)

1666/7: David Lewis impanelled as a member of a Grand Jury, 24 Jan. 1666/7. (B. Weisiger, York Co., Va. Records, 1665-1672, p. 53.)

1669: David Lewis died 8 Feb. 1669. (Charles Parish Register.)

1670: Will of David Lewis of New Poquoson Par., York Co. - To son John Lewis, all my land extending to the land of Christopher Garlington. To son David Lewis, housing, orchards and plantation I live on, to Richard Center's line. To wife Mary to live on land of my son David for Widowhood. If my sons die under age, then land to my wife for life, then to my friend John Knapton. Mares to my wife and sons. Sons not to divide estate until age 21. Executors: Wife and friend John Knapton. Wit.: James Turner, Richard Center (R), Edmund Watts. Signed David (U) Lewis. Recorded 10 Nov. 1670.

David Lewis Jr. Records:

1650: David Lewis b. 21 Oct. 1650? (Date partially illegible) (York Co. - Charles Parish Register.)

1685: David Lewis pats. 217 acs. N. side dams parting York & Warwick Cos., includes 99 acs. purchased by his father, David Lewis. Adj. Owen Davis. 20 Apr. 1685. (Nugent, C. & P. II., p. 288.)

1685: David Lewis sells 50 acs. 16 Sept. 1685, formerly Thos. Lilbourne's, to John Aires. (wit. by Gilbert & Joane Lewis) (York Co. Deeds, Wills and Orders, Bk 8, pp. 66-67.)

1688: Sarah Lewis, dau. of David by Ann, b. 28 Jan. 1688 (d. 28 Aug. 1693.) L.C. Bell, *op. cit.*, pp. 125, 229.)

1690/1: David Lewis, son of David by Ann, b. 29 Jan. 1690/1. (d. 2 May 1703.) L.C. Bell, *op. cit.*, pp. 125, 228.)

1690/1: A judgement was granted against David Lewis for Col. Lawrence Smith for 650 lbs. tobo. due per bill of 22 Jan. 1689/90. (York Co. Deeds, Wills, Orders Bk. 9, p. 2. 24 Feb. 1690/1.)

1692: John Lewis, son of David by Ann, b. 31 Aug. 1692. (L.C. Bell, *op. cit.*, p. 125.)

1700: Elias Lewis, son of David and Ann, b. 24 Nov. 1700. (L.C. Bell, *op. cit.*, p. 125.)

1702: Death of David Lewis 9 Mar. 1702. L.C. Bell, *op. cit.*, p. 228.

John Lewis, Son Of David Lewis, Sr. Records:

1663: John Lewis, son of David by Mary, b. 19 June 1663.1663. L.C. Bell, *op. cit.*, p. 125.)

1688: John Lewis, son of John by Jane, b. 1 Mar. 1688. (L.C. Bell, *op. cit.*, p. 125.)
Note: According to Tyler's Quarterly, Vol. 22, p. 167, John Lewis married Jane Mackintosh, dau. of Enos and Elizabeth Mackintosh of Charles Parish, York Co. and had one son. After the death of John, she married a Nobling, poss. Thos. Nobling, listed on the 1704 Quit Rent list of King and Queen Co., Va.

1688: Mr. Samuel Ranshaw 132 acs. in the Oaken Swp. in Warwick Co. in Denbigh Par. 20 Oct. 1688, p. 678. Beg. neer Shotbolt, cor. of Capt. Mathews to Thomas Wooton: his own, & land of John Lewis. (Nugent, C. & P. II, p. 327.)

1689: Thomas Branton, 33 acs. Warwick Co. in the Oaken Swp. 20 Apr. 1689, p. 704, Adj. Capt. Miles Cary, Mr. Tho. Harwood (Jr.); Thomas Platt; & John Lewis; on Howard & Woottons line; to Calvert's land. Note: "This patt. to be charged in York." (Nugent, C. & P. II, p. 332.)

1691: John Lewis and Edward Mosse owned lot 33 on a town plat in York Co. surveyed by Col. Lawrence Smith and recorded Sept. 1691. Owen Davis owned lot 13. (York Co., Va. Records, 1691.)
Note: For other patents showing the location of David, Jr. and his brother John's location see the following in Nugent, C. & P. II: Owen Davis, p. 384; Thos. Lilburne, p. 288; Garnett Corbitt, p. 300; and Samuell Singnall p. 310.

4. Robert Lewis (d. 1656) York Co., Va. Records:

Note: Since Col. Sorely, in *Lewis of Warner Hall*, stated that he thought this Robert Lewis was the ancestor of that family, I have tried to be as complete as possible. It appears to me very doubtful that he was their ancestor.

There were two Robert Lewises listed as coming to Virginia in 1635, one age 23 and one age 38. Since the records of this Robert Lewis show him buying a plantation in 1638, and marrying a woman already twice widowed, it seems more likely that he was the older one. There were two Robert Lewises christened in London in 1597: Robert Lewis, son of Edward Lewis, chr. 15 May 1597, St. Andrew Hubbard with St. Mary at Hill; and Robert Lewis, son of Griffin Lewis, chr. 7-Sept. 1597, Westminster, St. Margarets. (IGI 1988 p. 85, 417.) One of them may have been the Robert Lewis, age 28, who sailed from London for Virginia on the *Transport,* 4 July 1635. (Hotten, p. 103.)

1638: John Utie and Robert Bouth sold to Robert Lewis a plantation with all ground in same. Crop is let to Henry Wills. Lewis to have privelege of Creek parting Piney Neck and Queens Ck. Neck for 1060 lbs. tobaco. 12 Nov. 1638. (B. Weisiger. York Co. Records 1665-1672, p. 37.)

1644: Robert Lewis fined 200 lbs. tobo. for not rendering his guardians acct. in York Co. (Va. Mag. V. 17, p. 211.)

1645/6: The estate of Thos. Smallcomb owed Robert Lewis 100 lbs. tobo. 10 Mar. 1645/6. (Sorely, Lewis of Warner Hall, p. 21.)

1646: Robert Lewis and John Hansford appt'd. to make a census of Hamilton Parish, York Co. (Sorely, *ibid.,* p. 21.)

1652: Robert Booth pats. 400 acs. York Co. 3 July 1652 at Queens Cr. adj. Mr. Robert Vaus, Merchant, and John Uty's land now in occupation of Robert Lewis, Wm. Cooks and Geo. Gill. (Nugent, C. & P. I, p. 278.)

1656: Robert Lewis buys 500 acs. from John King that King had pat. 19 Nov. 1649, N. side York Riv., bounded by King's Cr. and Porpotanck Riv., which King assigned to Mary, widow of Robert Lewis. (Later assigned to his two daus. Alice & Mary.) (York Co. Record Book I, p. 41-42; Nugent, C. & P. I, p. 186.)
Note: Land was at mouth of Porpotanck Riv. on west side.

1656: Account of estate of Robert Lewis, dec'd. ordered by York Court, 25 Aug. 1656, from Capt. Ralph Langley who had married his widow, Mary. Recorded 30 Sept. 1656. (Fleet, Col. Va. Abs. Vol. 3, p. 130. 1988 ed.)

1658: Capt. Ralph Langley had custody of cattle belonging to Mary and Alice Lewis and Ann Holman which came to them through their deceased brother Henry Jones. 10 Sept. 1658. (Sorely, *op. cit.* p. 22.)

1660: York Co. Orphans' Court 11 Sept. 1660: Ann Hollman, dau. of Thos. Hollman, dec'd., lately married to Wm. Hill.... Ordered that Capt. Ralph Langley, guardian of sd. Ann deliver such cattle as belong to her...being a joint stock belonging to sd. Ann and to Mary Lewis by Henry Jones' death, their brother by their mother's side.... Account of the cattle of orphans of Robert Lewis, 10 Sept. 1660, including Ann Holman, Mary Lewis, rec'd for Mr. Sanderson for sd. orphans, 11 Sept. 1660 (signed) Ralph Langley. (B. Weisiger, York Co., Va. Records 1659-1662, p. 41-2.)

Note: There is a record of a Henry Jones with land at Queen's Ck. mentioned in the patent of John Bell of 1 Oct. 1639 (Nugent, C. & P. I, p. 114.) and a Thomas Hollman who pat. 100 acs. betw. Martin's Hundred and Kiskiake 24 Aug. 1639 (Nugent, C. & P. I, p. 30). These were probably the first two husbands of Robert Lewis' wife.

1666: Richard Roberts and Mary Roberts assign Queen's Ck. land of Robert Lewis to Col. Nathaniel Bacon. Land purchased by Robert Lewis from John Utye and Robert Bouth, which I, said Roberts, marrying the daughter and heiress of sd. Lewis sell with the consent of the sd. Mary. (B. Weisiger, York Co. Records 1665-1672, p. 37.)

1668: New Kent Co, 10 Sep 1668: A jury found Robert Lewis had died seized of 500 acs. purchased from John King, alias John LeRoy, who had died an alien, land escheats to the crown, 21 Feb. 1667/8. Thos. Ludwell, escheator General Writ. (In: Va. Genealogist, Vol. 19, p. 132.)

1668: Ben Lillington of Queens Ck., York Co. signs note of debt to Daniel Wild of same and Richard Roberts of 'Porobentanck' in New Kent Co., planter, for 2000 lbs. tobo. 27 Nov. 1668. (B. Weisiger, *ibid.*, p. 137.)

1669: 11 Nov.: Deposition of John Wing of London... that Richard Roberts of 'Porobentanke' New Kent Co., planter, became indebted by bond of 19 Oct. 1667 to Stephen Porter....and Overington Jeale....of London (Followed by another deposition that he became indebted to the same two by a bond of 9 Sept. 1668.) (P. Coldham, Compl. Bk. of Emigrants 1661 - 1699, p. 153.)

1704: In the Virginia Rent Roll of 1704 the following two entries may apply to Richard Roberts and his wife, Mary Lewis: Gloucester rent roll, Abbington Parish: Richard Roberts for wife: 300 acres. York County: Mary Roberts, 25 acres. (L. des Cognets, Jr., Engl. Dup. of Lost Va. Records, pp. 147 and 179.)

5. John Lewis Of New Kent (Hanover) Co. (D. 1726) Family Records:

　　Note: The tradition in this family is that their immigrant ancestor, John Lewis, lived with the Mostyn Family in Denbyshire, Wales, before coming to America and was born ca. 1635-1640. A comparison of the traditional birthdates of the children of John Lewis (D. 1726) with the actual baptismal dates from the St. Peter's Parish register shows that they were born, except for John Jr., much later than thought, and it would be very unusual for someone born in the sixteen-thirties to be having children in the sixteen-ninties. It is possible that two John Lewises, the immigrant and the one who died in 1726, were combined.

　　There are records of a John Lewis, born ca. 1633, who was associated with the Page family, who pat. land in the New Kent/Hanover Co. area. These records are as follows:

1659:　24 Oct.: Deposition of John Lewis, age about 26, says he brought no clothing or anything from the house of John Thomas (except old clothing the first master he had before John Thomas, bought him) into the house of Matthew Page, & that John Thomas detained a rug and a bed from him, which he brought with him; til his master Mr. Page, he never had a bed. (signed) John (O) Lewis. (B. Weisiger, York Co., Va. Records, 1659-1662, p. 17.)

1665:　26 Feb.: Admin. on estate of John Thomas, dec'd with will annexed, granted on oath of Wm. Gibbs and other wit. John Lewis to be sworn by Capt. Daniel Parke, is granted to Mr. Benj. Lillington, who married Katherine, the relict. To be appr. 12 Mar. & equally divided among the children by Capt. Richard Crowshaw et al. (B. Weisiger, York Co., Va. Records, 1665-167, p. 21.) Will of John Thomas, dtd. 3 Apr. 166_ (5)?: My houses and 250 acs. at Queens Cr. to my three sons, equally div. betw them & my wife for widowhood. All my land at 'Portupotamacke' (*sic,* Poropotancke), 490 acs. to them as above. Wit.: Wm. Gibbs, John (O) Lewis. Rec. 26 Feb. 1665/6. (*ibid.,* p. 24.)

　　Baptismal dates of children, fr. Parish Register:
　　Jno., son of Jno. Lewis, bapt. ye 27th of Febry 1686/7
　　David, son of John Lewis, bapt. the 5 May 1695
　　Abraham, son of John Lewis, planter, bapt. 27 Nov. 1698
　　William, son of John Lewis, baptz ye 22 Nov. 17__.
　　(Nat. Soc. of Col. Dames: Par. Reg. of St. Peter's New Kent Co., Va. 1680 - 1787, pp. 19, 20.)

1704:　Quit Rent List: John Lewis of New Kent Co.: 375 acs. (L. des Cognets, Engl. Dupl. of Lost Va. Records, p. 167.)

1726:　Will of John Lewis names the following children:
　　Mrs. Rebecca Lyndsay; Abraham; Sarah; Mrs. Angelica Fullove; David; John Jr.
　　Note: John Lewis, Jr. = Eliz. McGrath; David Lewis = (1) (ca. 1717) Ann Terrell (D. 1734); (2) = ?; (3) = Mary McGrath (W. T. Lewis, Gen. of the Lewis Family, pp. 56, 57.)

6. Nicholas Lewis (D. ?) Of St. Peter's Parish, New Kent Co.:
Note: The following records may apply to the family of this Nicholas Lewis:

I. NICHOLAS LEWIS OF YORK CO., VA.:

1659: 4 Apr.: Nicholas Lewis and Margaret Lewis listed as headrights for John Stannoff in a certificate for 700 acs. of land. (L. Duvall, York Co., Va. Wills, Deeds, Orders: 1657-1659, p. 69.)

1668: Morris Heard and wife Anne in Middletown Par. York Co., sell to Nicholas Lewis of Hampton Par. York Co. 50 acs. pt. of a divident bought of Wm. Gantlett, a mile fr. Skimino Cr. next to John Smith, Thos. Pinkethman and Nicholas Lewis....1 Oct. 1668. (B. Weisiger, York Co. Records 1665-1672, p. 165.)

1670: Thos. Meakins to Robt. Bartlight: 100 acs. York Co. Bounded by Mr. Pinkethman & Gantlett's line, John Smith's line & Mr. Hubertt (*sic,* Mathew Hubbard) 12 Feb. 1668. I assign this bill of sale to Nicholas Lewis. (signed) Robert (R) Bartlett 18 Jan. 1670/1. (*ibid.,* p. 229.)

1673: I, Wm. Eaton have sold & delivered to John Stevens all my right in estate formerly belonging to John Smith. 31 Mar. 1673. (signed) Wm. Eaton. Wit.: Nicholas (N) Lewis, Mary (M) Lewis. (B. Weisiger, York Co., Va. Records 1672-1676, p. ___.)

1675/6: 24 Jan.: Wm. Whitehead, servent to Nicholas Lewis, imported in the 'Barnaby' Capt. Matthew Rider, Commander, is adjudged age 15 and is to serve until 24. (*ibid.,* p. 147.)

II. NICHOLAS LEWIS OF PETSO. PARISH, GLOUCESTER CO. (D. 1699.):

1699: To Nathaniel Mills for keeping Nicholas Lewis' child 6 mos. 500 lbs. tobo. Nicholas Lewis, orphan, bound out to served Henry Morris of Stratton Major Par., King & Queen Co. until age 21 to learn the trade of Coopery. Henry Morris to provide him with one broad cloth suit, two shirts, hat, shoes and stockings. (Petsworth Par. Reg. p. 60.)

1700: 24 Apr. James Lewis, son of Nicholas, fatherless & motherless, 5 years old the 9th day of next month, bound to James Hayes to receive 3 yrs. schooling.

1700: 6 Nov.: John Lewis, orphan, age 9, bound to Nathaniel Mills until he reaches age 21. To receive 2 yrs. schooling.

1701: 8 Nov.: James Lewis, being an orphan boy of age 7, bound to John Day, formerly bound to James Hayes, now dec'd. and taken from his widow for want of maintenance. (Note: James Lewis continues to be mentioned in the parish records as receiving charity until his death in 1736. His widow, Elizabeth, received charity from 1739 through 1760.)

1704: Nicholas Lewis, orphan, listed in the Quit Rent list of Petsworth Par. Gloucester Co. as owning 350 acs. (L. des Cognets, Engl. Dupl. of Lost Va. Records, p. 141.)

III. NICHOLAS LEWIS OF ST. PETER'S PARISH, NEW KENT CO. (D. ?.):
Note: May be identical with Nicholas Lewis, orphan, of Petsworth Parish, Gloucester Co.

17__: 29 Oct.: Baptism of Edward, son of Nicho. Lewis. (p. 20)
1708/9: 16 Jan.: Baptism of Mary, Daughter of Nicho., Lewis (p. 20.)
1708: 20 March Birth of Angelico, dau of Nicho. Lewis, baptised 27 Apr. 1708 (p. 21.)
1715: 22 March, Birth of William, son of Nicho. Lewis by Eliz. his wife. (p. 32)
1717: 22 Nov.: John, son of Nicho. Lewis born (p. 89.)
1723/4: 9 March, James, son of Nicho, Lewis born. (p. 91)
(Nat. Soc. of Col. Dames of Amer. in the State of Va., Parish Register of St. Peter's, New Kent Co., Va., 1680-1789, pp. 20, 21, 32, 89, 91.)

IV. LEWIS FAMILIES ON THE
NORTH SIDE
OF THE
YORK RIVER

1. Records of Mr. John Lewis of Monmouthshire, Wales and Va. (1592-1657):

BASIC REFERENCE: Grace Moses, *The Welsh Lineage of John Lewis (1592-1657), Emigrant to Glouchester Va.* 1984. (Revised, with supplement, 1992.)

1591/2: Feb. 22: John, son of Lewis Rycketts (aka Prichard) baptised at St. Telio's church, Llantilio Pertholey, Mon. (Moses, p. 11.)

1610/1: Feb. 3: John Lewis Pricket marries Johane Lewis at St. Telios. (Moses, p. 11.)

1611/2: Feb. 5: Gwenllian, dau. of John and Johane Lewis bapt. at St. Telios. (Moses, p. 12.)

1615/6: Mar. 1: Lettus (Lettitia/Lydia), dau. of John and Johane Lewis bapt. at St. Telios. (Moses, p. 12.)

1615: Sept. 29: Burial of Catherine Prichard at St. Telio's. (Presumed mother of John Lewis.) (Moses, p. 11.)

1616: May 4: Burial of Lewis Prichard at St. Telios. (Presumed father of John Lewis.) (Moses, p. 11.)

1616: Sept. 6: John Lewis makes payment of 203 lbs. for 1 1/2 tenements on High St. Abergavenny to Stephen Hughes, Vintner, and his wife, Maria. (In records of the Lordship of Abergavenny-Moses, p. 18..)

1616: Oct. 6: Before the King's Justices at Westminster, Michaelmas Octaves 14 James I. John Lewis, Plaintiff, Stephen Hughes and Maria his wife, Deforciants, concerning one messuages, two gardens with appertenances in Abergavenny. Stephen Hughes and Maria agree property belongs to John Lewis.... John Lewis gives them 60 lbs. (Moses, p. 22.)

1617: Oct. 6: Westminister, Octave of Michaelmas, 15 James I: Rees Thomas Phillip and John Lewis, Plaintiffs, Henry Thomas Morgan and Margaret, his wife, and Morgan Thomas ap Thomas and Katherine, his wife, Deforciants, concerning two messuages, one barn, two gardens, one orchard, 20 acres of land, 12 acres of meadow, 10 pasture, and 30 acres of wood with appurtenances in Llantilio Pertholey and Aberystouth.... The property to be the right of Rees, as those which Rees and John received from them (all four named.) It is recognized that the properties shall be held by Rees and John and the heirs of Rees. Rees and John give them 60 lbs. (This appears to be the property known as Ty-Hir.) (Moses, p. 25.)

1621: Jan. 1: Watkin, son of John Lewis bapt. at St. Telios. (Moses, p. 12.)

1627: John Lewis, Mercer, included in a list of tenement rentals of Abergavenny and in a list of the Burgesses. (Moses, p. 19.)

1628: Apr. 18: Will of Richard Lewis of Llangatock, Crickhowell, Gent. proved. (dated March 15, 1627) Mentions sons: Edward Prichard and Thomas Prichard, and children of deceased sons Lewis (Prichard) and William (Lewis)*: Thomas Lewis, Maudelen Lewis, Marie Lewis, Dorite Lewis, Elizabeth Lewis, and John Lewis; Dau. (in-law) Eliz. Lewis (widow of eldest son, William Lewis*; grandson and heir, Richard Lewis (only one listed in the Lewis pedigree in J. A. Bradney, Hist. of Mon. Vol. I, p. 338-9.) *William Lewis, Atty, B.A., Oxford, St. Mary's Hall 1586/7; M.A., Oxford, Glouchester Hall, 1592/3; B.C.L. (Bachelor of Civil Law), 1596 (Moses, p. 34). William Lewis kept his father's last name as his surname, while the rest of the sons followed the Welsh tradition and used the father's first name as their last name. Will in: Brecon Probate Records, 1628-1653. (Moses, p. 9-10.)

Will Abstract of **Richard Lewis** of the parish of Langattock Juxta Crickhowell, gent.

Will dtd. 15 March 1627.

To Cathedral Church of St. David's - 2 shillings; for forgotten tithe - 3s. 4d.; for reparation of the parish church of Langattock Juxta Crickhowell - 10s; for reparation of the bridge between Langattock and Crickhowell - 10s; all lands purchased from William Vaughan Esq. and Charles Vaughan Esq. in parish of Langattock to son Edward Prichard and heirs until testator's heir Richard Lewis shall pay them the sum of £100; to Maudlen Lewis - £3 8s. 9d.;

To **Thomas Lewis** one of the sons of testator's son Lewis - £4 8s. 5d.;

To son **Thomas Prichard** - 2 oxen; to Lewis Thomas - 2 oxen; to grandchild Marie Lewis - 2 cows; to Elizabeth Lewis - 2 cows; to Doritie Lewis - 40s; to grandchild Maud verch Thomas - 4 cows and 10 sheep; to Marie verch Thomas - 1 cow and 4 sheep; to heir Richard Lewis - timber, corn, ploughs, etc.; to son Edward Prichard - £10; to William ap Ieuan Weelim of Llanelly - £10. (The above £20 is in the hand of Ieuan Thomas Weelim of Langattock Juxta Crickhowell.)

To Ieuan Thomas Weelim - 40s due on the above £20; to daughter Elizabeth Lewis - some silver, bed, bedding, 'bedsteed that is in the chamber in the oulde howese', pewter items, sundry household goods etc. (all specified,) 2 hives of bees and 2 sows; to heir Richard Lewis - 3 hives of bees;

To grandchild **John Lewis** - 4 sheep and 4 lambs and a 'ffyly black coult.' (Note: believed to be son of Lewis Prichard and ident. with John Lewis [1592-1657]);

To grandchild and heir **Richard Lewis** - all other household goods; to son Edward Prichard - a grey horse; to Anne Herbert, wife of John Watkin of Crickhowell - 10 lambs;

Son **Edward Prichard** to be executor.

Signed Rychard Lewis (very feeble signature - seal lost.)

Witnesses: James Morgan; John Meredith; Lewis Meredith; Edward Johns; Meredith Powell; Thomas ap Thomas; Tho. Harrys. Proved by the executor 19 Apr. 1628.

Inventory dtd. 16 Apr. 1628 appraised by John Meredith, David Howell, Thomas ap Thomas, James Morgan and William Jones. Detailed inventory (no helpful references except to £20 in hands of Ieuan Thomas William) total £113 6s.

1630: Nov. 21: John Lewis married Catherine Philip at St. Telio's (St. Telio's Parish Register.)

1633: Dec. 15: John Lewis son of John Lewis bapt. at St. Telio's. (Moses, p. 12.)

1638: Nov. 9: John Lewis listed as a Senior Burgess in the Charter of King Charles I to the town of Abergavenny. In: J. A. Bradney, Hist. of Mon. Vol. I, p. 153. (Moses, p. 18.)

1652: May 6: Deed of Ffeeoffment from John Prees of the Parish of Old Castle, Yeoman, to John Davies of the Parish of Llanfihangel Crucorney, Yeoman, for two messuages and two closes in Llanfihangel Crucorney, lately purchased from John Lewis and others. (This property, known as Upper Penbiddle was in the manor of Grossmount.) In: J. A. Bradney, Notes on Hist. of Mon. p. 66. (Moses, p. 2)

1653: July 1: Mr. John Lewis patents 250 acres on Poropotank Creek, Glouchester Co., Va. (now King and Queen Co.) The five headrights include: himself, Lydia, (prob. Letitia) Lewis William Lewis, Edward Lewis, and John Lewis Jr. (Nugent, Cavaliers and Pioneers, Vol. I, p. 229.)

1657: Aug. 21: Death of John Lewis of Monmouthshire and Poropotank Ck. (Harris, John Lewis 1594 1657); In: Va. Mag. of Hist. & Biog., Vol. 56 (1948), pp. 195-205.)

Records of Maj./Col. John Lewis (ca. 1633 - 1682):
1633: Dec. 15: John, son of John Lewis, bapt. at St. Telios, Llantilio Pertholey, Monmouthshire. (Parish Register of St. Telios.)

1653: July 1: John Lewis, Jr., headright of Mr. John Lewis for 250 acs. Lewis Branch, formerly Totopotomy's Branch, Poroporotank Ck. (Nugent: C. & P. I, p. 229.)

1655: Dec. 29: John Lewis Jr. pats. 250 acs. Glost. Co., beginning at the main swamp of Poropotank, running down same from land of Col. Richard Lee to the Beech Spring. (Nugent: C. & P. I. p. 323.)

1657: Nov. 10: Rice Williams of Brecon, Spinster, bound to serve John Lewis four years in Va. (Coldham, P. W. Complete Bk. of Emigrants 1607-1660, p. 365)

1658: Apr. 7: John Wood unto John Lewis Jr.: five cows with calves to be delivered 20 March next on the North side of the York River betw. Tindale's point and Mattapony. Signed John Wood, wit.: Wm. Bacon and Wm. Thomas. Recorded 17 May 1658. Westm. Co. Records, p. 104a. (In: Dorman: Westm. Co. Records 1658 1661, p. 11.) [1]

1663: Nov. 22: John Lewis pats. 1700 acs. at the head of Poropotank Ck. on both sides of the swamp to land of Mr. Major, to Papatico Br, to land of Tho. Hanckes.... to land of Geo. Austin and up Coals swamp to Col. Richard Lee's land. 120 acs. granted to Timothy Lowdwell and Thos. Broughton 13 Sep 1651 & assigned to said Lewis, and 1000 acs. pat. by Mr. Howell Price 5 Oct. 1656 and assigned to said Lewis and 600 acs. for transp. of 12 persons. (Nugent: C. & P. I, p. 484.)

1666: Nov. 6: Thomas Creeton and Hugh Roye pat. 2100 acs. New Kent Co. 1800 acs. viz.: 400 acs. marsh on N. side York River.... Land formerly John Duncomb and John Lewis': 1400 acs. purchased from said Lewis and Duncomb and 700 acs. for trans of 14 persons. (Nugent: C. & P. II, p. 4.) Note: In the above sale Duncomb sold 300 acs. and John Lewis sold 1100 acs. - see later. In all probability John Lewis used the money to purchase the 775 acs. of Chemokins alias Port Holy and lease the 1825 acs. that later escheated. - See Maj. Wm. Lewis records.

1667: Aug. 16: Mr. John Lewis pats. 2600 acs. (same size as Chemokins - Port Holy plantation Maj. Wm. Lewis patented.) New Kent and Glost. Cos. upon both sides of Poropotank Ck (Swp.) adj. Timothy Lowdell, John Leviston, Mattapony Swp, Richard Major, Geo Major, Popetico Swp, John Chamberline.... to John Fox, John Nettle, Geo Austin, Cole's Br. and br dividing this from land of Mr. Richard Lee.... 80 acs. purchased of sd. Lowdell, 1000 acs. of Mr. Howell Prise (Price), 600 acs. granted sd. Lewis 23 Nov. 1663, and 920 acs. for transp. of 19 persons. (Nugent: C. & P. II, p. 44.)

1667: Sept. 5: Birth of Edward Lewis, son of John Lewis, (Tombstone record, Poropotank Ck.)

---

[1] Two pats. in 1658 prob. his: 28 June J. L. & Robt. Jones, Gent. 2,000 acs. Westm. Co. (Nugent, C. & P. I, p. 367) Jones fr Poropotanck Cr. (Nugent, C. & P. I, p. 322) 8 Nov. J. L. & James Turner pat. 1,000 acs. N.K. Co. "Lewis Island" opp. Cohoke Cr. (Site of Maj. Wm. Lewis 50 ac. 1653 pat.) (Nugent C. & P. I, p. 379.)

1668: Apr. 22: Mr. John Lewis pats. 100 acs. New Kent Co. N.E. side of Cainhoe's swp. beginning at John Leviston's land. (Nugent: C. & P. II, p. 39.)

1669: Nov. 5: Mr. John Leviston pats. 780 acs. New Kent Co. adj. Mr. John Lewis... 400 acs. granted 16 Dec. 1653 and 380 acs. for transp. of 8 persons. (Nugent C. & P. II, p. 67.)

1669: Nov. 30: Birth of John Lewis (III) son of John Lewis Jr. (Tombstone Record Warner Hall.)

1673/4: Feb. 25: Lt. Col. John Smith, Mr. John Buckner, Mr. Philip Lightfoot, Mr. Thos. Royston, and Mr. John Lewis pat. 10,050 acs. New Kent Co. on Mattapony River adj. Mr. Thos, Hall and John Pigg and Herndon and Bagby. Transp, of 201 pers. (Nugent: C. & P. II, p. 149.)

1674: July 22: Maj. Richard Lee pats. 1140 acs. Glost. Co. known by the name of Paradise... nere Mr. John Lewis... 1000 acs. granted to sd. Lee by two pats. 140 acs. betw. sd. tracts for transp. of 3 persons. (Nugent: C. & P. II, p. 152.)

1675: Oct. 4: Major John Lewis and Mr. John Lane pat. 43 acs. 20 poles, New Kent Co. Stratton Major Parish on N.W. side of Assatine (Tastine) swp and ck. Adj. Nicholl's land, James Trite's and land of Mr. Henry Briggs. Transp. of one person. (Nugent: C. & P. II, p. 166.)

1675: Maj. John Lewis mentioned in a petition of Richard Young of Glost. Co. who requested that he be appointed by the court to make a survey in his behalf. (Cal. of Va. State Papers, Vol. I. p. 10.)

1675/6: Mar. 11: Susanna Wells, infant... heir of John Wells, decd. pats. 50 acs. Glost. Co... which was surveyed by Mr. John Lewis, surveyor, at the instance of Edw. Wells, father of the said John... (Nugent: C. & P. II, p. 171.)

1677: Feb.: Maj. John Lewis mentioned in regard to damages suffered from rebels in Bacons rebellion. (Va. Mag. Vol. 5, p. 67; Wm. & Mary Quart. (I), Vol. 9, p. 260.)

1677: Aug. 4: Maj. John Lewis donates 500 lbs. Tobacco to Petsworth Parish, Glost. Co. (Petsworth Parish Reg.)

1677: Sep. 13: First mention of John Lewis as Col. (Petsworth Parish Reg.) Note: John Lewis appears to have held the rank of Major and Col. of the Gloucester Co. militia and of Capt. in the New Kent Co. militia as he owned land in both bounties.

1678: Mar. 29: Will of James Miller of York Co. names loving brother Maj. John Lewis and his sister Mrs. Isabella Lewis, wife to Maj. John Lewis leaves her his entire estate and after her death 'to my two nephews, Edward Lewis and John Lewis the younger'. (York Co. Records: 1675 - 1684, p. 39.)

1679: Oct. 1: Mr. Matthew Kemp pats. 640 acs. New Kent Co. N.E. side Mattapony River, adj. Mr. Diggs, granted Mrs. Eliza Kemp for a greater quantity 24 Mar. 1664, and now resurveyed by Col. John Lewis, and due for transp. of 13 persons. (Nugent: C. & P. II, p. 202-203.)

1680: Apr. 26: Wm. Snapes pats. 75 acs. adj. Col. John Lewis, Glost. Co. Petsworth Parish. (Nugent: C. & P. II, p. 209.)

1681: Apr. 23: Maj. Robert Payton pats. 1,000 acs. New Kent Co., St. Stephens parish by order of Col. John Lewis (Nugent: C. & P. II, p. 219.) Note: At this period John Lewis was sheriff of New Kent Co. (L. des Cognets, *op. cit.,* p. 1.)

1681/2: Death of Col. John Lewis, probably on a voyage to England, as shown by the absence of a gravestone in the Poropotanck graveyard, and the following entry in the parish register of St. Mary's Church, Newington, Surrey: 1682, Oct. 16, married: Robert Yard and Isabella Lewis, late of Virginia. (New Eng. Hist. & Gen. Reg., V. 18, p. 81, 1864.)

1683: Apr. 16: Mr. Henry Fox, son & heir of John Fox, pats. 300 acs. New Kent and Glost. Cos.... nigh Col. John Lewis' quarter.... dividing this and land of Mr. Wm. Lynes.... (Nugent: C. & P. II, p. 255.)

1686: Oct. 30: Mr. John Stark merch. pats. 484 acs. New Kent Co., St. Stephens Parish.... adj. land formerly Col. Abrahall's to Mattapony River.... order to survy same.... by Col. John Lewis and George Morris, surveyor, in the present of a jury, 10 May 1673, which he sold to said Stark. (Nugent: C. & P. II, p. 301.)

1691: Apr. 28: Joshua Story pats. 7,440 acs. New Kent Co. N. side Mattapony river above the fork where the great run comes into Moroconick Ck., part of 10,050 acs. granted Lt. Col. John Smith.... and Mr. John Lewis 25 Feb. 1673/4, Due sd. Story by order 17 Oct. 1688 for transp. of 149 persons. (Nugent: C. & P. II, p. 358-359.)

1695: Oct. 25: Marg. Todd and Francis Todd, orphans of Mr. Wm. Todd, pat. 500 acs. King and Queen Co. in Stratton Major Parish on Peanketank Smp adj. David Brom. Granted George Durge 16 Apr. 1683, deserted.... granted Mr. Wm. Todd 29 Apr. 1693. Now survced according to the first survey made by Col. John Lewis. (Nugent: C. & P. III, p. 2-3.)

Land Records Of Edward And John Lewis (III), Sons Of Maj./Col. John Lewis Of Poropotanck Ck. (1633-1682)

1683: Sept. 20: Mr. John Lewis Jr. pats. 250 acs. New Kent Co. Granted to Charles Hawley 7 Apr. 1674, which he died seized of. Escheated by inquisition under Wm. Leigh, Deputy Escheator, 25 July 1681, and now granted by order. (Nugent: C. & P. II, p. 268.)

Note: Charles Hawley's pat. (Nugent: C. & P. II, p. 145.) identifies the land as being on the Tastine swamp. It was possibly part of the 600 acs. sold John Cosby by Maj. Wm. Lewis, and the following pat. was the other 350 acs. of it.

1690: Apr. 21: Mr. Edward and Mr. John Lewis pat. 352 acs. on a branch of the Assatine (Tastine) swamp... importation of 8 persons: Daniel Hay, John Butler, John Lewis, Roger Hay, Ann Hay, Eliza. Lovell, Wm. Morgan, Saml Holding. (Nugent: C. & P. II, p. 342.)

Note: The first six headrights of this list are identical in name and order with those in the Northumberland Co. pat. in 1678, by Richard Rice, who had previously resided in Rappa Co. near Edward Lewis of Totoskey Ck. The John Lewis in the list appears to be John Lewis (d. 1697) of Northumberland Co.

1690: Apr. 21: Capt. John Lane of New Kent Co., Stratton Major Parish, pats. 140 acs. adj. Mr. Green, Geo. Dillard, and Mr. Edward and John Lewis. (Nugent: C. & P. II, p. 341.)

1691: Oct. 20: Wm. Collins and Timothy Coniers pat. 620 acs. King and Queen Co. begin near Geo. Dillards to mouth of Cool Spr. Br. nigh Cornelius Vaughan to Tastine main swp.... 350 acs. (*sic*) granted Mr. Edward and John Lewis 21 Apr. 1690 who conveyed to the above mentioned 30 Mar. 1691. 268 acs. being overplush. Imp. of 6 persons. (Nugent: C. & P. II, p. 372.)

Note: The 268 acs. "overplush" apparently included the 250 ac. pat. of John Lewis Jr. 20 Sep 1683.

1704: Apr. 26: Edward Lewis pats. 400 acs. King and Queen Co. adj. Maj. Lewis, east on main swamp of Arsatians Ck. alias Tarsantian, adj. his own 640 acs. Behind land of Capt. Robert Abrahall. Granted Maj. Wm. Lewis 8 June 1655. Deserted and now granted for transp. of 8 persons. (Nugent: C. & P. III, p. 82.)

1711: Apr. 28: John Lewis Esq., John Smith of Purton, and John Washington Jr. of Westmoreland Co. Pat 46-1/2 acs. Glost. Co. Surv. by Lawrence Smith, Gent. late Surv. of Glost. Co. for Mr. George Warner, dec'd and is granted to sd. Lewis, Smith and Washington as heirs of sd. Warner. By order of the general court, 19 Apr. 1709. (Nugent: C. & P. III, p. 116.)

Note: John Washington Jr., refers to the eldest son (b. 1692) of Lawrence Washington (d. 1698) and Mildred (Warner) Washington (d. 1701) - prob. to distinguish him from his cousin and guardian, John Washington of Chotank, Stafford Co., Va.

CHART OF JOHN LEWIS (1592 - 1657) FAMILY

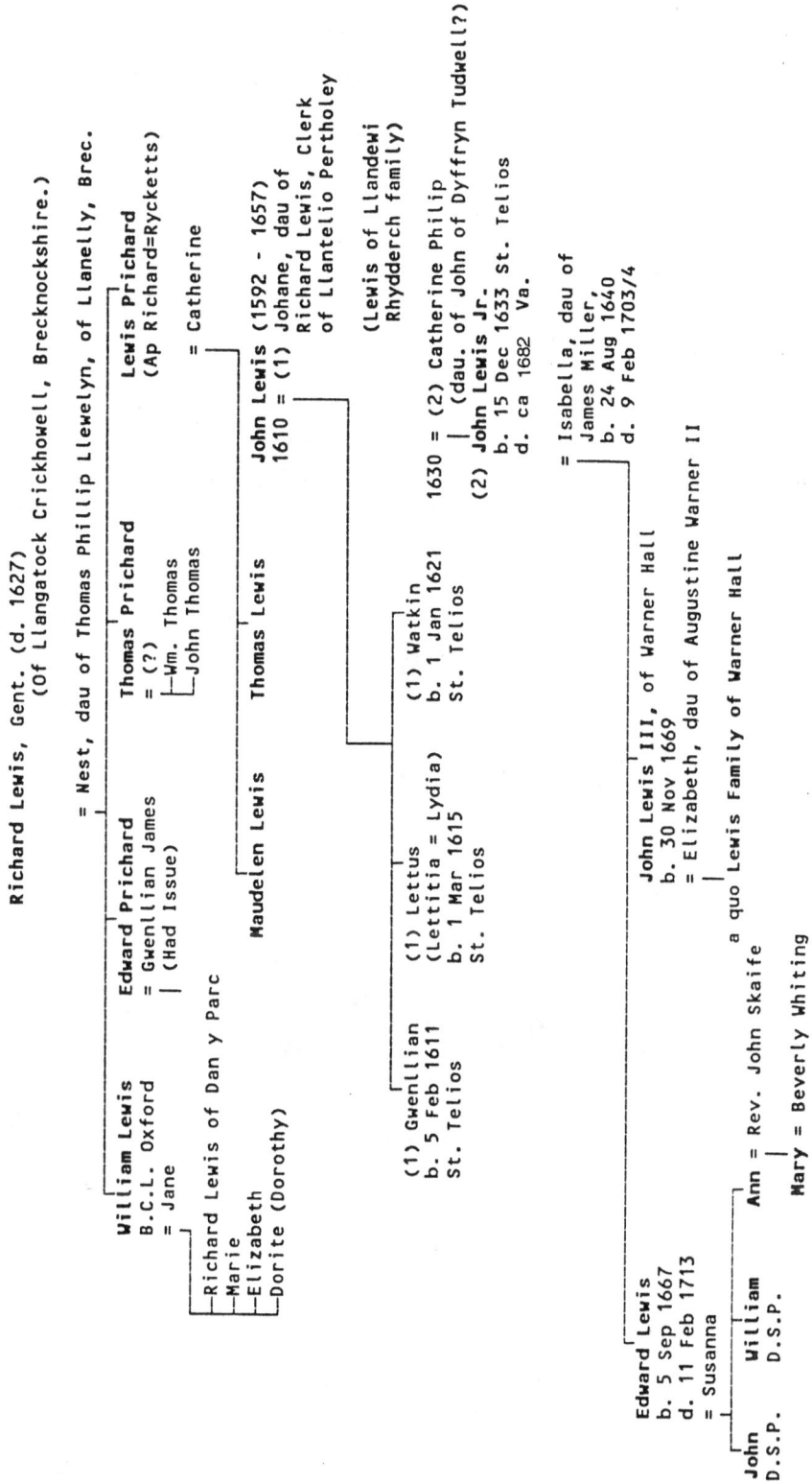

Richard Lewis, Gent. (d. 1627)
(Of Llangatock Crickhowell, Brecknockshire.)

= Nest, dau of Thomas Phillip Llewelyn, of Llanelly, Brec.

William Lewis
B.C.L. Oxford
= Jane

Richard Lewis of Dan y Parc
Marie
Elizabeth
Dorite (Dorothy)

Edward Prichard
= Gwenllian James
(Had Issue)

Maudelen Lewis

Thomas Prichard
= (?)
Wm. Thomas
John Thomas

Thomas Lewis

Lewis Prichard
(Ap Richard=Rycketts)

= Catherine

John Lewis (1592 - 1657)
1610 = (1) Johane, dau of
Richard Lewis, Clerk
of Llantelio Pertholey

(Lewis of Llandewi
Rhydderch family)

1630 = (2) Catherine Philip
(dau. of John of Dyffryn Tudwel(?))

(2) John Lewis Jr.
b. 15 Dec 1633 St. Telios
d. ca 1682 Va.

= Isabella, dau of
James Miller,
b. 24 Aug 1640
d. 9 Feb 1703/4

(1) Gwenllian
b. 5 Feb 1611
St. Telios

(1) Lettus
(Lettitia = Lydia)
b. 1 Mar 1615
St. Telios

(1) Watkin
b. 1 Jan 1621
St. Telios

John Lewis III, of Warner Hall
b. 30 Nov 1669
= Elizabeth, dau of Augustine Warner II

a quo Lewis Family of Warner Hall

Edward Lewis
b. 5 Sep 1667
d. 11 Feb 1713
= Susanna

William
D.S.P.

Ann = Rev. John Skaife

John
D.S.P.

Mary = Beverly Whiting

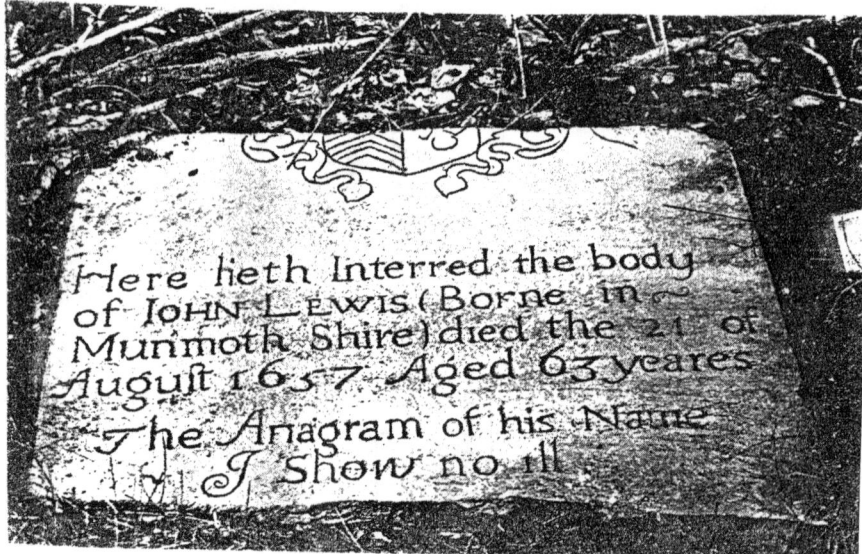

**Photo of Tombstone Arms of
John Lewis (D. 1657)**

--reproduced from photo in *Virginia Magazine of History & Biography*, vol. 56 p. 197

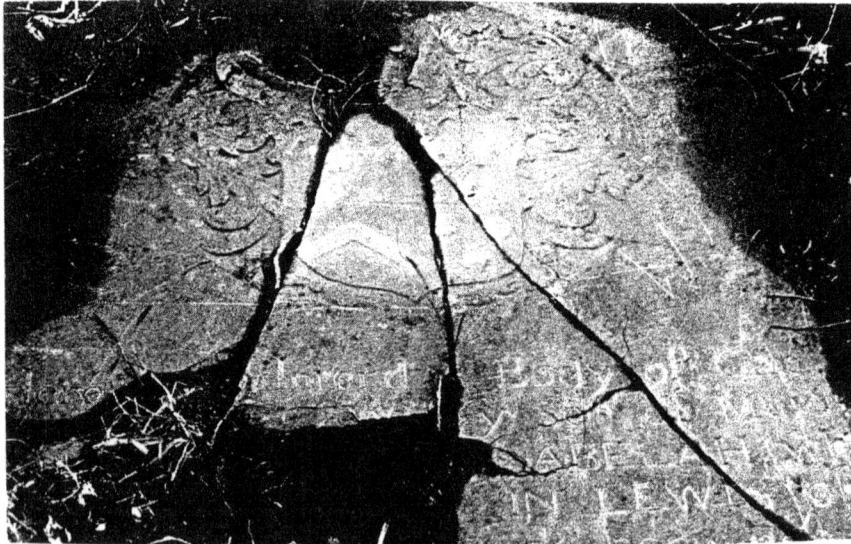

**Photo of Tombstone Arms of
Edward Lewis (D. 1713)**

--reproduced from photo in *Virginia Magazine of History & Biography*, vol. 62 p. 481

NOTE: Some members of the Morgan family of Llangenny, Brecknockshire - cousins of this family bore very similar arms. See: Hawkins, Cwrt-Y Gollen and Its Families, 1967. Publ. of the Brecknock Museum. pp. 11 and 15. (Arms of Lewis Morgan and John Morgan.)

2. Records of William Lewis of Kingston Parish (d. 1682/83):

1653: William Lewis, headright of David Fox, for land on S. side, Rappahannock Riv. (Nugent, C. & P. I, p. 263.)

1657: William Lewis, a headright of Lt. Col. Henry Fleet for land certificate. (Lancaster Co., Va. Orders Bk. I, p. 3.)

1662: William Lewis assigned land pat. for land in Balt. Co. Md. by Howell Powell, 10 Aug. 1662. (Balt Co. Deeds Liber RM HS, p. 10.)
Note: A group of Quakers from Lanc. Co., Va. had land warrants granted to them in Md. 16 July 1659. They included: Thomas Powell, 700 acs; Howell Powell, 300 acs.; Wm. Ball, 500 acs, Robert Ball, 500 acs. (both sons of Col. Wm. Ball); Robert Gorsuch, 300 acs.; Richard Gorsuch, 300 acs.; Walter Dickenson, 600 acs.; Wm. Clapham (or Chapman) Jr. 500 acs.; Hugh Kensey (Kinsey) 400 acs.; and Thomas Humphrey 400 acs. (In: Tyler's Quart. Vol. 30, p. 80-86.) William Lewis appears to have married Constant Harwood - listed as a headright of Wm. Shorte & Wm. Lippeate for 400 acs. Lancaster Co. 1 Sep. 1657. (Nugent, C. & P. I, p. 355.)

1662: William Lewis assigns this land to Mr. Richard Carter, (son of Col. Edw. Carter.) Wit. by Geo. Seatoune and Anthony Webb. (Balt. Co. Liber RM HS, p. 11.)

1663: Wm. Lewis and wife Constant appoint John Gwyn (son of Col. Hugh Gwyn) their Atty to have Howell Powell acknowledge the 300 acs, sold to me (W.L.) and by me sold to Mr. Richard Carter, signed by Wm. Lewis (WL) (Mark) and Constant Lewis, (X) (Mark). Wit. by Geo. Seatoune and Samuel Lake. 24 Mar. 1663. (Balt. Co. Liber RM HS, p. 11.)
Note: John Gwyn was later minister of Abingdon Parish, Glost. Co. Geo. Seaton was a rebel during Bacon's rebellion and was taken prisoner by Maj. Robt. Beverly and his goods seized. (Min. of the Council & Gen. Court of Va. dtd. 15 Mar. 1676.) He had been a Justice.

1668: Wm. Lewis' land adj. patent of Geo. Seatoune for 300 acs. on the head of Hugh Gwyn's development on the s. side of the Pyanketanck Riv. adj. land surv. for Col. Humphrey Higginson... running from Old Mans Cr. at Peanketancke unto Wm. Lewis. (Nugent, C. & P. II, p. 38.)

1684: Thos. Allomaine pats. 52 acs. Glost. Co. Kingston Parish, adj. Mr. Wm. Elliott, Wm. Lewis, and Lt. Col. John Armstead. (Nugent, C. & P. II, p. 274.)
Note: The wife of Thos. Allmain was cited for cutting tobacco plants in Glost. Co. on 24 May 1682. (Exec. Journals of the Council of Col. Va. Vol. I, p. 23, 24.) This was during the tobacco riots. Richard Bayly (Jr.), age 19 had been condemned to death, but was later pardoned. It is possible that Wm. Lewis died during this period. His land was re-patented four years later:

1686: Col. John Armstead pats. 130 acs. in Kingston Parish, Glost. Co. 30 Oct. 1686, beginning not far from the chapel adj. Mr. Wm. Elliot & Geo. Seaton. It was later repat to Henry Armstead 28 Oct. 1697. (Nugent, C. & P. II. p. 17.); and then to Robert Carter Esqr. ('King' Carter), on 30 Oct. 1702. (Nugent, C. & P. III. p. 64.)

1686: Col. John Armstead pat. 202-1/2 acs. with Mr. John Gwin, 30 Oct. 1686. (This pat. the same day as the one above and in the same location was also poss. Wm. Lewis'.) (Nugent, C. & P. II, p. 302.)

Issue: (?)

3. Records of Mr. Christopher Lewis of St. Stephen's Parish, New Kent Co.

1668: A Christopher Lewis on jury in the land escheat case of the land sold by John King, alias Le Roy, an alien, to Robert Lewis, on Poropotanck Cr. New Kent Co., 21 Feb. 1667/8. New Kent Co. (Va. Genealogist, Vol. 19, p. 132.)

1674: A Christopher Lewis a headright for Capt. Lawrence Smith and Capt. Robrt. Beverly for 6,500 acs. in Rappahannock (Essex) and New Kent Cos. (Nugent, C. & P. II, p. 160.)

1684: Mr. Christopher Lewis pats. 700 acs. New Kent Co. (King & Queen), St. Stephens Parish, in a fork of Pyanketanck Swp. by Axell's (Exoll's) Swamp. 500 ac. part purchased of Lt. Col. Thomas Claybourn; 200 acs. for transp. of four persons. (Nugent, C. & P. II, p. 279.)

1694: Mr. Zachary Lewis pats. 500 acs. King and Queen Co. (formerly New Kent) along land granted to Thos. Claybourne, now belonging to Mr. Christopher Lewis. (Nugent, C. & P. II, p. 386.)

1694: A Christopher Lewis, member of jury, 12 Nov. 1694, Essex Co. (Essex Order Bk I. p. 368.)

4. Zachary Lewis (D. 1719?) Of King and Queen Co.

Note: The records of Zachary Lewis I in King and Queen Co. are very sparce, due to the loss of county records. The most detailed early statement about the origin of the family is that of Rev. Iverson Lewis that "he was the son of John Lewis, whose father, Zachary Lewis came from Brecknock, Wales to Va. in 1692, at which time he settled in the Co. of King and Queen." (Hayden, Va. Genealogies, p. 380.)

1694: 20 Apr.: Mr. Zachery Lewis pats. 500 acs. King & Queen Co. Beg. near the Dragon Swp. along land granted to Thos. Clayborne, now belonging to Mr. Christopher Lewis... (Nugent, C. & P. II, p. 386.) Note: a Dorcas Lewis is among the headrights. See Christopher Lewis records for his patent.

1703: 23 Oct.: Zachary Lewis pats. 450 acs. King William Co. Betw. the Herring Crs. Beg. at mouth of Wolftrap Br. to Up. Herring Cr. to Mouth of run of Turkey Perch Br. (Nugent, C. & P. III, p. 75.) Note: Other pats. in this area included two of Ambrose Smith, whose descendants intermarried with those of Zachary Lewis. For a discussion of these lands see L. des Cognets, Engl. Dupl. of Lost Va. Records, pp. 57-63. An article on this Smith family and the crest on a large silver spoon owned by them is in Tyler's Quarterly, Vol. 4 (July 1922) p. 150-1. It will be discussed later in the section on the Zachary Lewis family coat of arms.

1704: Zachary Lewis' land listed in the Va. Quit Rent Lists:
King and Queen Co.:   350 acs. owned by Zachary Lewis
                      300 acs. listed under Dyley Quarles as Zachary Lewis land.
King William Co.: 450 acs. (L. des Cognets, *op. cit.,* pp. 152, 154, 160.)

1706: 10 Mar.: Deed fr. Francis Shackleford of S. Farnham Par. Essex Co. to John Shackleford of Petso. Par. Gloster Co. 150 acs... Power of Atty, same date: Sarah Shackleford to Zachary Lewis: "Sir, appear for me at the Essex court & relinquish my right of dower of 150 acs. of land... and you will oblige your loving sister. (Signed) Sarah (X) Shackleford." (Essex Co. Deeds 1704-1707 Bk. XII, p. 372.) Note: so little is known about Zachary Lewis I, that it is possible that she (Sarah) was his sister-in-law. The name of Zachary Lewis I appears as a wit. or atty. in many Essex Co. records up to 1719, which is probably the date of his death.

1708: 17 Jan.: Zachary Lewis was appointed deputy escheator general for Essex Co. by John Lewis Esqr. (of Warner Hall) who was escheator general for Gloucester, Middlesex, King & Queen, King William and Essex Cos. (Essex Co. Deeds and Wills, Bk XIII, p. 184.) Note: Zachary Lewis I was known to have had two sons, John, the eldest, and Zachary Lewis II. Their descendants are given in Hayden's Va. Genealogies, pp. 377-394.

DISCUSSION OF THE ZACHARY LEWIS FAMILY COAT OF ARMS:

In the book *Lewises, Meriwethers and their Kin,* by Sarah Travers Lewis (Scott) Anderson, pub. 1938, p. 355, she gives the coat of arms of the Zachary Lewis family as that of the Lewis family of Abernant Bychan, based on the crest of a horse's head, bridled, that was used by that family and which also appears on a large silver spoon owned by descendants of Zachary Lewis and the Ambrose Smith families who intermarried. In the article on this Smith family that appeared on pp. 150-1 of the July 1922 issue of *Tyler's Quarterly,* the spoon and crest are described, but no mention is made that it was a Lewis crest. The question is whether there was any Smith family that used that crest and the answer is yes. *Burke's General Armory,* pp. 937 and 945 lists a Smith/Smyth family of Credehill, Co. Hereford; Co. Hertford; Askham, Co. Nottingham; and Overton, Co. Salop; Arms granted 1590: Argent, on a mount vert in base a lion statant reguardant proper. Crest: A horse's head, roan color, mane sable, bridle or. (Another bears the crest sable.) Ambrose Smith pat. land adj. to Zachary Lewis in King Wm. Co.: 600 acs. 23 Apr. 1703 & 200 acs. 23 Oct. 1703. (Nugent, C. & P. III, pp. 74, 76.) He is prob. the Ambrose Smith listed as a shipper along with John Weith, fr. London to Va. via the *York Merchant*, 27 Nov. - 16 Dec. 1697. (P. Coldham, Compl. Bk. of Imm. 1661 -1699, p. 681.) Ambrose Smith must have died before the 1704 Quit Rent List was compiled, since the 800 acs. in King Wm. Co. is listed as belonging to Christopher Smith, who is also listed with 200 acs. in King and Queen Co. (L. des Cognets, *op. cit.,* pp. 154, 160.) This leaves the question of which family the crest originally belonged to unresolved.

Another coat of arms, crest and motto appear as the frontispiece in pamphlet commemorating the 200th anniversary of this family's residence in Virginia at the Lewis Congress held 4 Sept. 1894 at Bel-Air plantation, Spotsylvania Co., Va. It was published at Frankfort, Ky. 1894, by Geo. A. Lewis. There is no explanation of the arms in the pamphlet, but the publisher was a grandson of John Lewis of "Llangollen" who was very interested in the family's origin. It may have even been registered at the College of Arms and it would be very interesting to have their records checked. The crest is a calvary cross; the shield is gold with two sable bars, and on the gold are six sable martlets 3, 2, and 1, all facing to the shield's left. The motto in Latin, is: Deus meumque jus. (God and my right.[*]) I will not comment further except to say that a comparison of this with the Arms and pedigree of Sir William de Valence is very suggestive. (See Lewis of Llandewi Rhydderch in pt. one; Burke, *Gen. Armory*, p. 1047.)

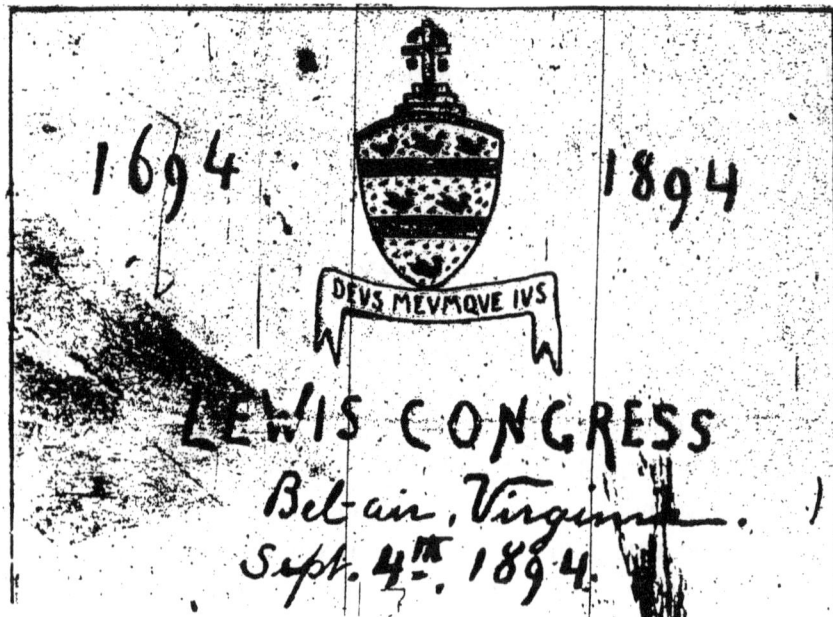

---

[*] Note: The motto is the same as that used by the Scottish Rite Masons.

V. LEWIS FAMILIES
ON THE SOUTH SIDE
OF THE RAPPAHANNOCK RIVER

1. Records of Richard Lewis (d. ca. 1667) Family of Lancaster (Middlesex) Co., Va.

1638: (?) Richard Lewis, headright of Capt. Christopher Wormley for 1420 acs. on Wormley's Cr. adj. New Poquoson. Transported the second year (i.e. after Wormley's arrival ca 1636/37). (Nugent, C. & P. I, p. 99.)

1649: (?) Richard Lewis, headright of Richard Kemp, Esqr. (Sec. of State) at Mobjack Bay. (Kemp had married Eliza., dau of Christopher Wormley.) (Nugent, C. & P. I, p. 182.)

1649: Richard Lewis, headright of Ralph Wormley for land at Rosegill Cr. Lancaster Co. (Nugent, C. & P. I, p. 206.)

1652: Richard Lewis pats. 300 acs. on Nymcock Cr. Lanc. Co. (Nugent, C. & P. I, p. 284.)

1653/4: Richard Lewis assigns this land to Thos. Willis and Richard Watkins. (Jan 4: Lanc. Deed Bk. I, p. 155.)

1653: Richard Lewis to pay levy on 2 tithables to Mr. Richard Perrot. (Lanc. Orders I, p. 93.)

1654/5: Feb. 5: Richard Lewis to pay levy on 3 tith. to Mr. Richard Perrot. (Lanc. Orders I, p. 174.)

1655: Richard Lewis again assigns land at Nimcock to Willis and Watkins, 20 Aug. (Nugent, C. & P. I, p. 313.)

1655: Richard Lewis to pay levy on 2 tith. to Abraham Weeks, 7 Dec. (Lanc. Co. Orders I, p. 237.)

1656: Richard Lewis signs inventory of estate of John Johnson Jr. (Lanc. Co. Record Bk. II, p. 50; In Fleet, Col. Va. Abs. Vol. I.)

1658: Oct. 7: Richard Lewis pats. 500 acs. on Sunderland Cr., alias Burnham's Cr. - Voided by a pat. of Cuthbert Potter 2 hours earlier. (Nugent, C. & P. I, p. 370.)

1658/9: Jan. 16: Richard Lewis pat. 500 acs. on Coplands Cr. adj. Robert Kemp (bro. of Richard & Edmond Kemp). (Nugent, C. & P. I, p. 384.)

1658/9: Jan. 16th: Richard Lewis pats. 200 acs. on Sunderland Cr. adj. Cuthbert Potter and Thos. Willis. (Nugent, C. & P. I, p. 384.)

1659: Mar. 30: Richard Lewis appointed Constable in the place of Thos. Willis. (Lanc. Co. Orders. In Duvall, Va. Col. Abs. Ser. 2, p. 7.)

1662: Feb. 2: Richard Lewis pats. 190 acs. Obert's Cr. Lanc Co. Granted to Capt. Wm. Brocas (married Mary Adams, widow of Christopher Wormley) who assigned to Sir Henry Chichily (Gov.) who assigns to Richard Lewis. (Nugent C. & P. I, p. 245 & p. 422.)

1662: Aug. 20: Richard Lewis sells 100 acs. adj. Cutbert Potter to Thos. Tushwell (Tugwell.) Signed by Richard Lewis and his wife, Frances. (Lanc. Co. Rec. Bk. II, 1654-1664, p. 248.)

1664: Dec. 2: Richard Lewis, Planter, sells 200 acs. adj. Robt. Kemp to Wm. Pue. (Lanc. Rec. Bk. II, p. 294. In: Fleet Col. Va. Abs. Vol. 1.)

1668: Richard Lewis in list of Tith. with 5 Tith. (In: Duvall, Col. Va. Abs. Ser. 2, Vol. 2, p. 93.) (Last year in list.)

1675: Mar. 21: Mr. Richard Lewis mentioned as deceased in pat. to Robert Price for 450 acs. adj. orphans of Mr. Richard Lewis. (Nugent, C. & P. II, p. 175.)

Records Of William Lewis (D. 1683), Son Of Richard Lewis

1683: Grace Lewis Exec. of Wm. Lewis, son of Richard Lewis. (In Middlesex Co., Va, Orders Bk. 2, p. 151)

2. John Lewis (D. 1705?), carpenter, of Stratton Major Par., New Kent Co. and Christ Church Par., Middlesex Co.

(Note: Poss. connected with Richard Lewis [D. 1667/8?] family of Middlesex.)

1681: 24 Oct.: John Lewis of New Kent Co. and Elizabeth O'Brissell of this Parish married, 24th of Oct. 1681. (Christ Church Par. Register, p. 20.)

1686: 2 Aug.: Indenture betw. John Bourk of the Par. of Christ Church in the Co. of Middlesex, planter, and Mary his wife of one pt. and John Lewis of the Parish of Stratton Major in the Co. of New Kent, Carpenter, of the other part. For 1200 lbs. tobo. & cask... 50 acs., part of 190 acs. granted to sd. John Bourk in Mdx. Co. on the main swp. of Sunderland, alias Burnham's Cr....adj. Thomas O'Brissels' plantation. (Middlesex Co. Deed Bk. 2, pp. 229-230.) (In Sparacio, Middlesex Co. Deeds 1679-1688, pp. 69.)
Note: John Burk's pat. for 191 acs., Mdx. Co. 30 Oct. 1686, Begin. at Thomas O'Brissel's near head of Green Br... (Nugent, C. & P. II, p. 301.) From the location this could certainly be ident. with the 190 acs. pat. by Richard Lewis 2 Feb. 1662. (Nugent, C. & P. I, pp. 245, 422.)
This John Lewis could be the same as, or, more likely, a son of the John Lewis mentioned as a servant in the will of Rowland Burnham, dtd. 12 Feb. 1655/6: "I leave

Family Chart of Richard Lewis (D. ca 1668)
of Lancaster/Middlesex Co. Va.

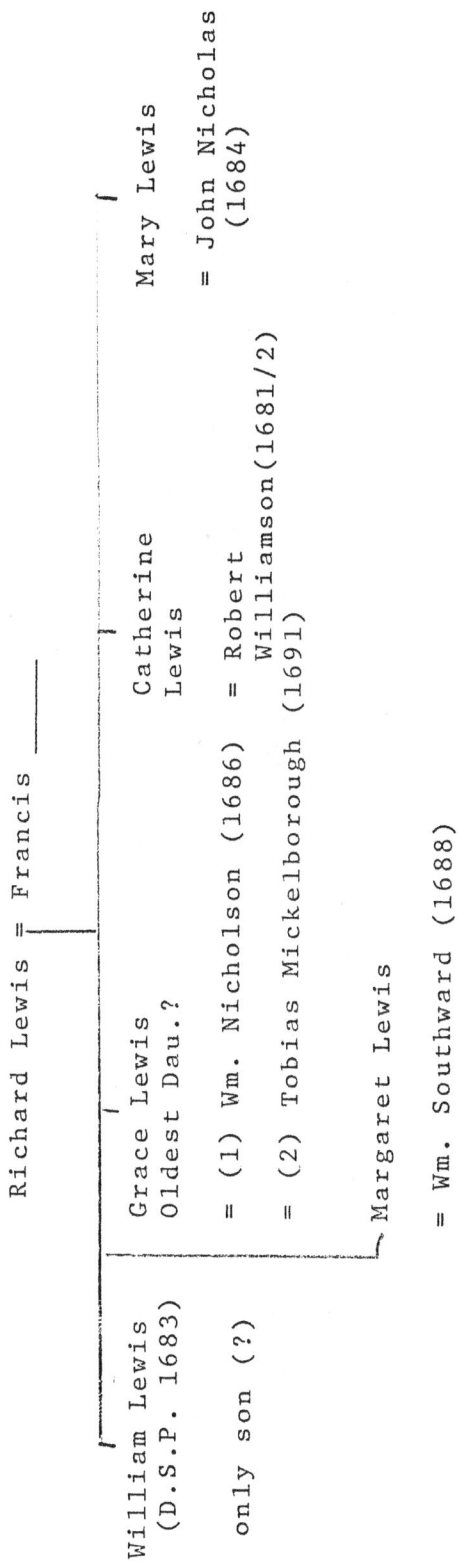

Richard Lewis = Francis _____

William Lewis
(D.S.P. 1683)

only son (?)

Grace Lewis
Oldest Dau.?

= (1) Wm. Nicholson (1686)

= (2) Tobias Mickelborough (1691)

Margaret Lewis

= Wm. Southward (1688)

Catherine
Lewis

= Robert
Williamson(1681/2)

Mary Lewis

= John Nicholas
(1684)

to my dau. Elleanor Burnham and to my son, Francis Burnham, three English servents called John Henley, David Watkins, and John Lewys..." (Lanc. Co. Deeds & Wills 1654-1661, pp. 46-49.) (In Sparacio, Lanc. Co. Deeds & Wills 1654-1661, pp. 22-24.) After the death of Rowland Burnham, his widow, Alice, nee Eltonhead, married Henry Corbin, whose pat. for 700 acs. of land "on the N.E. side of the Mattapony Riv. about 25 miles up the Great Swamp" (Dragon Swamp at the head of the Peankatanck Riv) would place it in Stratton Major Parish.) The patent includes the names of John Henley, David Watkins, John Lewis and John "Birk" dtd. 15 Sept. 1658. (Nugent, C. & P. I, p. 369.)

Records of the children of John Lewis and Elizabeth O'Brissell from the Christ Church Parish Register:

1691: 26 July: Thomas, son of John and Elizabeth Lewis Bapt. (p. 50.)

1691: 28 Sep.: Griffin, the son of John and Elizabeth Lewis, buried (p. 53.) Griffin, John (D. 1748) and any other children of John & Elizabeth were probably bapt. in Stratton Major Par., whose records have not survived. Only those named for O'Brissells appear in the Christ Church Reg.

1693/4: Eusebius Lewis, son of John and Elizabeth Lewis, born 22 Jan. and Bapt. 4 March (p. 52.) (He was named for the Eusebius O'Brissell who was buried 7 Mar. 1689/90) (p. 39.)

The later records of Middlesex Co. mention only John Lewis (D. 1748) who probably inherited the 50 acs. of his father, and Eusebius Lewis who was left 100 acs. by the will of Thomas O'Brissell, dtd. 11 Dec. 1698, plus an additional 100 acs. after the death of his wife, Ann. Thomas Lewis (B.1691) was also left the 100 acs. and the additional 100 acs., but does not appear in any further records. (In J.W. Boyd, A Fam. Hist...p. 257-8.)

1705: Poss. death date of John Lewis, since John Aldin was security on the admin. bond of John Lewis this year.

Children of John Lewis (D. 1748) and wife Elizabeth from the Christ Church Parish Register:

1710: Mary, Dau. of John and Eliza. Lewis, bapt. 3 Jan. 1710. (p. 75.)
(This may be the Mary Lewis, d. 24 Aug., Bur. 25 Aug. 1720) (p. 176.)
1713: Elizabeth, Dau. of John and Eliza. Lewis, Bapt. 7 Mar. (p. 88.)
(She married Griggs Yarborough 27 June 1735. (p. 169.)
1717: Susanna, dau. of John and Eliza. Lewis, b. 23 Apr., Bapt.26 May. (p. 97) (She married Valentine Ball 31 Jan. 1733.) (p. 168.)
1719: John, son of John and Eliza. Lewis, b. 11 Apr., Bapt. 3 May. (p. 98) He married an Elizabeth and died in 1758. See below.)
1720: Thomas, son of John and Eliza. Lewis, b. 3 Jan., Bapt. 29 Jan. (p. 106.)
1722: Margaret, dau. of John and Eliza. Lewis, b. 25 Jan., Bapt.17 Feb. (p. 112.)
1724: Richard, son of John and Eliza. Lewis, b. 10 Nov., Bapt. 6 Dec. (p. 116.)
1728: Mary, dau. of John and Eliza. Lewis, b. 10 Nov., Bapt. 1 Dec. (p. 125.)

1711: 3 July: John Lewis (D. 1748) buys a tract of land from Powell Stamper of Middlesex (acs. not given.) (Middlesex Deeds Bk. 3 p. 268.)

1748: The Will of John Lewis (D. 1748) mentioned his 3 sons: John, Thomas, and Richard; leaving each of them 100 acs.; his grandchildren, Griffin and Sarah Yarborough; the residue to his wife Elizabeth for life, then divided equally among all children now living. (In J.W. Boyd, *ibid.,* cites Middlesex Co. L.W.B. p. 79.)
Note: In 1755 on 25 July Thomas Lewis, then of Henrico Co. sold his 100 acs. to Wm. Brooks of Middlesex Co. (Middlesex Deed Bk. 8, pp. 68-70.)

1758: The will of John Lewis (1719-1758) mentions sons: William, John, and Thomas; wife, Elizabeth, if she remarries, whole estate to be divided equally betw. loving wife and five children: Wm., John, Thos., Ann and Mary. (In: J.W. Boyd *ibid.,* p. 253. Cites Middlesex L.W.C. p. 15.)

Children of this John Lewis (1719-1758) and his wife Elizabeth listed in the Christ Church Parish reg. are:
William Lewis, b. 31 July, Bapt. 2 Sept. 1750. (p. 299)
Ann Lewis, b. 3 Aug., Bapt. 28 Aug. 17__ (p. 298)
John Lewis, b. 17 Feb., Bapt. 30 March 1755 (p. 286)
Note: In Apr., 1774, Wm. Lewis then of Goochland Co. and wife Sally sold his land, 100 acs. to Robt. Stamper of Middlesex (Middlesex Deeds Bk 9, pp. 264-66.)
On 30 Oct., 1779, Thos. Lewis then of Ware Co., N.C., sold his land, 84 acs., to Robt Stamper (Middlesex Deeds Bk. 9A, p. 410)

Records of Eusebius Lewis (B. 1694) from the Christ Church Parish Register:
1716: Eusebius Lewis married Mary Loyall, 5 Apr. (p. 83)
1716: William, son of Eusebius and Mary Lewis, b. 26 Nov., Bapt. 2 Dec. (p. 95)
1717: John, son of same, b. 8 Dec., Bapt. 19 Jan. 1717/18. (p. 98)
1720: Anne, dau. of same, b. 4 May, Bapt. 29 May 1720. (p. 105)
1722: Usebius, son of same, b. 10 Oct., Bapt. 11 Nov. (p. 111)
1725: Mary, dau. of same, b. 10 Apr., Bapt. 2 May. (p. 117)
1728: William (II) (The first Wm. d. 8 Dec. 1716 - p. 172.) Son of same, b. 3 Jul, Bapt.18 Aug. 1728 (p. 124).
1730: Matthew, son of same, b. 23 Nov., Bapt. 28 Dec. 1730 (p. 130). He died 16 Dec. 1732 (p. 188.)
1733: Sarah, dau. of same, b. 28 May, Bapt. 1 July 1733 (p. 136). (She died 4 Nov. 1733, p. 189.)
1735: Death of Eusebius Lewis Sr. 21 Nov. 1735 (p. 190.)

Records of Eusebius Lewis, Jr. (1722-1760):
1760: Will of Eusebius Lewis dtd. 4 Feb. 1760: mentions wife, Martha Lewis, children: Richard, Dorothy, Mary, Gabriel, and Elizabeth. (In: J. W. Boyd, A Family History: Wright-Lewis-Moore and Connected Families, Early Settlers Greene Co. Georgia, 1968, p. 257, cited as Middlesex L.W.C. pp. 36, 37.)

Family Chart of John Lewis (D. 1705?),
Carpenter, of Stratton Major Parish,
New Kent Co. & Christ Church Parish,
Middlesex Co. Va.

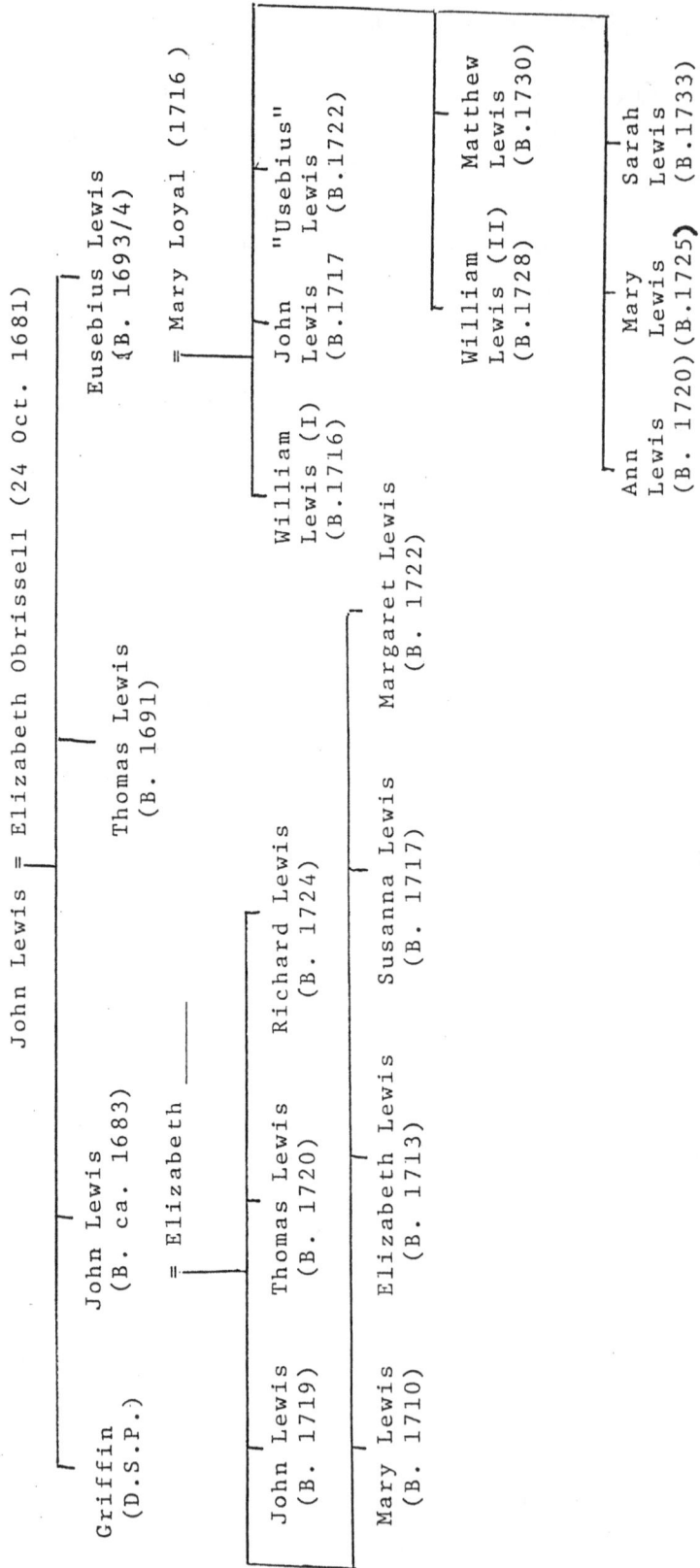

John Lewis = Elizabeth Obrissell (24 Oct. 1681)

Eusebius Lewis
(B. 1693/4)

= Mary Loyal (1716)

Thomas Lewis
(B. 1691)

John "Usebius"
Lewis Lewis
(B.1717 (B.1722)

William
Lewis (I)
(B.1716)

William Matthew
Lewis (II) Lewis
(B.1728) (B.1730)

Ann Mary Sarah
Lewis Lewis Lewis
(B. 1720)(B.1725)(B.1733)

John Lewis
(B. ca. 1683)

= Elizabeth

Griffin
(D.S.P.)

Richard Lewis
(B. 1724)

Margaret Lewis
(B. 1722)

Thomas Lewis
(B. 1720)

Susanna Lewis
(B. 1717)

Elizabeth Lewis
(B. 1713)

John Lewis
(B. 1719)

Mary Lewis
(B. 1710)

3. Records of James Lewis (d. ca 1720) Middlesex Co., Va.

1714: James Lewis an appraiser of the estate of John Wats, Dec'd. 1 Feb. 1714. (Middlesex Co. Will Bk., 1713-1734, p. 31.)

1720: Will of James Lewis dtd. 13 Sep 1715, prob. 7 July 1720: Wife Joanna (Joan) dau of Wm. Kilbee. Children: James, Edmond, Katherine, Zebulon, Jasewa (Joshua.) (Middlesex Co. Will Bk. 1713, 1734, pp. 134-5.)

Issue: (With dates from Christ Church Par. Reg.)

Edmond (Not in Register)

Katherine (Not in Register)

James: chr. 30 Nov. 1690, p. 41.

Thomas: chr. 5 Nov. 1693, p. 42. (D.S.P?)

Zebulun: chr. 22 Oct. 1699, p. 46 (d. 1738 Isle of Wight = Jane, sister of Benj. Cooper. (Bodie, Southside Va. Fam. Vol. 1, p. 316.)

Joshua: b. 27 Dec. 1702, p. 60 (d. 1760) Isle of Wight Co. = Martha, dau of John Marsden. (Bodie, Southside Va. Fam. Vol. 1, p. 315-316.)

Note: James Lewis may have been the son of the Edmond Lewis who died in Lancaster/Middlesex Co in 1663.

VI. LEWIS FAMILIES ON THE
NORTH SIDE
OF THE
RAPPAHANNOCK RIVER

1. Records Of Edward (ap) Lewis (D. 1697):

1656: Edward ap Lewis a headright of Mr. Humphrey Booth on a land certificate granted 6 June 1656. (Sparacio, Lanc. Co. Deeds & Wills 1652-1657, p. 109.) Note: The names on this certificate appear on the land pat. of John Suggett, 20 Feb. 1662, in Nugent, C. & P. I, p. 481.

1660: Edward Lewis buys 400 acs. fr. John Williams, carpenter, and wife Mary of Farnham Cr. (Sparacio, Rappahannock Deeds & Wills, 1654-1661, p. 94.)

1662: Edward Lewis ordered to remove quarter he built betw. the woods and the (Morattico) Indians. (Sparacio, *ibid.,* St. 2, pp. 6-7.)

1662/3: Tho. Robinson and Edward Lewis pat. 1140 acs. Rappahannock Co. 20 Feb. 1662/3. (Nugent C. & P. I, p. 470.)

1663: Edward Lewis pats. 498 acs. a mile up Ewd main Br. of Totoskey Cr. on Swd. side called the Cross Cr. 1 June 1663. Running to line of James Samford. (Nugent, C. & P. I, p. 486.)

1664: Wm. Barber of Totoskey Cr. Sells Roger Williams 200 acs. on S. Br. of Tot. Cr. adj. Edw. Lewis. (Sparacio, *op. cit.,* p. 78.)

1664: Edw. Lewis and wife Mary sell James Biddlecomb 400 acs. of land. 4 July 1664, wit. by Wm. Barber and Thos. Freshwater. (Sparacio, *op. cit.,* pp. 79-80.)

1664: Wm Barber sells Fran. Settle 400 acs. Tot. Cr. adj. Edw. Lewis. (Sparacio, *op. cit.,* p. 85.)

1664: 13 Oct.: James Samford sells Quintan Sherman 200 acs. adj. Edw. Lewis and Roger Williams. (Sparacio, *op. cit.,* p. 105.)

1665: 1 Nov.: Humphrey Booth gives deed of gift (2 cows) to Edw. Lewis, son of Edward Lewis. (Sparacio, Rappahannock Deeds & Wills I, pp. 76-7.)

1666: 14 Nov. Edw. Lewis sells Giles Cale 200 of 498 acs. on Tot. Cr. Adj. Roger Williams incl. his old plantation house. (Sparacio, Rappahannock Deed Bk. 3, 1663-1668, pp. 29-30.)

1666: 14 Nov. Wm. Landman sells 1/2 of tract of 1140 acs. pat. by Edw. Lewis & Thos. Robinson & sold by them to Samuel Man & Wm. Landman, to Eliza. Man of Northumberland Co. for her lifetime & then divided by John Knott & Mary, dau. of Sam. & Eliza. Man. (Sparacio, *ibid.,* p. 34.)

1666/7: 1 Jan.: Wm. Moseley sells 5.798 acs. adj. Thos. Robinson & Edw. Lewis pat. to Mr. John Hull. (Sparacio, *ibid.,* p. 36.)

1666/7: 5 Mar: Edw. Lewis gives Quintillian Sherman pow. of Atty. in suite of Miles Hugill. Wit. by Johanna Freshwater. (Sparacio, *ibid.,* p. 53.)

1667: 6 Nov.: Indenture to farm betw. Edw. Lewis and David Thomas, Yeoman, land on Tot. Cr. known as David's Quarter. (Sparacio, *ibid.,* p. 74-5.)

1668: 6 May: Thomas Robinson gives Deed of Gift (one heifer & its incr.) to Mary, dau. of Edw. Lewis. (Sparacio, *ibid.,* p. 107.)

1668: 3 July: James Biddlecomb sells 200 acs. of land to Anth. Lancaster, adj. Wm. Barber and Thos. Coley, sold to him by Edw. Lewis. (Sparacio, *ibid.,* p. 124.)

1669: 7 May: Edw. Lewis wit. deed of gift of Geo. Nichols & Mat. Wilcoxe for division of 4,000 acs. of land with gift of 1,000 acs. to daus. Anne & Mary Nichols. (Sparacio, *ibid.*)

1670: 27 Aug.: Will of David Thomas gives estate to Edw. Lewis. (Sparacio, Rappahannock Deeds & Wills 1665-1677, p. 42-3.)

1671: 5 July: Edw. Lewis Deed of Gift to Zachary, son of Geo. Nichols. One heifer. (Sparacio, Rappahannock Deeds & Wills 4, pt. 2, p. 68.)

1674: 8 Mar. Elizabeth, dau. of Edw. Lewis bapt.

1676: Joanna, dau. of Edw. Lewis bapt. Sept. 8th.

1678: 31 Aug.: Robt. Wood sells Edw. Lewis 200 acs. adj. Geo. Nichols and Matthew Wilcocks. (Land formerly Thos. Freshwaters.) (Sparacio, Rappahannock Deeds & Wills 1677-1682, pt. 1, p. 106.)

1681: 19 Dec.: Samuel Griffin sells 200 acs. to Philip Hunning, formerly sold by Edw. Lewis to Giles Cale. (Sparacio, *ibid.,* pt. 2, p. 90.)

1682: 13 Jan.: Philip Hunnings sells land bought fr Sam. Griffin to Richard Jasper. (Sparacio, Rappahannock Deed Bk. 1682-1686, p. 9.)

1682/3: Edw. & Mary Lewis sell Thos. George, Gent., 298 acs. One mile up eastern br. of Tot. Cr. (Note: Thos. George was formerly a Justice of Middlesex Co., Va.)

1683: 17 Aug.: Will of Thos. George, Gent., leaves land he bought fr. Edw. Lewis on Tot. Cr. to dau. Margaret or if she prefers 20,000 lbs. tobo., land to son, Leroy George. Sparacio, Rappahannock Co. Wills, 1682-1687, pp. 17-18.)

1683/4: 6 Mar.: Judgement to Edw. Lewis ag. estate of Thos. George, dec'd, for 9,212 lbs. tobo. & cask for bal. of bill. (Sparacio, Rappahannock Co. Orders 1685-1687, p. 8.)

1685/6: 3 Mar.: Edw. Lewis & three others to lay out land belonging to Lunn & Beedelcomb orphans. (Sparacio, Rappahannock Co. Order Bk 1685-1687, p. 29.)

1690: 29 Apr.: John Landman of Westmoreland Co. sells Wm. Hassell of Rappahannock Co. 100 acs., part of tract pur. by his father, W. Landman fr. Edw. Lewis. (Sparacio, Rappahannock Deeds 1688 - 1692, p. 71.)

1691: Edw. & Thos. Lewis of Rappahannock Co. Cert. for 528 acs. in Rappahannock & Northumb. Cos. on a br. of the Yeocomico dtd. 15 June. (Northern Neck Land Bk I, pp. 12 & 59.)

1691: 16 June: Edw. & Thos Lewis of Rappahannock Co.: certification for 2 parcels of land in N. Farnham Par. one of 101 acs. & one of 330 acs. (*ibid.*, p. 61.)

1691: 21 Aug.: Edw. & Thos. Lewis and Wm. Morgan of Rappahannock Co., Cert. for 321 acs. and Cert. for 360 acs. (*op. cit.,* pp. 97 - 98.)

1691/2: 2 Mar.: Wm. Morgan assns. his interest in the 360 acs. to Edw. & Thos. Lewis. (Richmond Co. Deed Bk. I, pp. 182-186.)

1692: 11 Apr. Deed fr. Edw. Lewis, Thos. Lewis and John Landman to Thomas Walker. 92 1/2 acs. near Tot. Cr. adj. Geo. Eale and Wm. Smith and land of Thos. Walker. The John Landman part cont. 16 acs. taken fr. the Edw. & Thos. Lewis part of two overplus within the old lines of the Thos. Robinson & Edw. Lewis pat. of 1140 acs., leaving it entire. (Sparacio, Rich. Co. Deeds 1692-1694, pp. 6-7.)

1692: 2 May: Mary Lewis, wife of Edw. Lewis appts. John Morgan Atty for sale. (Sparacio, *ibid.,* p. 7.) Note: The mark of this Mary is different from the previous Mary who was the first wife of Edw. Lewis. Her life also seems to have been more exciting.

1692: 6 Oct.: Edw. Lewis and Mary his wife brought action of trespass upon battery ag. Danl. Swillivant who assaulted her body on 25 Dec. last, through her into the clay hole and did evely intreat her until she made her escape into the house, but sd. Danll. pursued, breaking open the house door, reviling her with names as calling her French Bitch, and beating and abusing her to the danger of her life, if in time rescue had not been made, for which craves damages and costs. The Deft. by his atty. says he cannot plead for want of certainty. Court ordered case dismissed. Plaint. appealed to the Genl Court. Danll. Swillivant and Saml. Samford posted 5000 lbs. tobo bond to Col. John Stone, High Sheriff, and Edw. Lewis and Henry Clark did the same. (Sparacio, Rich. Co. Orders 1692-1694, p. 28)

1692: 6 Oct.: Action of Edw. Lewis ag. Edw. Read who married Exx. of Thos. George, dec'd is dismissed. (Sparacio, *ibid.*, p. 30.)

1692/3: 4 Jan.: Edw. Lewis confessed judgement to Capt. Wm. Moseley for 400 lbs. tobo & cask- 1/2 of bill passed to Plt. by Thos. and the sd. Edw. Lewis bearing date 18 Mar. 1691/2. (Sparacio, *op. cit.*, p. 39.)

1693: 30 July: Birth of Jane, dau. of Edw. and Mary Lewis. (King, Regs. of Rich. Co., Va., p. 115.)

1693-1695: Numerous suits in the Rich. Co. Orders re: Edw. Lewis suing and being sued.

1695: 30 Sep.: Birth of Lewis ap Lewis Lewis, son of Edw. and Mary Lewis. (King, Regs. of Rich. Co., Va., p. 116.)

1697: 2 June: Action brought by James Orchard ag. Edw. Lewis abates, deft. being dead. (Sparacio, Rich. Co. Orders 1697-1699, p. 5.)

1697: 8 Oct.: Ref. betw. Wm. Colston, Plt. and John Lewis, Deft. til next court: John Lewis hath possesed himself of the estate of Edw. Lewis of this Co. who dyed intestate, without being lawfully empowered thereunto - John Lewis summoned to appear at next court and show cause why letters of Admin. are not taken out, (Sparacio, *ibid.*, p. 23.)

1698: 1 June: Order of Admin. is granted to Martin Hammond and his wife Mary as nearest of kin upon estate of Edw. Lewis dec'd. Security bond of 5,000 lbs. tobo posted by Martin Hammond, Rich. Jesper, and Samll. Samford. (Sparacio, *ibid.*, p. 36.)

1698: 1 June: Ordered that Edw. Jones and Charles Barber inventory estate of Edw. Lewis, dec'd, at his house. (Sparacio, *ibid.*, p. 37.)

1698/9: 1 Mar. Judgement granted to Wm. Colston ag. estate of Edw. Lewis, dec'd, in hands of Martin Hammond and Mary his wife, Admx. of the estate, for 357 lbs. tobo. (Sparacio, *op. cit.*, p. 73.)

1701/2: 4 Mar.: Upon petition of Mary Lewis, widow and relict of Edw. Lewis, ordered that Wm. Morgan be summoned next to show cause why by force he debarrs Mary of her right of dower to the land mentioned by her in her sd. petiton. (Sparacio, Rich. Co. Orders 1699-1701, p. 93.)

1701/2: 5 Mar.: Action brought by guardians and trustees of Est. Of Capt. Arthur Spicer, dec'd ag. Martin Hammond and Mary his wife, Admx. of Edw. Lewis dec'd is dismissed - no prosecution. (Sparacio, *ibid.,* p. 100.)

1702: 1 July: According to complaint of Mary Lewis, widow and relict of Edw. Lewis, ordered that sheriff assn. sd. Mary her dower or third part of all the lands, houses, and tenements formerly in the possession of her sd. husband. (Sparacio, Rich. Co. Orders 1702-1704, p. 17.)

1704/5: 8 Mar.: The daughters of Edw. Lewis and their husbands: Simon Tayler & wife Elizabeth, Thomas Jesper and wife Anne, Christopher Pridham and wife Mary (Form. wife of Martin Hammond) of one party and Joseph Deek (husband of Katherine) and William Linton (Lynton) (husband of Joanna) of the other part. rights to land sold by Thos. Lewis to John Lewis. (360 acs. and 528 acs.) Note: John Lewis was the full brother of these five sisters, and appears to have died intestate before this date. (Sparacio, Rich. Co. Deeds, pp. 98-99.)

Known issue of Edward Lewis:
  By first wife, Mary:
    Edward, b. before 1 Nov. 1665. Prob. died young.
    John, no birth record, d. s. p. ca. 1704.
    Mary, b. before 6 May 1668 = (1) Martin Hammond, = (2) Christopher Pridham.
    Elizabeth, b. 8 Mar. 1674 = Simon Tailor
    Joanna, b. 8 Sept. 1676 = William Linton (of Copley par. Westm. Co.)
    Anne, no birth record = Thomas Jesper
    Katherine, no birth record = Joseph Deeke (Dike)

  By second wife, Mary (of French extraction?)
    Jane, b. 30 July 1693. May have married James Lamkin of Northum. Co.
    Lewis, known as Lewis ap Lewis Lewis b. 30 Sept. 1695. resided Northumberland Co., Va. D. by 15 May 1734 est. admin. by James Lamkin. (Lewis & Booker, Northumb. Co. Va Wills & Admins. 1713-1749, p. 90.) He left two daus.: Mary and Jane. (Jett, Records of Northumb. Co., Va., pp. 78, 85-6.) No other known issue.

Family Chart of Edward (ap) Lewis (D. 1696)
Of Old Rappahanock/Richmond Co. Va.

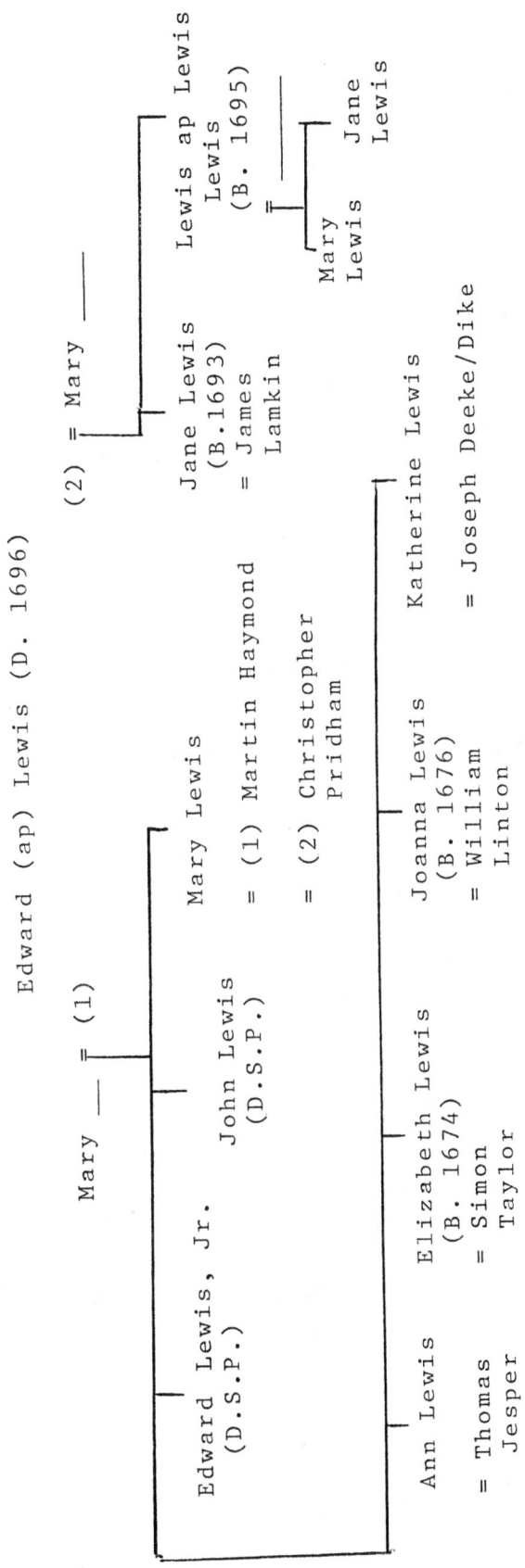

Edward (ap) Lewis (D. 1696)

Mary ——— (1)

(2) = Mary ———

Edward Lewis, Jr.
(D.S.P.)

John Lewis
(D.S.P.)

Mary Lewis
= (1) Martin Haymond
= (2) Christopher
      Pridham

Jane Lewis
(B.1693)
= James
  Lamkin

Lewis ap Lewis
Lewis
(B. 1695)

Mary   Jane
Lewis   Lewis

Ann Lewis
= Thomas
  Jesper

Elizabeth Lewis
(B. 1674)
= Simon
  Taylor

Joanna Lewis
(B. 1676)
= William
  Linton

Katherine Lewis
= Joseph Deeke/Dike

2. (Mr.) Thomas Lewis (D. 1709) Records:

1680: 27 Sep.: Thomas Lewis is a witness to the will of Thomas Goose, along with Richard Glover, age 44, Henry Clark, and Mary Glover. (Sparacio, Rappahannock Deeds & Wills, 1677-1682, Pt. I, pp. 50-51.)

1683: 19 July: Thomas Lewis ag. James Baker. Whereas an attach. was awarded Thomas Lewis ag. the estate of James Baker for 1600 lbs. tobo. and caske, which attach. is returned executed on a mare now running at the plantation of Col. Thos. Brereton, and whereas sd. Thomas hath this court made his debt appear due... judgement is granted the sd. Lewis for the sd. mare. (Northumberland Co. Orders 1678-1698, p. 192.)

1684: 7 May: Judgement granted Thos. Lewis ag. John Fulcher for 500 lbs. tobo and cask, due on sealed bill dtd. 19 June, 1683. (Sparacio, Rappahannock Co. Orders 1683-1685, p. 21.)

1685: 7 May: Non-suite granted Mrs. Eliz. George, Exrx. of Mr. Thomas George, dec'd, ag. Thomas Lewis, he not appearing to prosecute. (Sparacio, *ibid.,* p. 83.)

1685: 4 Sep.: Ref. granted betw. John Sherlock, Plt. & Thos. Lewis, deft. til next court. (Sparacio, Rappahannock Co. Orders 1685-1687, p. 11.)

1685: 10 Sept.: Benjamin, son of Thos. Lewis born. (King, Reg. of North Farnham Par. Rich. Co., Va., p. 115.)

1685: 21 Dec.: John Sherlock and Thomas Lewis appt. to appraise goods of Wm. Shepards estate in the suite of Wm. Davis (Sparacio, *op. cit.,* p. 23.)

1685/6: 3 Mar.: Judgement granted Mr. James Stanford ag. estate of Mr. Abraham Kenyon in hands of Thos. Lewis for 400 lbs. tobo. (Sparacio, *op. cit.,* p. 31.)

1687/8: 16 Feb.: Deed fr. John Overton, planter & wife Penelope to Thos. Lewis for 9,000 lbs. tobo and cask. Plantation of 252 acs. in Totuskey Cr. to on a point whereof now standeth the ferry house, adj. Mr. Davis and land of Leonard Jones. Land escheated and granted Edw. Eustace & by him sold to sd. Overton by deed dtd. 1 Jan. 1683. (Sparacio, Rappahannock Co. Deeds 1686-1688, pp. 92-93.)

1688: 2 July: Power of Atty fr. Penelope Overton to Rawleigh Travers for land Thos. Lewis bought of husband John Overton, formerly in possession of John De Younge. (Sparacio, *ibid.,* p. 93.)

1688: 2 May: Ordered that Thos. Lewis, John Morgan & James Collins be paid 4 days attendance by Angel Jacobus...in his suite with Ralph Whiting. (Sparacio, Rappahannock Co. Orders 1687-1689, p. 25-26.)

1689: 29 June: Indenture betw. Thos. Lewis & wife Mary and Henry Webster. They sell Henry Webster 70 acs. - pt. of land he bought fr. John Overton 16 Feb. 1687. (Sparacio, Rappahannock Deed Bk. 1688-1692, pp. 24-25.)

1689: 3 July: Mary Lewis appts Henry Lewis Atty. to ackn. above deed. (Sparacio, *ibid.,* p. 25.)

1689: 3 July Indent. Betw. Saml. Bayley & Phil. Hunning for 1/3 vessell *Dolphin* Bayley sells Hunning 450 acs. Chingatege Cr. adj. Ralph Whiting. Wit. by Thos. Lewis & Ralph Witings. (Sparacio, *op. cit.,* p. 21-22.)

1689: 28 Sep.: Thos. Lewis wit. deed of Abraham Cooke to Thos. Gladman for 50 acs. w. side of Tot. Cr. (Sparacio, *op. cit.,* p. 44.)

1689: 10 Oct.: Henry Webster sells back to Thos. Lewis the 70 acs. he bought fr. him previously. (Sparacio. *op. cit.,* pp. 53-54.)

1689: 20 Oct.: Leonard Jones of river Nanticock of Md. appts. Thos. Lewis Atty for deed of sale fr. Jones to Richard Bramham. (Sparacio, *op. cit.,* p. 58.)

1689: 2 Nov.: Deed of exchange betw. Thos. Lewis, ferryman, and Wm. Davis, planter: Lewis gives Davis 40 acs. - Pt. of land purchased fr. John Overton in exchange for 40 acs. Davis bought of John De Younge & Thos. Freshwater, dec'd. (Sparacio, *op. cit.,* pp. 55-56.)

1689/90: 20 Feb.: Thos. Lewis and Deborah Bramham wit. deed of sale of land to John Morgan, blacksmith, for 50 acs. on Tot. Cr. (Sparacio, *op. cit.,* p. 74.)

1690/1: 19 Feb.: Cert. to Thos. Lewis of Rappahannock Co. for 477 acs. in sd. Co., surveyed 29 Sept. 1683 for Edw. Eustace & Wm. Davis. Beg. at a white oak near the line of John Shurlock & Leonard Jones, N. bank of Tot. Cr. above Madam Hull's store. (Nugent, C & P. Suppl., Northern Neck Grants No. 1, 1690 - 1692, p. 3.) Note: This appears to be the land pat. by John De Young 3 Nov. 1664 and later escheated. (Nugent, C. & P. I, p. 514.)

1691: 21 Aug.: Certs. to Thos. & Edw. Lewis & Wm. Morgan for 2 tracts of land: 321 acs. on W. br. of Tot. Cr. adj. Miles Hughgott, John Shurlock & Thos. Freshwater; 360 acs. in Rappahannock & Northumb. Cos. adj. Thos. Freshwater & Zacariah Nichols, formerly Henry Corbin's. (Nugent, *op. cit.,* p. 6.)

1692: 15 June: Thos. & Edw. Lewis, of Rappahannock Co., 528 acs. in Rappahannock & Northumb. Cos. beg. in N. line of Thos. Freshwater by br. of Yeocormaco Riv. binding on land form. granted to Thos. Robinson.... (Nugent, *ibid.,* p. 4.)

1692: 16 June: To same: two parcels of land in North Farnham Par. in Rappahannock Co. On W. side of N. br. of Tot. Cr. cont. 101 acs. beg. on W. side of Ferry Rd. nr. plant. of Wm. Clayton. 230 acs. beg. at pat. of Thos. Robinson & Edw. Lewis.... (Nugent, *op. cit.,* p. 4.) Note: The same page lists various documents relating to the 477 acs. that Thos. Lewis purchased fr. John Overton in 1687.

1692: 5 Dec.: Thomas Lewis, son of Thomas Lewis and Mary born. (King, Reg. of North Farnham Par. Rich. Co., Va., p. 115.)

1693: 4 Oct.: Thomas Lewis ag. Danll. Swillivant for breaking the bottom out of his ferry boat as it was passing Mr. John Loyd's landing on Tot. Cr. Jury granted non-suit to Danll. Swillivant to be payed with cost of suit.

1694: 7 Oct.: Ordered that Thomas Lewis be payed at next court levy 5,000 lbs. tobo for keeping Totuskey Ferry and the way through the marsh in good repair. (Sparacio, Rich. Co. Orders 1694-1697, p. 12.) Note: this order was repeated every year to at least 1703, with the amt. fr. 4500 to 5,000 lbs. tobo annually.

1694/5: 6 Mar.: Order ag. the sheriff to Henry Lewis for the non-appearance of Thos. Lewis. (Sparacio, *ibid.,* p. 33.)

1695: 1 May: Order granted last court to Henry Lewis ag. sheriff for the non-appearance of Thomas Lewis for 600 lbs. tobo and cask upon bill is confirmed and ordered to be paid. (Sparacio, *ibid.,* p. 36.)

1695: 9 Sep.: William Lewis son of Thomas and Mary Lewis, born. (King, *op. cit.,* p. 155.

1696: 3 June: Thos. Lewis makes over to John Lewis of Northumberland Co. (son of Edward Lewis) his interest in the 360 acs. of land that he, Edw. Lewis & Wm. Morgan pat. 21 Aug. 1691; and in the 528 acs. adj. above that he and Edw. Lewis pat. 15 June 1691. (Sparacio, Rich. Co. Deeds 1695-1701, pp. 25-27.)

1696/7: 3 Feb.: Last will & Test. of Leonard Robinson, dec'd., presented by Ex. Mr. Joseph Dike (Deeke) & proved by oaths of Thos. Lewis & John Wakeman. (Sparacio, Rich. Co. Orders 1694-1697, p. 120.)

1697/8: 11 Feb.: Thos. Lewis wit. deed of gift of Charity Webster to her dau. Ann. (Sparacio, Rich. Co. Deeds 1695-1701.)

1698: 3 Nov.: Ordered that Thos. Lewis be licensed to keep an ordinary for next year at his house near Totuskey Ferry, and gives bond to keep good order within sd. house. (Sparacio, Rich. Co. Orders 1697-1699, p. 63.)

1701: 7 May: Thos. Lewis accepts Tobias Pursell, son of David Pursell, dec'd, to keep until 18 years old as a servant from the churchwardens of N. Farnham Par. (Sparacio, Rich. Co. Orders 1699-1701, p. 66.)

1701: 3 Dec.: The last will & test. of John Evans was proved by the oaths of Thomas Lewis and Benjamin Lewis. (Sparacio, Rich. Co. Orders 1699-1701, p. 80.)

1701/2: 6 Feb.: A jury was impaneled that incl. Mr. Thos. Lewis. (Sparacio, *ibid.,* p. 89.) Note: this was the first time that Thos. Lewis was given the title of Mr. and may indicate that he was serving as a vestryman of North Farnham Parish at this time.

1703/4: 1 Mar.: A certificate granted Thos. Lewis for 100 acs. of land due for importation of two persons into this colony by name Thos. Lewis and Chas. Coner, the sd. Thos. making oath that neither he nor any to his knowledge had received certificate for the same, the right of which in court he assns. to Capt. Chas. Smith, (Sparacio, Rich. Co. Orders 1702-1704, p. 96.) Note: the entry following this was a cert. granted to Rich. Clifton for 100 acs. for the imp. of John Defferrick and Joane Rowling which Clifton assn. to Capt. Chas. Smith. These four rights were used in a pat. of John May for 191 acs. in Essex Co., St. Mary's Par. 26 Apr. 1704. Chas. Coner was deceased by this time as Maj. David Gwin had been paid 133 lbs. tobo for an inquest on him 1 Jan. 1700/1 (Sparacio, Rich. Co. Orders 1699-1701, p. 49.) This entry would indicate that Thos. Lewis had paid the cost of his own and Chas. Coner's immigration to Va. rather than coming as an indentured servant. If so, he waited a long time to claim the land rights due him.

1703: 30 Aug.: Mr. Thos. Lewis owed 900 lbs. tobo fr. the estate of Wm. Brockenbough, dec'd. (B. Fleet, Va. Col. Abs. V. I, p. 280.)

1705: 4 Dec.: Benjamin Lewis (son of Thomas) wit. Power of Atty. of Deborah Bramham. (Sparacio, Rich. Co. Deeds 1705-1708, p. 16.) Note: This is the last record of Benjamin in Rich. Co. He probably moved to St. Paul's Parish, Stafford Co. about this time, where his later records are found.

1706: 2 Aug.: Thos. Lewis sells Thos. Thorne, Gent., 431 acs. granted Thos. Lewis and Edw. Lewis, late dec'd, in joint tenancy, 16 June 1691 in two parcels: 101 acs. & 330 acs. Mary Lewis gives James Coward her power of atty. for sale. (Sparacio, *ibid.,* pp. 32-33.)

1709: 20 May: Will of Thos. Lewis, proved 1 June 1709: To son Thos., Jr. all land & plantation house etc. If he dies without issue, to dau. Deborah Pound. To son Thos., all wearing apparel, best hat, black horse, Smoaker, trooping saddle, pistols, sword, holster, feather bed and furniture. Rest of estate divided equally betw. Thos., Jr. & Deborah Pound. She and husband to live on plantation with Thos. and keep estate undivided until he is 21. Thos., Jr. and son-in-law John Pound to be at equal costs & charges in keeping ferry. (Rich. Co. Will Bk. 1699-1709, pp. 129b - 130b.)

Issue of Thomas Lewis:
  1. Benjamin (b. 10 Sept. 1685): Of St. Paul's Par. Staff. Co. (D. 1735)

one known son: Thomas who married Elizabeth Mealy, dau of Daniel Mealy of Staff. Co., son of Patrick Mealy of Northumb. Co. Thos & Eliza. had two sons, Benjamin & Daniel. See St. Paul Par. Reg. & will of Daniel Mealy, Staff. Co. Records.

2. Thomas, Jr. (b. 5 Dec. 1692) of Tot. Cr. (D. 1744)
   Married Joyce Hammon (d) 1730. Had: John, b. 1713, d. young.
   Thomas, b. 1715, d.1720; Mary, b. 1720; Thomas,b.1726
   Winifred, b. 1728/9.
   Thomas = (2) Ann. Had: Jesse, b. 1731; Mary Ann, b. 1733.

3. Surles (b. ca. 1690.) Of Washington Parish, Westmoreland Co. (d. 1736) Believed to be a son of Thos. Lewis for the following reasons: His name, a surname, indicates he was a second son. The only place this spelling of Searles/Sorrel was being used was in Rappahannock Co. in the 1689-1690 period. See Records of John Searls/Surles/Sorrel who married Dorcas Ingram, Rappahannock/ Essex Co.; Secondly, he named his eldest son Thomas; Thirdly, he resided at Little Ferry on the Upper Matchotick Cr., which was then the boundary betw. Westmoreland & Stafford Cos., where he leased 160 acs. fr. Capt. Anthony Thornton of St. Paul's Parish; and is thought to have operated the ferry there; Fourthly, the mill on Totuskey Cr. was owned by the Newton family who intermarried with the Berryman family who had the mill on Upper Matchotick Cr. adj. Little Ferry. Surles married (1) Unknown, and had Thomas, Surles Jr., and Sarah. He married, secondly, Elizabeth Rousseau, dau of Wm. Linton & Joanna Lewis, (Edw's dau.) and widow of Hillaire Rousseau, a Huguenot immigrant. By her Surles had James and John. Of Surles' children, Thos. (D. 1771) leased land at Ravenworth plantation in Fairfax Co. and was overseer there for Henry Fitzhugh, and later for Thomas Ludwell Lee. (Had many children.) Surles, Jr. later moved to the Carolinas, as did his half brother, John, died 1757 Fairfield Co. S.C., who first lived in Caroline Co. Va.; Sarah married a Render of Orange Co. Va.; and James died without issue on land in Pr. Wm. Co. given him by his mother and inherited by his brother, John.

4. William: may be the William who married Sarah and had the following issue: (fr. the N. Farnham par. reg.)
   John, b. 26 Dec. 1724; Elizabeth, b. 29 Jan. 1726/7; Mary, b. 26 Jan. 1728/9, Anne, b. 19 June 1731; Margaret, b. 24 Feb. 1736.

5. Deborah: married John Pound, Jr. and had issue: For their descendants, see: *The Family History of a Lot of Pounds,* by Walter C. Pounds, Jr. Heritage Books, Inc. 1995.

3. Henry Lewis (D. 1698) Records:

Note: While it does not appear that Henry Lewis had issue, his will was not recorded. Also his links with Thomas Lewis and Mr. Joseph Lewis may be important in tracing their origins.

1685: 3 Nov.: Henry Lewis & Geo. Bruce wit. a deed of John Stewart and a bond of same. (Sparacio, Rappahannock Deed Bk. 1682-1686, p. 98.)

1686: 5 May: Henry Lewis appointed Constable in the place of & in the Precinct of Angel Jacobus for ensuing year. (Sparacio, Rappahannock Orders 1685-1687, p. 41.)

1687: 5 May: Ordered Walter Davey Constable in room and precincts of Henry Lewis. (Sparacio, *ibid.*, p. 78.)

1688: 3 May: Ordered Henry Lewis take out of his bill passed to John Talbott 67 lbs. tobo for sd. Talbots levy. (Sparacio, Rappahannock Orders 1687-1688, p. 31.)

1689: 6 Nov.: Ordered Sheriff take John Talbott in custody til he gives peace bond towards Henry Lewis. (Sparacio, *ibid.*, p. 93.)

1688: 13 Apr.: Deed betw. Angell and Eliz. Jacobus & Francis Gower of one pt. and Henry Lewis of the other pt.: For 2,000 lbs. tobo. tract on lower side of Rappahannock Cr. adj. John Essex, Col. Walker, Maj. Price & Col. Wm. Lloyd - 96 acs. sold by Geo. Bruce to Mr. Henry Clark, father-in-law of Ang. Jacobus & Fran. Gower. Wit.: Geo. Eale & Thos. Ward. (Sparacio, Rappahannock Co. Deed Bk. 1688-1692, pp. 2-3.)

1688/9: 6 Mar.: Eliz. Jacobus signs power of Atty for above parcel of 96 acs. Henry Lewis bought of her brother, John Clark, dec'd, adj. Geo. Bruce and Luke Thornton. (Sparacio, *ibid.*, p. 3.)

1689/90: 5 Mar.: Henry Lewis swears he goes in fear and danger of his life fr. John Talbott. Court orders John Talbott detained until he posts peace bond toward Henry Lewis. (Sparacio, Rappahannock Orders 1689 1692, pp. 6-7.)

1689: 3 July: Mary Lewis, wife of Thos. Lewis appts. Henry Lewis Atty. to ack. deed of Thos. Lewis to Henry Webster. (See Thos. Lewis records.) (Sparacio, Rappahannock Deeds, 1688-1692, p. 25.)

1690: 1 July: Henry Lewis sells tract of 96 acs, to Benj. Tucker. (Sparacio, Rappahannock Deeds 1688-1692, p. 84.)

1690: 5 Nov.: Henry Lewis confesses judgement to parish of N. Farnum for 509 lbs. tobo & cask - fine due from Mary Lewis for committing sin of fornication. Note: this was sometimes charged a husband and wife if they had a baby seven months or earlier after their marriage. (Sparacio, Rappahannock Orders 1689-1692, p. 42.)

1690/91: 8 Jan.: Benj. "Tacker" sells tract of 96 acs. back to Henry Lewis. (Sparacio, Rappa Deeds *op. cit.,* p. 101.)

1692: 3 Nov.: Non-suite granted Henry Lewis ag. Joseph Lewis as assignee of Capt. Wm. Hardidge, he not appearing (Sparacio, Rich. Co. Orders 1692-1694, p. 35.)

1693: Apr. 5: Judgement granted Joseph Lewis, assignee of Capt. Wm. Hardidge ag. Henry Lewis for 1400 lbs. tobo. (Sparacio, Ibid p. 45.)

1694: Apr. 4: James Orchard and Henry Lewis bound over ag. complaint of John Baker for stealing a Negro girl named Judith found in their custody. Compl. dismissed. (Sparacio, *op. cit.,* p. 82.)

1694: 1 Oct: Grant to Henry Lewis of 160 acs. (part missing) adj. Wm. Pierce, Luke Thornton, Col. John Walker. (Gray, Va. N. Neck Ld. Grants 1694-1742, p. 1.)

1695: 6 Mar.: Order granted Henry Lewis ag. James Orchard for 200 lbs. tobo. proved by Mary Lewis, wife of Henry for accomodating a Negro girl named Judith, there placed by sd. Orchard. Confirmed. Order granted ag. sheriff by Henry Lewis for non-appearance of Thos. Lewis. (Sparacio, Rich. Co. Orders 1694-1697, pp. 32-33.)

1697: 2 June: Mary Banks absented herself fr. service of Henry Lewis, her master, for ten days. To serve 24 days after her time expires. (Sparacio, Rich. Co. Orders 1697-1699, p. 4.)

1697/8: 3 Mar.: Action brought by Henry Lewis ag. John Wright (of Westm. Co., blacksmith, for not delivering one pr. of andirons) dismissed. Plt. not prosecuting. (Sparacio, *ibid.,* pp. 18, 28.)

1698: 6 July: Last will and test. of Henry Lewis presented to court by Mary, his widow & Extx. Proved by oath of Wm. Smith. (Sparacio, *ibid.,* p. 44.)

1698/9: 3 Mar.: Judgement granted Dr. Richard Pemberton ag. Thos. Dickerson as marrying Mary Lewis, extx. of Henry Lewis, dec'd, for 1200 lbs. tobo. Action brought by Edw. Barrow ag. Thos. Dickson as marrying Mary Lewis, extx of Henry Lewis, dismissed. (Sparacio *ibid.,* pp. 81-2.)

1699: 8 June: Action brought by Dr. Rich. Pemberton ag. Thomas Dickinson as marrying Mary Lewis, extx of Henry Lewis is dismissed. (Sparacio, *ibid.,* p. 95.)

1699: 2 Nov.: Judgement to Mrs. Ann Brent, Admx of Robert Brent, dec'd, ag. estate of Henry Lewis, dec'd in hands of Philip Hunnings and Jane his wife, exers of sd. deceased for 11011 lbs. tobo. (Sparacio, *ibid.,* p. 127.)

1718: 2 Sept.: Marmaduk Beckwith of Rich. Co. on behalf of Metcalf Dickinson, son of Thos. Dickinson dec'd, set forth that Henry Lewis poss. 167 acs. granted 1 Oct. 1694 and by will dtd. 11 Apr. 1698 rec. in Rich. Co. Records 6 July 1698 devised to his wife Mary Lewis. Mary m. Thos. Dickinson and died without disposing of same. Land escheats. Mary Brookenbough who formerly desired the escheat m. John Spicer & relinquished their right. Grant to Metcalf Dickinson: 167 acs. on Rappahannock Cr. in Richmond Co. adj. Col. John Stone, Col. Wm. Peirce, Luke Thornton, Col. John Walker. (Gray, Va. N. Neck Land Grants 1694-1742, p. 66.) Note: Thos. Dickinson wit. the will of Thos. Lewis in 1709, along with Thos. Lewis' servant, Tobias Purcell. He was Clerk of the Court for Richmond Co. for several years.

Note: there are three early records in Rappahannock Co, which may pertain to this Henry Lewis, as the Henry Lewis who witnessed them signed with the same mark (H) as this Henry:

1671: 1 Jan: John Dyke (= Dike/Deeke), deed of gift to John Forth, Jr. of Rappahannock Co. (a heifer.) Wit. by Henry Lewis (H) and Thos. Jones. (Sparacio, Rappahannock Deeds 1672-1676, pt. 1, p. 40.)

1673: 12 Dec.: John Cole, wife Ann and sister-in-law Margaret Gantlett, dau. of Mr. Wm. Gantlett, dec'd, sell John Froth 135 acs. pt. of dividend of land Col. Wm. Clayburn sold Mr. Wm. Gantlett, who left to his four daus. Wit. by Dennis Conners and Henry Lewis (H). (Sparacio, Rappahannock Deeds 1672 - 1676, pt. 2, p. 1.)

1673/4: 3 Feb.: Power of atty of Ann Cole to ack. sale of above 50/70 acs. of land to her bro. in law John Froth. Wit. by Henry Lewis and John Symons. (Sparacio, *ibid.,* p. 2.)

Note: Because of the location of Henry Lewis land near that of Angel Jacobus, Richard Metcalf, and the orphans of Col. Moore Fauntleroy, See Gray, ibid., grant 2-181, p. 14, and grant B-64, p. 89, it is possible that the Henry Lewis who bought 400 acs. on the Ta river in 1744 from Griffin Fauntleroy, Jr. of Northumberland Co., in Spotsylvania Co. was a descendant or relative of this Henry Lewis (D. 1698.) (The records of this Henry Lewis of Spotsylvania Co. and his descendants are given in Cook, Pioneer Lewis Families, Vol. IV, p. 521.)

4. Mr. Joseph Lewis Of Bristol And Richmond Co., Va. (D ?)

1676: 4 Feb.: John Evans apprenticed in Bristol to Moses Jones 4 yrs. Va. via "Rochelle Merchant" Master Joseph Lewis. (Coldham, Compl. Bk. of Emigrants, 1661-1699, p. 262.)

1681: 18 Aug.: Joseph Lewis ag. James Moore, referred to next court. (Northumberland Co., Va., Orders 1678-1698, p. 102.)

1681: 19 Oct.: Court finds there is due to Mr. Joseph Lewis fr. James Moor upon bal. of acct. 180 lbs. tobo & cask. Judgment is granted sd. Lewis ag. sd. Moore for sd. sum. (*ibid.,* p. 104.)

1688/9: 1 Jan.: Deed fr. Wm. Cooper & wife Elizabeth to Joseph Lewis of Bristol for 160 acs. N. side Rappahannock Riv. Betw. Mr. Patton and Lane. (Sparacio, Rappahannock Deed Bk. 8, 1688-1692, pp. 1-2.) Note: This is immed. followed by the deed fr. Jacobus & Gower to Henry Lewis.

1692: 5 May: Joseph Lewis and Alexr. Swann wit. deed fr. Edwin Conway to Wm. Reynolds. (Sparacio, Rich. Co. Deed Bk. 1, 1692-1694, pp. 2-22.)

1692: 4 May: Joseph Lewis assumes bond of 100 lbs. Sterling for Nicholas Lott. (Sparacio, Rich. Co. Orders 1692-1694, p. 2.)

1692: 5 May: Arbitrators betw. Nicholas Lott and Samuel Bayly to meet at the house of Joseph Lewis. (Sparacio, *ibid.,* p. 10.)

1692: 1 June: Nich. Lott & Joseph Lewis ack. themselves indebted to Col. John Stone, high sheriff, for 10,000 lbs. tobo. if Lott doesn't answer an appeal fr. Bayly. (Sparacio, *ibid.,* p. 12.)

1692: 3 Nov. Nonsuite is granted Henry Lewis ag. Joseph Lewis as assignee of Capt. Wm. Hardige - He not appearing to prosecute. (Sparacio, *ibid.,* p. 35.)

1693: 5 Apr.: Judgement granted to Joseph Lewis as assignee of Capt. Wm. Hardige ag. Henry Lewis for 1,400 lbs. tobo. (Sparacio, *ibid.,* p. 45.)

1694: 2 Aug.: Judgement granted to Joseph Lewis ag. estate of David Pursell, dec'd, in hands of Excx for 770 lbs. tobo. (Sparacio, Rich. Co. Orders 1694-1697, p. 1.)

1694: 6 Sep.: Judgement granted to Wm. Colston ag. Mr. Joseph Lewis for 309 lbs. tobo. (Sparacio, *ibid.,* p. 9.)

1716: 26 Oct.: Will of Thomas Edwards leaves a bequest to Thomas Lewis, his cousin, son of Joseph Lewis. (Essex Co. Deeds & Wills, Bk. 14 , p. 686.)

Note: The following entry is copied from *America Heraldica*, ed by F. de V. Vermont, p. 26 and appears to be that of the descendants of Mr. Joseph Lewis: LEWIS: The Maryland family of Lewis has always used the arms we give, and occupied important social rank in Va., Md., and Pa. The early settler of the name arr. in Amer. before 1700 and married a Thomas of the Md. Thomases.

He settled in Fairfax Co., Va., (*sic*) where his son Joseph Lewis was born in 1713. From there Joseph Lewis moved to Calvert Co., Md., and later to Baltimore Co. in the same colony. His son, Capt. Jsoeph Lewis, born 1747, served with distinction in the Revolutionary War. (Note: the DAR Patriot Register lists a Lt. Joseph Lewis, b. 17 Apr. 1753, d. 9 Mar. 1791; mar. Eliz. Duncan, Md.) His son, Elisha Lewis (b. 1792) was a volunteer during the War of 1812 and promoted to officer rank on the field of battle.... The Maryland Lewises belonged originally to the co. Monmouth, Eng., Lewises, the arms of whom they bore ever since their arrival in the new world. They descend fr. Sir Robert Wallis, Knt. Lord of of Llanarth, temp. Edward III. (A description of the Arms of Lewis of Llandewi Rhydderch follows and they are illustrated on plate XXI of the same work.)

VII. LEWIS FAMILIES ON THE
SOUTH SIDE
OF THE
POTOMAC RIVER

1. Major William Lewis Of York And Westmoreland Cos., Va.

Note: Maj. Wm. Lewis was a surveyor. He surveyed and pat. land in many counties: York; - areas which became New Kent and King and Queen Cos., and Westmoreland Co. He appears to have resided in Westmoreland Co. in the last records of him in Virginia. He could be identical with or the father of William Lewis of Talbot Co. Md. (D. 1669). He appears to have some connection with the Lewis family of Poropotanck Cr., and may have brought them with him when he returned fr. England in 1649/50. Col. John Lewis (D. 1681/2) of Poropotanck Cr., who was also a surveyor, may have been his apprentice, as he seemed to make a point of buying land originally owned by Maj. Wm. Lewis.

1635: 7 Aug.: Persons transported to Va. fr. London on the *Globe* include William Lewis, age 25; Edward Lewis, age 21; Nicholas Jernew, age 28; Richard Townsend, age 28, and his wife, Frances, age 21, and son, Francis, age 2. (Hotten, Orig. Lists..., pp. 119-121.) Note: Nicholas Jernew was also a surveyor who eventually resided on land on Lower Matchotick Cr. where he surv. and pat. 900 acs. in 1650. At the same time Maj. Wm. Lewis was surveying on the Upper Matchotick Cr. where he was listed as a headright by Mrs. Francis Townsend, widow, and also by Thos. Blagg. His trip to England in 1649 may have had some connection with the death of Richard Townsend. Maj. Wm. Lewis prob. picked out the 800 acs. here that he pat. 31 Mar. 1654. Lower Matchotick was the boundary betw. Westmoreland and Northumberland Cos., while, for many years, Upper Matchotick was the boundary betw. Stafford and Westmoreland Cos.

1649: William Lewis was in England - Deposition of Daniel Roberts, age 26, 20 Sept. 1656: That in 1649 Wm. Lewis of Va. being in England brought a bill of exchange from Va. of Everard Roberts for 25 lbs. sterling to the father of said Everard and that Lewis said at that time to Mr. John Roberts, father of said Everard, that that was all that he (Everard) owed him (Lewis) that he was paid and satisfied. Northumberland Co. Bk. 14, 1652-58, p. 89. (In: Fleet, Col. Va. Abs. Vol. 19, p. 47.)
Note: This Roberts family appears to be that of Cornhill Ward. London, originally of Wardley in Co. Rutland. John Roberts was a haberdasher. Everard was 12 years old at the time of the Visitation. (Harlean Soc. Vol. XVII: Visit. of London 1633-35, p. 203.)

1650: Jan. 30: William Lewis, headright of Thomas Blagg for 500 acs. S.W. on Upper Mattchotick Ck. (Northumberland, later Westmoreland, later Stafford, later King George Co.) (Nugent: C. & P. I, p. 207.)

1650: Feb. 7: William Lewis, headright of Mrs. Francis Townsend, widow, 2,200 acs. Northumberland Co. East side of Chotank and west side of Upper Mattchotick Neck. (Nugent, C. & P. I, p. 208.)

1653: July 1: A William Lewis headright of Mr. John Lewis for 250 acs. on Lewis, formerly Totopotomy, Br. of Poropotank Ck., Glouchester Co. (Nugent: C. & P. I, p. 229.)

1653: July 1: Major Wm. Lewis pats. 362 acs. on south side of the freshes of York River (Pamunkey River), right against Totopotomy, his fort called Asiskewincke. (Nugent: C. & P. I, p. 235.)
Note: By resurvey this was found to be 312 acs. which Wm. Lewis or Walter Broadhurst appears to have exchanged with Giles Brent Jr. for Brent's 300 acs. in Westmoreland Co. at Nominy. Brent repatented this land on the Pamunkey 4 Sept. 1661 or 1662. (Nugent: C. & P. I, p. 398-99.) The additional 50 acs. was patented as the following:

1653: Oct. 14: Maj. Wm. Lewis pats. 50 acs. York Co. on S.S.W. side of York River freshes (Pamunkey River) opposite to land of John Pownsey (Pounsey) and N.W. to Chohoake Ck. (Nugent, C. & P. I, p. 251.)
Note: The entire island on which this patent was located was repatented as 1000 acs. by John Lewis, and James Turner, on 8 Nov. 1658, as Lewis Island. (Nugent, C. & P. I, p. 379.) It now appears on maps as West Island, and is adjacent to the Pamunkey Indian reservation.

1654: Mar. 31: Maj. Wm. Lewis pats. 800 acs. in Northumberland Co. upon the eastward side and towards to head of Upper Machoticks Ck. near land of Thomas Blagg, and northly into the woods upon branches of Chotanke. (Nugent, C. & P. I, p. 241-2.)

1654: May25: Maj. Wm. Lewis pats. 3 tracts in the Tastine swamp area, then in New Kent, now in King and Queen Co. 640 acs. behind land of Mr. Arthur Price and Mr. Wm. Wyatt. (Nugent, C. & P. I, p. 284.)
Note: Assigned to Thomas Hickman before 6 Oct. 1658. (Nugent, C. & P. I, p. 379.)
1200 acs. - incomplete pat. (Nugent, C. & P. I, p. 284.) Repatented. (Nugent, C. & P. I, p. 335.)
200 acs. adj. Ralph Green (Nugent, C. & P. I, p. 284.)
Note: Sold as part of 600 acs. to John Cosby 5 Jan 1656. (C. & P. I, p. 335.)

1654: Dec. 23: Wm. Lewis witnesses a deed of gift from Joseph Crowshaw to dau Rachel and her husband Ralph Graves of 1,000 acs. on S. side of Mattapony River adj. Capt. John West on the east, Col. Wm. Claybourne on the S. Lt. Palmer on the west and the Mattapony River on the North. (York Co. Records Bk. I, p. 290)

1654/5: 2 Jan, Wm. Lewis and Geo. Morris wit. a deed of Thos. Smith, carpenter, to James Harris, planter, of land on N. side of Mill Swp., part of 700 acs. purchased by me of

Joseph Crowshaw, Gent. (York Co. Records 1659-1662, B. Weisiger, p. 25.) (Note: Harris & wife sold to Mr. Daniel Wild 13 Apr. 1660.)

1655: Mar. 26: Wm. Lewis and John Mattro (m)? headrights of Saml. Solace and Robert Troliver on Poropotank Ck. (Nugent, C. & P. I, p. 307)

1655: Jun 8: Maj. Wm. Lewis pats. 400 acs. N.E. side Mattapony River. Tastine Swamp, adj. his own land and behind Capt. Robert Abrall (Abrahall). (Nugent, C. & P. I., p. 311.)

1655: Jun 28: Maj. Wm Lewis pats. 2,000 acs. New Kent Co. (Later King and Queen) N.E. side Mattapony River bounded by "Mama Sheement" on N.W. and near head of said river. (Nugent, C. & P. I, p. 208.)
Note: By tracing adjacent patents it appears this land was next to that of Dr. Giles Moody (Nugent, C. & P. II, p. 63) and was repat. as 3,000 acs. by Mr. Leonard Claybourne, 1 Apr. 1671. (Nugent, C. & P. II, p. 92.)

1656: Jan. 5: John Cosby buys 600 acs. from Maj. Wm. Lewis - but entered no rights for it. (Nugent, C. & P. I, p. 335.)
Note: This appears to be the 200 acs. of 25 May 1654, and the 400 acs. of 8 June 1655.

1656: Jan. 14: Maj. Wm. Lewis repats. his 1200 acs. pat. of 25 May 1654. (Nugent, C. & P. I, p. 335.)
Note: Maj. Wm. Lewis assigned this land to Josiah Parsons, it lapsed and was later regranted to Col. Robert Abrahall, 20 Oct. 1675. (Nugent, C. & P. II, p. 169.)

1656: Jan. 20: Maj. Wm. Lewis pats. 2,600 acs. S.W. side of the freshes of the York River (Pamunkey River): One half the development called Port Holy, alias Chymahocens (Chemokens), containing 1550 acs. purchased from Col. John West, from mouth of Mattadequin Ck. S.S.W. toward head of Tanx Weyoake Run to Mr. Joseph Crawshaws (Croshaws) line to Chimahokans: 775 acs. purchased of Col. John West and 1825 acs. for transportation of 37 persons. (Nugent, C. & P. I, p. 336.)
Note: This was later a plantation of Col. John Lewis of Warner Hall before he and his wife, Elizabeth Warner, moved to Warner Hall. It appears from the land records that it may have been purchased from Maj. Wm. Lewis ca 1666 by John Lewis Jr. of Poropotank Ck.
On 6 Nov. 1666, John Lewis Jr. sold 1100 of the 1700 acs. he had pat. 23 Nov. 1663 (Nugent, C. & P. II, p. 4). He retained the 600 acs. that included his father's 250 ac. pat. of 1 July 1653, and his own 250 ac. pat. of 2 Dec. 1655 (Nugent, C. & P. I, pp. 229, 323). - This would have enabled him to buy the 775 ac. part and lease the 1825 acs. The 1825 acs. did escheat after his death and was repat. by John Smith of Purton (Nugent, C. & P. III, p. 17) on 28 Oct. 1697. - The year following his sale of land, John Lewis was able to pat. enough land to bring his Poropotank Ck. holding up to the identical size of the other: 2600 acs. (Nugent, C. & P. II, p. 44.)

Note: It is listed as 2600 acs. owned by John Lewis, Esqr. in the 1704 Quit Rent List of New Kent Co. (L. Des Cognants, Engl. Dupl. of Lost Va. Records, p. 167).

1656: Feb. 6: Maj. Wm. Lewis and Robert Hubbard (former Clerk of the Council) pat. 2,000 acs. in Westmoreland Co. behind the head of Nominy River on back of land of John Rosier, Clerke. (Nugent, C. & P. I, p. 340.)

Note: This land consisted of two earlier pats. of 1,000 acs. ea.: Wm. Lewis' had been pat. by Wm. Hardidge 16 Sept. 1651; Robert Hubbard's part was pat. by Thomas Speke 16 Sept. 1651. In 1658, Wm. Lewis apparently sold his back to Wm. Hardage, who repat. 19 Oct. 1658 and 9 Dec. 1662 (Nugent, C. & P. I, p. 420).

A 300 ac. tract adj. to this land on the west had been pat. by Walter Broadhurst and then repat. by Capt. Giles Brent Jr. 4 May 1653 - who assigned it to Edmond Brent. Edmond died, leaving it to his dau. Katherine Brent who repat. 9 Dec. 1662, along with the 1,050 acs. that John Rosier had pat. 14 Jan. 1656 and sold to Edmond Brent the same day. (Nugent, C. & P. I, p. 420-421.) Maj. Wm. Lewis may have exchanged his 312 ac. Totopotomy Ck. pat. for this, as Capt. Giles Brent Jr. repat. the Totopotomy land in 1661 or 1662. (Nugent, C. & P. I, p. 398-399.) Maj. Lewis appears to have owned the 300 acs. until it was repat. by Ann Brett, nee Broadhurst, later Washington, on 1 Oct. 1667. (Nugent, C. & P. II, p.) He mentioned as owning the land in Nugent, C. & P. II, p. 5, and p. 22. The Lewis and Hubbard 2,000 ac. pat. was later part of a 2,500 ac. pat. to John Lord and Wm. Horton on 9 Feb. 1663. (Nugent, C. & P. I, p. 483.)

1657: Mar. 24: Maj. Wm. Lewis petitioned the House of Burgesses to commission two young men to carry on explorations to the west of the existing settlements. (Journal of the House of Burgesses 1619-1659/60, p. 106.)
(Note: Maj. Wm. Lewis may have resigned his commission at this time.)

1657: June 1: Wm. Lewis and John Rosier witness a document in which John Knott acquits John Hillier of all debts. (John Hillier was John Rosier's father-in-law.) (Westmoreland Deeds, Wills, Pats., Etc. 1653-1659 p. 79 - In Fleet: Col. Va. Abs. Vol. 23, p. 73.)

1657: July 19: Survey by Maj. Wm. Lewis for Mr. Jas. Baldridge. Westm. Deeds. (Fleet, Col. Va. Abs. Vol. 23, p. 76.)

1657: 30 Nov.: Letter fr. Richard Webley to the Gov., states that Mr. Joseph Crowshaw, late high Sheriff took a list of tithables to his own use, and also allowed a survey given him by a surveyor whereby he gained 1,030 acs. of land with out any authority and satisfaction for it. Followed by dep. of Daniel Parke aged 28: In Oct. last Maj. Wm. Lewis & Mr. Morecraft concerning the delivery to Maj. Corshaw (*sic*) of a survey of 2700 acs. and concerning a dif. of 100 acs. of Maj Wm. Lewis dtd 27 Nov. 1657. (Duvall, York Co., Va., Deeds, Wills, Orders 1657-1659, p. 7).

1658/9: 11 Mar.: Maj. Wm. Lewis granted 2,000 acs. New Kent (later King William) Co. in the freshes of the York Riv. - Assn to Geo. Chapman, who assn. to Wm. Pullen, who repat. 21 Oct. 1662. (Sparacio, King William Co., Va., Recoreds, 1702-1703, p. 2.)

1658/9: List of the Disposal of the Leview (Levy) collected for the Co. of Westmoreland Anno 1658: To Mr. Rosier for Mr. (Major)? Lewis' levies the last year: 053 (lbs. Tobacco.) Westm. Deeds, Wills I p. 126-126/A. (In: Dorman, Westmoreland Co. Records, 1658-1661. p. 29-30.)

1660: Estate account of John Hillier: Payment to Maj. Lewis, signed by John Rosier. In: Dorman, Westmoreland Co. Records 1658-1661, p. 55.

1666: Oct. 26: Land of Maj. Lewis mentioned in a pat. of Richard Sturman for 1004 acs. in Westm. Co. (Nugent, C. & P. II, p. 5.)

1667: Apr. 17: Land of Maj. Lewis mentioned in a pat. of Capt. John Lord and Mr. Wm. Horton for 1544 acs. Westm. Co.: 800 acs. upon lands of Maj. Lewis and Thomas Dyas (Dios); 744 acs. upon land surveyed for Henry Durant and land of Maj. (Wm.) Pierce. (Nugent, C. & P. II, p. 22.)

1667: May 9: Thomas Gerrard, Esq., of St. Clement's Manor, Md. sells Richard Foster two-thirds of the neck, incl. St. Margaret's Island, laid out by Maj. Lewis for 700 acs. (Md. Arch. Vol. 57, p. 330 - Prov. Ct. Proc. 1668.)

1667: Oct. 1: Ann Brett dau of Walter Broadhurst, repats. the 300 acs. in Westm. Co. (She was later the 2d wife of Col John Washington.) (Nugent, C. & P. II, p. 30.)

1671: Apr. 1: Mr. Leonard Claybourn pats. 3,000 acs. New Kent Co. (included the 2,000 acs. pat. by Maj. Wm. Lewis on 28 June 1655.) (Nugent C. & P. II, p. 92.)

2. John Lewis (d. ca. 1694) of Northumberland Co., Va.

(?) 1662: John Lewis, servant to Capt. Peter Ashton, adjudged eleven years old 20 Jan. 1661/2. (Born ca. 1650.) (Northumberland Co. Order Bk. 2, p. 149 (In: W. P. Haynie, Rec. of Indent. Svts. and or Certs. of Land, Northumb. Co., Va., 1650-1795. Item No. 205.) (Note: This could refer to John Lewis [D. 1697] of Northumberland Co., Va.)

1678: John Lewis mentioned as brother-in-law of John Muttoone Jr. 26 Sept. 1678. (Northumberland Co. Order Bk. 1666-1678, p. 260.)

1679/80: 21 Jan.: Whereas Francis (sic) Lewis did complain that Abraham Morris, svt. to Clement Lattimore, had violently assaulted her and broke her head so grievously that the sd. wound cost her for the cure 500 lbs. tobo... Ct. ordered sd. Morris after time of service, pay sd. Francis 1200 lbs. tobo. (Northumb. Orders, 1678-98, p. 54.)

1681: John Lewis, who married Frances, the dau of John Muttoone, dec'd, complains that John Muttoone by will left legacies to the rest of his children but nothing to his (J.L.'s) wife. Ordered that (four men named) make inquiry into estate given sd. Frances by her father at the time of her marriage and make equal portions with the rest of the daus out of the whole. 21 Apr. 1681. (Northumberland Orders, 1678-1698, p. 93.)

1694/5: John Nickless, who married Frances, exs. of John Lewis dec'd is granted probate of the will. Proved by the oaths of Wm. Havett and John Nickless, wit. to sd. will, 16 Jan. 1694/5. (Northumberland Orders, 1678-1698, p. 682.)

1706: Mutton Lewis with the consent of his brother-in-law, (step-brother) John Nickless, aged sixteen, to serve Richard Swanson until twenty-one. 18 Sept. 1706. (Northumb. Co. Orders, 1699-1713, p. 396.)

1713: Mutton Lewis pet. the court that his dec'd father, John Lewis, left a part of his estate to him by will, which came into the possession of John Nickless, dec'd, whose relict Robert Gordon intermarried and legacy remains in his custody. Sd. Mutton produced his father's will, whereby it appears that he gave to his son one short gun and two cows, and Gordon denies he had same. Ordered that sd. Gordon deliver the legacy. (Northumb, Orders, 1699-1713, p. 823.)

1728: Land of Mutton Lewis adj. Frances Michael pat. of 400 acs. Spotsylvania Co. St. George Parish. 28 Sept. 1728. (Nugent, C. & P. III, p. 370.)
Issue: Unknown if any.

3. Records of Edward Lewis (D. ?) of St. Stephen's Parish, Northumberland Co.

(?) 1678: 26 Sept.: An Edward Lewis is a headright of Wm. Seargant and Joane Clark for 1583.3 acs. Rappa. Co. / adj. Capt. Lord and John Butler. (Nugent, C. & P. II, pp. 188-9.)

1690: 21 May: Edward Lewis, being a poor impotent person, is excluded from paying any levy. (Northumb. Co. Orders, 1678-1698, p. 506.)

1693/4: 21 Mar.: Wm. Lewis, son of Edward and Ann Leiwis, through the charity of Thomas Flynt and Anne his wife maintained two years. The sd. Anne, now the widow of Thomas Flynt moved that the child might serve her until 21. (*ibid.*, p. 648-9.)

1694: 18 May: Ordered upon petition of Edw. Lewis that Mrs. Anne Flynt deliver up to him his son named William Lewis which he affirms she detains from him. (*Ibid.*, p. 658.)

1696/7: 17 Mar.: Lucretia Lewis, dau. of Ann and Edward Lewis, 7 years old the 9th of June last, to serve Thomas Hughlett and Mary his wife, by consent of her mother. (*ibid.*, p. 759)

1698: 20 Apr.: Charles and Edward Lewis, sons of Edward and Mary Lewis to serve James John until 21. (With consent of their mother.) (*Ibid.*, p. 816.)

Records of the sons of Edward Lewis:

1. William Lewis:
   1733: William Lewis' will, 13 Dec. 1733, rec. 9 Jan. 1733/4: Leaves Capt. Geo. Heale "my farm in Gt. Britain containing 48 acs. called Websterhall in the Parish of Poles Warden, (*sic,* St. Paul's Walden) in the Co. of Hartfordshire, given me by my great grandfather, Charles Lewis. (Note: Capt. Geo. Heale was formerly of Cherry Point, Northumb. Co. See his will 1736, Lanc. Co. Wills. p. 111.) (In: Abs. of Lanc. Co., Va. Wills 1653-1800.) (Lanc. Will Bk. 12, p. 289.)

2. Edward Lewis:
   1714/15: 17 Mar.: John Baskafield, a poor distempered man having complained to this Court that he hath been unlawfully detained (by Philiip Bustle [*sic*-Bussell], Edward Lewis & others) as a servant under pretensions of curing his malady....

3. Charles Lewis:
   1712: Charles Lewis pats. 200 acs. Richmond Co. 26 May 1712. (Northern Neck Land Bk. 4, p. 83.)

   1726:17 Nov. Will of Charles Lewis, probate 1 Feb. 1726/7: Mentions: Sons: Charles and Edward, Daus.: Catherine and Betty; Wife and five children. (Rich. Co. Will Bk. 5, p. 32.)
   Children: Names and dates (fr. the North Farnham Par. Reg.)
   Joyce, b. 26 July 1712

Catherine, b. 1 Aug. 1715

Edward, b. 12 Feb. 1718

Charles, b. 4 Aug. 1720

Betty, b. 5 Sept. 1722

Note: Charles Lewis married Mary, dau. of Wm. Barber. (Another Lewis, William, grandson of John Lewis (D. 1697) of Cherry Point. married Ann, dau. of Wm. and Joyce Barber.) The will of a Charles Lewis, who may have been the one b. in 1720, or his son, was probated 19 Oct. 1805 in Pittsylvania Co. Va. (Will Bk. 11, p. 279.) listing the following children: Sons: Edward, Charles, Zachariah, James, John and William; Daus.: Lucretia and Mary, which covers all the names of these two Cherry Pt. families.

Family Chart of Edward Lewis, (D. ?) of Cherry Point,
Northumberland Co. Virginia

Charles Lewis of Webster Hall Farm, St. Paul's Waldon, Herts.

William Lewis (?)

Edward Lewis (D. ?)

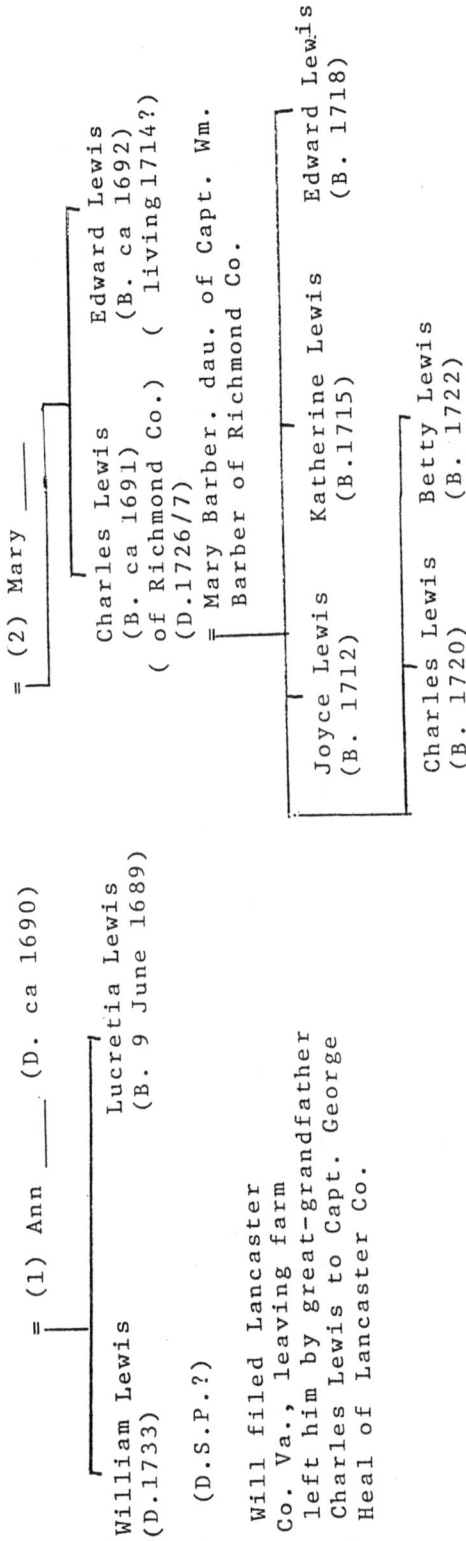

= (1) Ann _____ (D. ca 1690)

= (2) Mary _____

William Lewis
(D.1733)

(D.S.P.?)

Will filed Lancaster
Co. Va., leaving farm
left him by great-grandfather
Charles Lewis to Capt. George
Heal of Lancaster Co.

Lucretia Lewis
(B. 9 June 1689)

Charles Lewis
(B. ca 1691)
(of Richmond Co.)
(D.1726/7)
= Mary Barber. dau. of Capt. Wm.
Barber of Richmond Co.

Edward Lewis
(B. ca 1692)
(living 1714?)

Joyce Lewis
(B. 1712)

Katherine Lewis
(B.1715)

Edward Lewis
(B. 1718)

Charles Lewis
(B. 1720)

Betty Lewis
(B. 1722)

4. Records of John Lewis (d. 1697) of Cherry Pt. St. Stephens Parish, Northumberland. Co., Va.

(?) 1663: John Lewis headright of John Hughlet, Northumb. Co. (In: W.P. Haynie, *op. cit.,* Item 271).

(?) 1679/80: Jan. 21: John 'Lowes', headright of Richard Rice for 300 acs. in Northumberland Co. (Northumberland Co. Orders, p. 54.)

1682/3: Feb. 21: John Lewis, in behalf of his wife, ye relict of Geo. Courtnell, did move the court for a third of the lands belonging to Cortnell.... etc. (Northumberland Orders, 1678-1698, p. 164.) (Note: John Lewis married Mary, widow of Geo. Courtnell, Jr., and dau of John Gerner/Gardiner, b. 1633, son of Richard Gardiner/Garnet, who imm to Md. in 1637. (Skordas Early Settlers of Md.)

1683: Sept. 30: John, son of John Lewis, bapt. (St. Stephen's Reg.)

1685: Jan. 9: William, son of John Lewis bapt. (St. Stephen's Reg.)

1686: May 20: John Lewis appointed Constable for Cherry Point. (Northumberland Orders, 1678-1698, p. 268.)

1689: May 15: Nicholas Powell, son of Edmond and Sarah, being three years old the 13th of Dec. next, with mother's consent to serve John Lewis and his wife until 21. (Northumberland Orders, 1678-1698, p. 462.)

1689: Nov. 6: Probate of the will of Nicholas Owen, by oaths of John Lewis, Thos. Banks, Mrs. Eliza. Banks, and Eliza. Smith to Thomas Bushrod. (Northumberland Orders, 1678-1698, p. 478.)

1690: Apr. 21: John Lewis headright for land pat. by Mr. Edw. and John Lewis in New Kent. Co., (orig. pat. by Maj. Wm. Lewis) and prob. had flaw in title of his sale to John Cosby, who entered no headrights for it. (Nugent: C. & P. II, p. 342.) (Same names in R. Rice list of 1679/80.)

1690: Sept. 13: John Lewis buys 150 acs. at Cherry Point from Ann, widow of James Gallian. (Northern Neck Land Bk. 2, p. 144-146.)

1691: June 18: John Lewis and Mary his wife vs. Thos. Bushrod. (Northumberland Orders, 1678-1698, p. 558.)

1694: May 18: John Lewis and Mary his wife, exs. of Geo. Courtnell, dec'd, vs. Roger Williams. (Northumberland Co. Orders, 1678-1698, p. 660.)

1697: May 19: Last will of John Lewis proved by Vincent Garner and Philip Aherne. (Northumberland Orders, 1678-1698, p. 769.)

1705: May 16: Eliza. Lewis, orphan of John Lewis, chose Thos. Byram to be her guardian. (Northumberland Co. Orders, 1699-1713, p. 769.) (In: Duvall, Col. Va. Abs. Ser. 2, Vol. 1, p. 101.)

1719: Dec. 17: John Lewis (Jr.) Repatents the 150 acs. at Cherry Point. (Northern Neck Land Bk. 5, pp. 218-219.)

Note: Some of the generations of this family from John Lewis, (d. 1697) and his wife, Mary, nee Garner, widow Courtnell, have been documented in *John Lewis: The Lost Pioneer,* by D. R. Long, 1971.

CHART OF JOHN LEWIS (d. 1697) FAMILY

OF NORTHUMBERLAND CO. VA.

John Lewis (d. 1697) (Resided Coan River, Northum. Co.)
= (ca 1682) Mary Garner Courtnell, dau of John Garner and
widow of Geo. Courtnell Jr. of Coan Riv.

(After death of John Lewis she = (3) Richard Price.)
Her will dtd 26 Dec 1724. Proved 20 Apr 1726.

John   William   James   Mary   Elizabeth
(b. 30 Sep 1683)   (b. 9 Jan 1685)   (d. 11 Jan 1747)

= (1) Eliza.   = Eliza.   = Hannah
(Christopher?)   dau of
                    Vincent
                    Cox   Peter William James Joanna Mary Sarah

Issue: Vincent Eliza. Ann

└ John (b. ca 1714)   = Ann, dau of John Longworth
                                        (Had Issue)
William (b. ca 1716)   To Loudon Co. Va.
= (1) Ann Barber

= (2) Mary (She = (2) Wm. Hughlet.)

Issue:
├ Griffin: (Had Issue)
└ Corbin (D.S.P.)

(For further information on this family, see: D. R. Long, *John Lewis, The Lost Pioneer*, 1971.)

VIII. THE LEWIS FAMILY OF THE
EASTERN SHORE OF
VIRGINIA

1. Records of John Lewis of Accomac Co. (d. 1697):

(Poss. the John Lewis b. 27 Jun 1619 & = Mary Gardiner 24 Jul 1632 Both at St. Martins in the Fields, London. (I.G.I. in England, Lond. 1988.)

1635: John Lewis a passenger on the *Thomas* to Va., age 16. (Hotten, p. 126)

1636: John Lewis a headright for John Furbush for 100 acs. Accomac Co. 20 June 1636. (Nugent, C. & P. I, p. 43.)

1654: John Lewis, aged about 35, states he had been a servant of Mr. John Neale about 15 or 16 years ago. Because of a debt owed by Neale to merchants of London, his cattle were taken from him and turned over to Col. Edmund Scarburgh. He had since entered the service of Col. Scarburgh as an overseer. Dated 20 Aug. 1654. (Northampton Co. Order Bk. 5, p. 10.)

1655: John Lewis gave a deposition, dtd. 30 Jan. 1654/55, saying that in 1652 he had been overseer of Mr. Scarburgh's servants at Occahannock. (Northampton Co. Order Bk. 5, p. 65.)

1658: John Lewis purchased 300 acs. in Accomac Co. adj. Chas. Scarboro's 3050 acs. pat. from George Freshwater, who had bought the tract from Ann Gardiner, the widow of July Gardiner, who had pat. it in 1652. (Nugent C. & P. I, p. 260.) (Whitlaw, Va's Eastern Shore, Vol. 2 [A54] p. 806.)

1664: John Lewis pats. 1,000 acs. on the N. side of Hunting Cr., Accomac Co. (Nugent, C. & P. I, p. 483.)

1690: John Lewis writes will, dtd. 15 Aug. 1690: Leaves land to his three sons, John, Robert and Richard. At death of John Jr. his land to his two sons William and John (III.)

1697: Recording of the will 3 Mar. 1696/7 (Accomac Wills 1692-1715, p. 154.) (Indicated that he signed (X) and had a seal.)

1697: Affadavit of Robert Lewis, Richard Lewis and Elizabeth, widow of John Lewis Jr. that they were the only living issue of John Lewis Sr. dtd. 9 Dec. 1697. (Accomac Wills 1692-1715, p. 186.)

Note: More records on this family can be found in: *G(eorge) R(obert) Lewis, A Brief History of the Lewis Family 1619-1971*, privately printed, 1971. Also in M.L. Cook's *Pioneer Lewis Families,* Vol. IV, pp. 693-695. Cook Publications, 1986.

CHART OF DESCENDANTS OF JOHN LEWIS (D.1697)
OF ACCOMAC CO., VIRGINIA

Sources: G. R. Lewis, A Brief History of the Lewis Family of Accomac Co. Va.
(1619 - 1971). Washington, D.C. 1972.

Mark C. Lewis: His Notes on the Lewis Family. At Accomac Public Library.
County Deed and Will Books: Cecil and Worcester Cos., Md.

John Lewis (ca 1619 - 1697)

(1) = Mary Gardiner(?)   (2)= ?   (3) = Lucretia Pott, dau. of John Pott, Jr.

John Lewis,Jr.   Mary Lewis
= Elizabeth Rudolphus   = (1) Isaac Dix
  dau. of Wm. Rudolphus   = (2) Wm. Groton

John
Lewis III
*

William
Lewis

Eliza.
=
Mr.
Scott

Comfort
.=
Wunney
Rue

= Eliza.
= (1) Susanna (Hill)?
= (2) Ann Tabatha
= (3) Martha

John IV   Daniel   Joshua(Josiah)
= Eliza.   = Sarah   (Left 70 acs or proceeds
                        of by his grandmother-in
                        Somerset, later Wor. Co. Md.

Robert   Richard
Lewis   Lewis
(1651-   (1652-1719(?)
1704+)   (Living 1709
              when he sold
              his Accomac land)

= (?)
 ┌ .Lucretia
 │ =Wm. Sherwood
 └ 2. Margaret
      =Joseph Thomas

Alexander Lewis
(1663-1678)
(D.S.P.-to Calvert
Co., Md. with John
Pott III).

(Poss. same as Richard Lewis of
Cecil Co. Md. who married Anna
and had Richard Jr. of St. John's,
Manor, Cecil Co. Md. and John,
who married Martha   and had
John Jr. who married (H)Ester,
dau. of John Pennington.

William, Jr.   Thomas   Isaac   JOhn(D.1762)
= Amy   = Betty   = Johanna
  Turnall   Taylor
                 Thomas, Jr.   Chandler

James (Sr.) ? Levin (I)
             = Margaret Major
(Prob. same James Lewis   (Founded Lewis Family
who pur. land in Wor. Co.   of Lewis' Warf, Dor.
Md. in 1764. His desc.   Co. Md. See G. R.
traced by Marg.H. Freas   Lewis. Op. Cit.
RR#1 Box 379, Felton,Pa.   for descendants.
17322.)

* See also the Lewis entries in Ruth T.
Dryden : Land Records of Wicomico Co.
Md. 1666 - 1810. (N.D.)

PART 3

EARLY LEWIS FAMILIES

OF

MARYLAND

I. LEWIS FAMILIES ON THE
NORTH SIDE
OF THE
POTOMAC RIVER

1. Thomas Lewis Of St. Mary's (& Poss. Calvert) Co. Md.

Note: This Thomas Lewis was an early immigrant to Md. and appears to be associated with the Puritan party there. As far as I can tell his fate, and whether or not he left issue is unknown, but his records are too interesting to omit.

1642: 1 July: Thomas Lewis was a headright of Mrs. Frances White for 1000 acs. granted in Md. (Md. Land Bks., Liber ABH, fol. 59; Liber I, fol. 24.) Note: Francis White was the sister of Jerome White, later surveyor general of Md., and George White, a justice of A.A. Co. She married Richard Wells, orig. of Va. & then of A.A. Co. Md. She had come first to Va. ca. 1637. (See Barnes, Balt. Co. Fam. 1659-1759, p. 685.) There were four Thomas Lewises listed in the Va. Land Pats. before 1642, and he may have been one of these:
Thos. Harwood pat. of 7 July 1635 (Nugent, C. & P. I, p. 25; Hannah Boyse pat., 11 Nov. 1635 (*ibid.*, p. 40); Francis Osborne pat. 14 July 1637 (*ibid.*, p. 60-1); and the Geo. Mynifie pat. 19 Apr. 1638 (*ibid.*, p. 118).

1646: Jan. 19: Thos. Sturman, Francis Gray, John Hampton, Robt. Sedgrave and John Sturman, ea. bound for 2,000 lbs. of tobo. in cask in case they leave the county of St. Maries without telling the Gov., or entertain secret intelligence with John Mott, Thos. Yewell, Thos. Lewis or Robert Smith, or anyone coming from them or harboring them, or know of their coming and not tell the Gov. (Md. Arch: Proceedings of the Council, 1636-1647, p. 176.)

1646: Jan. 19: Whereas Robert Smith, Thos. Yewell, and Thos. Lewis, being inhabitants of this province have secretly fled... and joined themselves to persons hostiley affected against this province and do hence return into this province by night as enemies and robbers and kill and carry away the cattle of the inhabitants. These are to summon the sd. Robt. Smith, Thos. Yewell and Thomas Lewis to surrender themselves to the sheriff of St. Maries Co. or at St. Inigo's fort afore the 4th Feb. next upon peril to be proclaimed rebels and robbers... (Md. Arch.: Proceedings of the Council, 1636-1647, p. 178.)
Note: The Sturmans, Francis Gray and Thomas Yewell were later of Westmoreland Co. Va. Thos. Yewell, Jr. later pat. land in Talbot. Co. Robt. Smith may be the Robt. Smith, Esqr. who later pat. much land in Talbot Co.

These next records may or may not apply to the same Thomas Lewis:

1649: Thomas Lewis has a year added to his service by Cornelius Lloyd. (Norfolk Co. Record Bk. B: Lower Norfolk Co. 1646-1651/2, p. 135A.) Note: Cornelius Lloyd was the brother of Edward Lloyd, later of Talbot Co. Md.

1653: 15 Apr.: Certificate granted to Lt. Col. Cornelius Loyd for six persons: "Will ye Souldier," Thomas Lewis, Lewes Morgan, two Scotchmen & Susana, a maide servent: These six assn. to Bartholomew Hoskins. (In N.E.H.G.R. Vol. 47, p. 194.)

1654: 6 Sep.: Some of these same headrights show up in the pat. of Robert Yeo for 650 acs. in Westmoreland Co., Va. adj. the land of Maj. George Read: Augimye, a Scot, Dubo, a Scotchman, Wm. Claybourne (Will ye souldier?), and Thomas Lewis. (Nugent, C. & P. I, p. 292.)

1655: Thomas Lewis listed as a headright transported in 1655 to Calvert Co. Md. by William Parker (form. of Low. Norf. Co. Va. & an assoc. of Va. Gov. Richard Bennett). His widow, Grace, later married Edward Lloyd. (Md. Land Bk.: Liber 5, fol. 259.)

1656: Thomas Lewis gave unto Ishmael Wright, Jr. one sow shoat... (Calvert Co. Ct. & Test. Bus. Md. Prov. Ct. Recs. 1656, p. 202.)

1666: Oct: Wm. Wheeler being ordered by the Commissioners of Calvert Co. to be bound over by the sheriff of that Co. to prosecute Thomas Lewis upon suspicion of theft at this Prov. Ct., Who is now again ordered to make his appearance next Prov. Ct. -to testify... Whereupon John Tucker came into Ct. and tendered himself to be security for the sd. Wheeler... accepted & bound by recognizance in ten pounds sterling... (Md. Prov. Ct. Rec., Prov. Ct. Proc. 1666, p. 128) Note: There seems to have been nothing further on this matter in the records.

Issue?

2. Records of James Lewis of St. Mary's Co. Maryland (d. 1691)

1641: James Lewis' year of birth according to his deposition, age 22, Chas. Co. Md. Court 11 Apr. 1663. (Md. Archives Vol. 53, p. 495.)

1659: James Lewis a headright of Dr. (Capt.) Luke Barber for 1400 acs. of land in Md. (Md. Land Bk. 4, p. 11.)

1662: James Lewis and Luke Barber tobacco receipt, March 1, 1662. (Md. Arch. Vol. 49, pp. 52-3.)

1662: James Lewis pats. "The French Lewis" Chas. Co. Md.

1663: Deposition of James Lewis, age 22, Chas. Co. Ct. (Md. Arch. Vol. 53, p. 495.)

1664: James Lewis signs note for 700 lbs. of Tobo. as James Lewis of St. Mary's, planter. (IL.) 21 May 1664. (Md. Arch. Vol. 53, p. 517-8.)

(?) 1664: 17 Nov.: James Lewis, a headright of Col. Edmond Scarboro, Accomac Co. (J. R. McKey, Acc. Co. Va. Ct. Order Abs. Vol. 1, p. 102.)

1665: Attachment granted to Mr. John Meeks for 500 lbs. Tobo and Mr. Richard Randall for 748 lbs. Tobo. against estate of James Lewis, who has absented himself out of the Province. (Md. Arch. Vol. 53, p. 571 & 584.)

1666: James Lewis and wife Mary register their cattle mark. (Md. Arch. Vol. 49, p. 569.)

1671: James Lewis of St. Mary's Co. charged with seditious words. 23 Oct. 1671. (Md. Arch. Vol. 65, p. xxiii.)

1672: A jury in Oct. presented James Lewis with calling the gov., the chancellor, and Col. (Wm.) Calvert all rogues, and that the Col. was a bastard. Found guilty and sentenced to 39 lashes on his bare back. (Md. Arch. Vol. 65, pp. xxiii, 39, 40.)

1672: James Lewis had to post bond of 10,000 lbs. Tobo. 8 Oct. for good behavior. (Md. Arch. Vol. 65, p. 42)

1673: Two of James Lewis' servants petitioned the court that they had served their time and that he refused to free them. (Md. Arch. Vol. 65, p. 179.)

1675: John Quigley stated 12 Feb. 1675, that on 3 Mar. 1673 James Lewis obligated himself to pay Quigley 1275 lbs. of Tobo in cask to be paid the 12 day of this instant. March in consideration of his passage from Barbadoes to Md. (Md. Arch. Vol. 66. p. 82-3)

1679/80: A servant of James Lewis accused him of cruelty and abuse resulting in the death of another servant by stomping on his throat after he took some food. (Md. Arch. Vol. 69. pp. 413-14.) (Note: For this he was branded on the hand for manslaughter, and claimed it was so ill done that it interfered with his signing documents.)

1693/4: James Lewis' inventory was filed in St. Mary's Co. (St. Mary Co. Liber 13 A Fol. 10.)

Issue: (?)

(?) 1711: A John Lewis and Ann Lewis wit. the will of Edw. Enloes of St. Mary's Co. 21 Apr. 1711. Rec. 14 June 1711. (Md. Cal. of Wills. Vol. 4, p. 195.)

(?) 1718: Will of John Coode of St. Mary's Co. dtd. 20 Apr. 1718, leaves Frog Hall to James Lewis and his heirs, provided he pays the sum of 7,500 lbs. Tobo to Coode's estate. (Md. Cal. of Wills Vol. 4, p. 171.)

Note: John Coode had resided in Virginia for a period before returning to Md. This record could refer to "Frog Hall" in Westmoreland Co., Va. If so, the James Lewis in the will was prob. the son of John Lewis (d. 1697) of Northumberland Co., Va.

3. David And Henry Lewis Of St. Mary's And Charles Cos., Md.

1668: 9 Sep.: Apprenticed in Bristol: David Lewis to George Marks, 4 yrs., Va.; Henry Lewis to same, 4 yrs. Va. (P. Coldham, Comp. Bk. of Emigrants 1661-1699, p. 132.)

1671: 16 May: David Lewis and Henry Lewis imported 1668 by George Marks, mate of the *Francis and Mary*. (Md. Land Records, Liber 13, Fol. 111.)

1673: 19 Apr.: David Lewis and Henry Lewis assign rights for service to Edward Williams of Talbot Co. (Md. Land Records, Liber 17, Fol. 416.)

1681: 25 Aug.: Dep. of Abraham Rhoad aged 36 yrs....saith upon 15th instant Roger Towle told dep. that John Rye, the miller at my Lords Mill told some man on St. Georges side that Thos. Courtney had forbid him, the sd. Miller, to go to the church on St. George hundred....
Henry Lewis aged forty years...he heard the sd. Roger Towle say that he heard that Thos. Courtney should forewarn the miller aforesaid from coming to church and bid him, the sd. miller go well armed if he did go least he come short home.
Henry Lewis aged forty yrs...saith that upon Tues. the 16th instant he heard Abraham Rhoad say that the people on St. Georges side talked largely and said that they did not know whither the people at Point Looke out were killed by Papists or the Indians, but named no particular person that reported it. Henry (X) Lewis, his mark. (Md. Arch. V. 17, p. 50.) Note: St. Georges Hundred in St. Mary's Co. is on the west side of St. Mary's River.

1682: 5 Apr.: David Lewis and Henry Lewis assigned 100 acs., "Asquith's Folly" from Wm. Asquith (pat. by him in St. Mary's Co. 13 Jan. 1682). (P. Coldham, Settlers of Md. 1679-1700, pp. 5, 105.) Note: "Asquith's Folly" appears of the Tract Map of St. Mary's Co., 1705, Chronicles of St. Mary's Vol. 21, No. 5, May 1973. It is located at the head of & East of St. Mary's River.

Bapt. Records of the children of David Lewis, Pyckyawaxon Parish, Charles Co., Md.:
Henry Lewis, b. 16 Oct. 1687
Isabel Lewis, b. 4 Aug. 1690
Mary Lewis, b. 8 Nov. 1692
David Lewis, b. 14 Dec. 1694
(M. Mickley, Charles Co. Liber P, No. 1, pp. 9, 11, 13, 16.)

4. Thomas Lewis (D. 1696) Of Charles And Pr. George's Cos.

1664: 9 Apr.: The name Thomas Lewis appears among 26 people entered as rights for 1300 acs. by Thomas Vaughan. (Md. Land Records, Liber 6, fol. 294.)

1671/2: 9 Jan.: Thos. "Lues," age 20 yrs., servant of Richard Edelen. (Chas. Co. Ct. & Land Rec. Liber E, No. 1, p. 52.) Note: Thos. Lewis may have named his eldest son Richard for Richard Edelen.

1687: Thos. Lewis, Geo. Leet and Henry Franklings register cattle marks. (Chas. Co. rec. Liber N, p. 288.)

1687: 6 Dec.: Will of Giles Blyzard (Date miscopied as 1678.) Rec. 17 May 1688: To wife Mary (2nd wife) "Cane's Purchase" and part of "Buplane" (*sic*); to dau. Susanna (by 1st wife), "Cane's Purchase" at death of wife to residue of "Buplaine"; to dau. Ann (by 2nd wife) "St. James"; to Thomas Lewis and Katherine his wife (dau. of 2nd wife by a prev. marriage), and their son Richard, a lease of 200 acs... (Md. Cal. of Wills, Vol. 6, p. 27.) Note: Giles Blyzard was listed as a carpenter of St. Mary's Co. in 1675/6, 22 Mar. when Raymond Stapleford of Dorchester Co. assigned him 100 acs. 'Reserve' below Robsons Cr. in Dor. Co. (Md. Arch. V. 66, pp. 128-130). On 6 Apr. 1676 Giles Blyzard, late of Cal. Co., otherwise called Giles Blyzard of Gt. Choptanck Riv. in Talbot Co. was found to owe John Ingram 3,560 lbs. tobo. (*ibid.,* p. 211.) On 7 Jan. 1677/8, Giles Blyzard wit. the power of atty of Mary Doodes in Middlesex Co., Va. (Middlesex Order Bk. 1677-1680, p. 113-113a.) On 21 Aug. 1684, Giles Blyzard married Susanna, dau. of John Cane (OCaine) and was granted 1,000 acs. "Buplaine" (Blewplaine) as a marriage settlement. (Chas. Co. Land Rec., Liber S, p. 286.)

1686: Giles Blizzard petitions the Council for a license to trade with the Indians for furs to make beaver hats and castors. Lic. granted 5 May 1686. (Md. Arch. Proc. of the Council, 1684-89, p. 471-2.)
On 8 Mar. 1691, Robt. Thompson binds himself to Ann, dau. of Giles & Mary Blizard for 20,000 lbs. tobo (Chas Co. Ct. & Land Rec. Liber Q, No. 1, p. 54).
On 21 Feb. 1693, Susanna, dau. of Giles Blyzard, dec'd. was to remain in custody of her mother-in-law (Stepmother) Mary Thompson (Chas. Co. Ct. & Land Rec. Liber S, No.1, p. 24.)

1713: 19 May: Indent. betw. Nath. Magruder of P.G. Co. & Susanna, his wife to John Fraser, clerk of P.G. Co. & Anne his wife: Susanna & Anne, daus. & coheirs of Giles Blyzard of Chas Co. inher. 1,000 acs: "Blew Plaine," 700 acs., "St. James," both in P.G. Co. "Caine's Purchase" in Chas. Co., 600 acs. in Balt. Co. called "Athelborough".... (Chas. Co. Land Rec. Liber F. Old Series, 5, p. 241 ff.) Note: Mary, wife of Giles was married to James Smallwood by 1715, and to Alex. Herbert, Gent. by 1722. (*ibid.,* p. 440, Liber I, p. 326.)

1692: 19 July: Thomas Lewis buys half of the tract "Battessey" (Battersea) fr. Philip Mason, planter, & wife Mary, 250 acs. (Chas. Co. Land Rec. Liber S, pp. 48-9.)

1694: 5 Mar.: Indent Fr. Wm. Thompson, planter, to Rich Gambrah, planter, half the parcel of land called "Batterzee" which Rich. Hes. and Philip Mason pur. fr. Rich. "Hawke" (sic - Fowke) ... Lately in poss. of Wm. Thompson and Thomas Lewis... (Chas Co. Land Rec., Liber Q, p. 67.)

1695: 22 Mar.: Will of Thomas Lewis of Pr. Geo. Co. Md. Rec. 3 June 1696: To wife, Catherine, life interest in his land; To son, Richard: 100 acs.; To son, Thomas: 100 acs.; To son John: 50 acs. adj. Thomas. (Md. Cal. of Wills, Liber 7, fol. 150.)

RECORDS OF THE SONS OF THOMAS LEWIS:
1703: 19 June: Will of John Watkins, Pr. Geo. Co.: to Dau. in law (Stepdau.) Ann Lewis; sons-in-law Thos. & John Lewis... Wife Mary & son-in-law Richard Lewis to be jt. exs. (Md. Cal. of Wills Vol. 11, p. 373.) (Note: Apparently, Mary, the widow of Giles Blyzrary, married John Watkins before she married James Smallwood, and had married Robt. Thompson before whe married John Watkins.)

I. RECORD OF RICHARD LEWIS, SON OF THOS. SR.:
1709: 29 July: Fr. Richard Lewis of P.G. Co., planter, to Wm. Tyler, carpenter of P.G. Co.: For 14,000 lbs. tobo. 100 acs. given Lewis by will of his father Thos. Lewis called Battersey, form. in Chas. Co. now in P.G. Co. bounded by Clash Cr. (P.G. Co. Liber F, fol. 5.) Note: He may have moved to Va. with his nephews and culd have been the Richard Lewis who was sexton of Pohick Church.

II. RECORD OF JOHN LEWIS, SON OF THOMAS SR.:
1703: 30 July: Indenture fr. John Soaper, cooper, of P.G. Co. to John Lewis, planter, of P.G. Co. land on W. br. of Patuxent Riv. called "Marborow's Plains." (P.G. Co. Liber C, fol. 71a.)

1711: 20 Aug.: Fr. John Lewis, planter, of P.G. Co. to Thos. Stonestreet, planter, P.G. Co.: For 5,000 lbs. tobo. 50 acs. land form. in Chas. Co. now in P.G. Co. left to John Lewis by his father, Thos. Lewis, orig. tract called Buttersy, bounded by Thos. Lewis, Jr. (P.G. Co. Liber F, fol.101.)

1711: Death of John Lewis (Will dtd. 5 Mar. 1710) Estate to wife, Elizabeth.

1711: 27 Sep.: Indent. fr. Henry Cox of Cal. Co., Gent. to Eliza. Lewis, widow, of P.G. Co. for the moyety of a tract of 113 acs. called "Good Luck" on N. br. of Patuxent, containing 200 acs. form. owned by Thos. Houser (sic, Horner) dec'd. land desc. to Eliz. Lewis and Mary Soaper, jt. heirs of Thos. Houser (Horner). (P.G. Co. Liber F, fol. 141.)

1711/12: 4 Feb.: Deed of gift of Eliz. Lewis, widow of P.G. Co. to John Lewis, her son, moyety of land on N. Br. of Patuxent Riv. called "Batterson's Vineyard," lately sold my sister, Mary Soaper, wife of John Soaper, by Henry Cox. (*ibid.*, fol. 153.) Same date: Deed of gift to children fr. Eliz. Lewis, widow, of P.G. Co.: To: Son Thomas, a bay mare, Bonny; To son John: a dark bay mare; To son Stephen, the 1st increase of the mare given John; To dau. Sarah, the next increase; to dau. Priscilla, the next increase: To son, Samuel, the next increase; to grandson, John Davis, child of my dau. Jane. (*ibid.,* fol. 154.)

1722: 26 Nov.: Fr. John Lewis of the colony of Va. to Eliz. Watters of Anne Arundel Co. Land cont. 113 acs. called "Batterson's Vineyard" laid out for John Soaper. Payment of 15 Pounds. (P.G. Co. Lib. F, fol. 463.)
Note: Of the four sons of John Lewis, three: Thomas, John Jr., and Stephen, moved to Stafford, later Fairfax Co., Va., while Samuel remained in Md.

III. RECORDS OF THOMAS LEWIS, JR.:
1712/13: 24 Feb.: Indent. fr. Thos. Lewis, his wife, and Mabel Timothy to Geo. Bennet, Sr.... A parcel called "Putney" (S) (S) Thos. Lewis (Mark) Rececca Lewis (Mark) Mabel Timothy (Mark). (Chas. Co. Land Records, Liber D #2, p. 14.)

1713/14: 9 Mar.: Indent. fr. Thos. Stonestreet of Pr. Geo. Co., planter, and Christina his wife - to Thos. Lewis for 5,000 lbs. Tobo. A parcel called "Birch Den" containing 100 acs. (Chas. Co. Land Records Liber D #2, p. 84.)
Note: "Birch Den," 150 acs., was a gift fr. Thos. Stonestreet Sr. To his son, Thos. Jr. (Chas. Co. Land Records Liber C #2, p, 7) in 1706.

1726: Inventory of Thomas Lewis, widow Rebecca of Charles Co., Md. Thought to be son of Thomas (D. 1696). (Md. Inventories Chas. Co. Liber XI, fol. 507.)

1739: 12 June: Jos. Hunt, of P.G. Co. & wife Mary; Jos. Fry of P.G. Co. & wife Eliz. & Wm. Robins of P.G. Co. & wife Ann, all daus. of Thos. Lewis, dec'd. convey tract "Birch Den" 150 acs. which form. belonged to Thos. Lewis. (Chas. Co. Land Rec. Liber 0, No. 2, fol. 402.) Note: in 1741: 10 Mar. Wm. McQueen & wife, Kath. co-heir with other sisters to "Birch Den" convey to Hump. Deaverson. (*ibid.,* fol. 464.)
Note: The site of the Lewis house at "Battersea" was excavated and was the subject of a Washington Post art. 17 June 1986, sec. D., pp. 1 & 9. Headline: "Area's oldest house is unearthed in Pr. Georges." Photos show shards of pottery, beads for trading with Indians and pipe stems. Hist. of "Batterzee" tract: Humphrey Hagget pat. 500 acs. 27 Sept. 1662. His widow = Richard Fowke, son of Col. Gerrard Fowke of Gunston Hall, who repat. 18 Sept. 1668. Sold or leased to Henry Acton, 250 acs. Thos. Stonestreet got poss. of all 500 acs. by 1726 and built Harmony Hall. (Md. Rent Roll Bks. Liber 4, fol. 372.)

Family Chart of Thomas Lewis (D. 1696)
of Charles/Pr. Georges Co. Md.

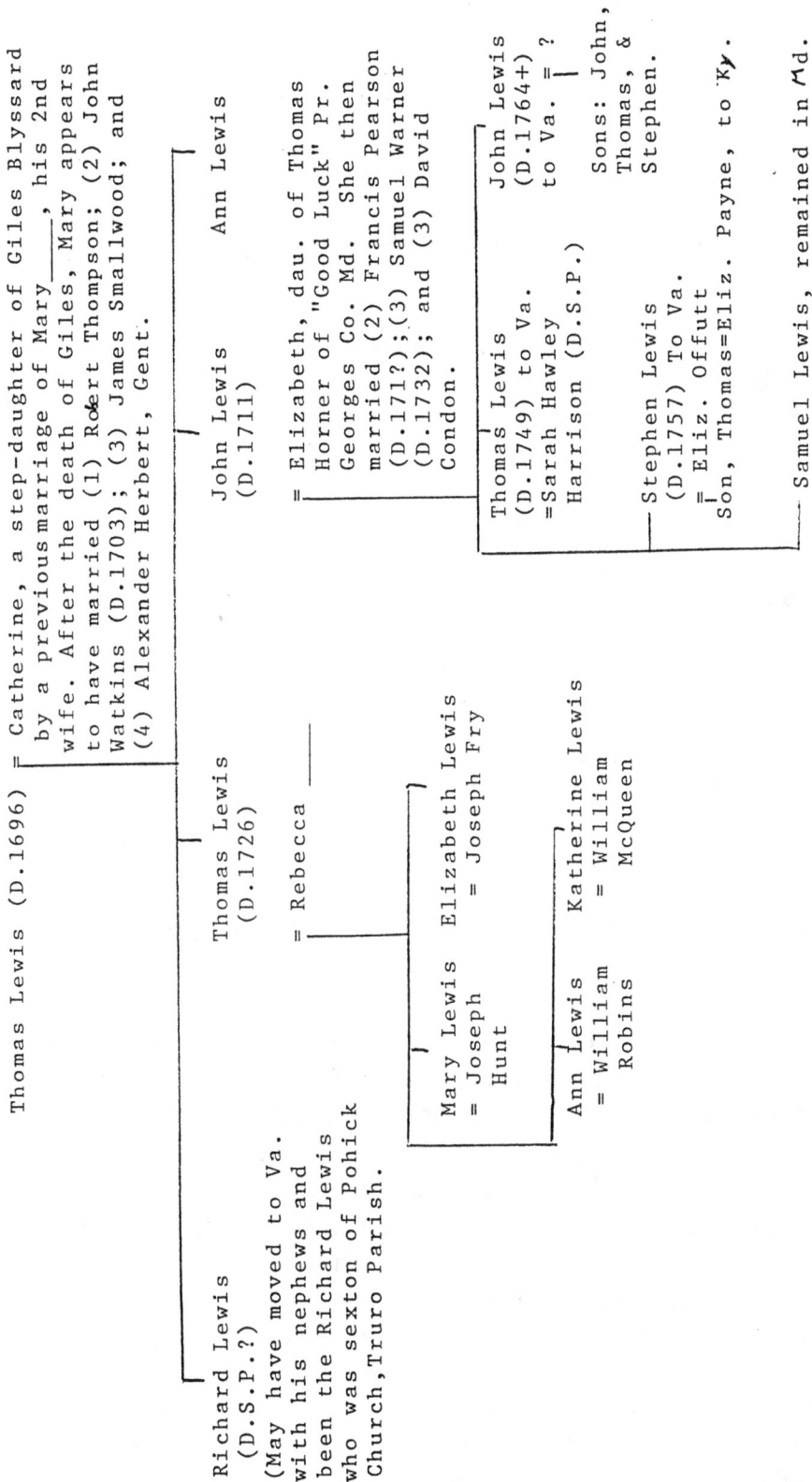

Thomas Lewis (D.1696) = Catherine, a step-daughter of Giles Blyssard by a previous marriage of Mary _____, his 2nd wife. After the death of Giles, Mary appears to have married (1) Robert Thompson; (2) John Watkins (D.1703); (3) James Smallwood; and (4) Alexander Herbert, Gent.

Richard Lewis (D.S.P.?) (May have moved to Va. with his nephews and been the Richard Lewis who was sexton of Pohick Church, Truro Parish.)

Thomas Lewis (D.1726) = Rebecca _____

Mary Lewis = Joseph Hunt

Elizabeth Lewis = Joseph Fry

Ann Lewis = William Robins

Katherine Lewis = William McQueen

John Lewis (D.1711) = Elizabeth, dau. of Thomas Horner of "Good Luck" Pr. Georges Co. Md. She then married (2) Francis Pearson (D.1712?); (3) Samuel Warner (D.1732); and (3) David Condon.

Thomas Lewis (D.1749) to Va. = Sarah Hawley Harrison (D.S.P.)

John Lewis (D.1764+) to Va. = ? Sons: John, Thomas, & Stephen.

Stephen Lewis (D.1757) To Va. = Eliz. Offutt Son, Thomas=Eliz. Payne, to Ky.

Samuel Lewis, remained in Md.

Ann Lewis

5. Jonathan Lewis Of Pr. Georges Co., Md. (D. 1724):

Note: Most Lewis researchers have assumed that he was a descendant of Thomas Lewis (D. 1696). However, he is not mentioned in the will of Thos. Lewis (D. 1696), or in any of the records of the John Lewis (D. 1711) family. The records pertaining to him are as follows:

1724: 13 Feb.: Inventory of Jonathan Lewis filed by Edw. Holmes and Samuel Brashers. (P.G. Co. Inventories, Box 6, folder 20; Rec. in Pr. Geo. Co. Inventories, Liber XI, fol. 222.)

1726: 29 June: Account of Jonathan Lewis filed by Joseph Belt, his Administrator. (P.G. Co. Accounts Bk, Liber 7, fol. 443.)
Children of Jonathan Lewis and wife Mary from St. Barnabas Church, Queen Anne Parish, Register:
Thomas Lewis, b. 11 July 1706
William Lewis, b. 13 Aug. 1708
Jonathan Lewis, b. 29 Aug. 1711
John Lewis, b. 30 Nov. 1713
Daniel Lewis, b. 6 Aug. 1715
Twins: Jonathan Lewis (II or III), b. 7 Aug. 1718
              David Lewis, b. 7 Aug. 1718
Mary Lewis, b. 8 July 1720
(Note: this list is given in Cook, Pioneer Lewis Families, Vol. IV., p. 996, where he adds a Jeremiah Lewis, b. 1722, who does not appear in the records. As a C.G. he should have known better.)

1730: Jonathan Lewis (Jr.) sells 100 acs. "Cox's Rest" which he had recieved from his father to Richard Lanham of P.G. Co.
Note: This record is given in Cook, *ibid.*, p. 995, without a citation. There are two problems with it: first, I could find no ref. to a Cox's Rest in any of the Pr. Geo. Records that have been published through 1727. There was a "Coxon's Rest" however, that had been pat. by Jon Wilcoxon. Second, Jonathan Lewis Jr. was born in 1718, and would not have been of age in 1730, nor was he the eldest son. It is poss. that it was sold by Thos. Lewis, who was the eldest and would have been of age. This Thomas Lewis is thought by many Lewis researchers to be the same Thomas Lewis who moved to Difficult Run, Fairfax, later Loudon Co. Va.
He is mentioned in a codicil to the will of Thomas Lewis (D. 1749), son of John Lewis (D. 1711): "I give and bequeath to my dear friend, Thomas Lewis of Fairfax Co., my right to a parcel of land whereupon he and Wm. Trammell now lives..." Dtd. 13 Sep. 1749. (Fairfax Co. Va. Will Bk. A, No. 1, p. 291.) Thomas Lewis of Difficult Run, (D. 1788), sold this land to John Stonestreet of Pr. Geo. Co. Md., on 22 Mar 1780 - Loudon Co. Land Bk, N, p, 197. Thos. Lewis' will dtd. 7 June 1788, doesn't mention Thomas Lewis, Jr., who is listed in the above deed, but does list sons William Lewis, Daniel Lewis and Levi Lewis. The will was wit. by John Stonestreet, James Hopper, Walter Bayne and Thomas Lewis, (Jr.)? (Loudon Co. Deeds & Wills, Book Q, p. 321.)

II. LEWIS FAMILIES ON THE
EASTERN SHORE OF
MARYLAND

1. Mr. William Lewis (D. 1669) Of Talbot Co. Md.

Note: This William Lewis appears in the Maryland Records in 1658, about the time that Maj. Wm. Lewis of Va. stops appearing in those records, except for land boundary refs. Other people, such as Thomas Yowell, Jr. of Westmoreland Co., Va. were pat. land in Talbot Co. at this time. This could be a son of Maj. Wm. Lewis, or the same person.

1659: William Lewis and wife Sarah granted 100 acs. for Service, Land called "Lewes." (Md. Land Records Liber 4, fol. 57.)

1661: 14 Nov. Wm. Lewis buys "Webley" fr. Edward Lloyd, 300 acs. pat by Edmund Webb 7 Jan. 1659. (Talbot Co. Land Records Liber R.F. #12, fol. 103.)

1661/2: 19 Mar.: Wm. Lewis pats. "Sarah's Neck" 50 acs. adj. Webley. (Md. Land Records, Liber 5, fol. 130, 145).

1664: Aug. 16: Mr. Wm. Lewis a jury member. (Tal. Co. Ct. Proc.: In Md. Archives Vol. 53, p. 372.)

1665/6 Mar. 19: Thos. Bolton, planter, to Wm. Lewis, planter, - 450 acs., "Boylton's Neck at head of Nanticoke River." (Tal. Co. Land Bk. I, p. 12.) (Dorchester Co.)

1667: July 15: Samuel Winsloe to Wm. Lewis, planter, 200 acs. called "Providence" S. side Chester River, E. side S.W. br. of Coursey Ck. (One third of 600 acs. laid out for Andrew Skinner, Henry Parker and Samuel Winsloe.) (Tal. Co. Land Bk. I, p. 28.)

1667/8: Jan. 27: John Burgis, servant to Wm. Lewis, judged to serve seven years, being about 16 years of age. (Tal. Co. Ct. Proc. In: Md. Arch. Vol. 53, p. 416.)

1667/8: Feb. 16: Wm. Lewis brought his servant Eliza. Bailey to have judgement of the court. She is judged to serve six years. (Tal. Co. Ct. Proc. In: Md. Arch. Vol. 53, p. 430.)

1668: Oct. 10: Joseph Winslow of Kequotan, Eliza. City Co., Va., Mariner, to Capt. Francis Armstrong to convey to Samual Winsloe of Talbot, Mariner, 680 acs, "Boston Clift" (pat. 4 Aug. 1665) adj. Daniel Jennifer and James Rigby, and 200 acs., "Plaindealing" in the western Br. of Tredhaven Ck. (pat 26 July 1664.) (Tal. Co. Land Bk. I, p. 53.) (Bond for 30,000 lbs. of Tobo. fr. Joseph Winsloe to Samual Winsloe for sale of above two properties follows on p. 54.)

1668/9: Feb. 16: Wm. Smith, planter, to John Garbly 100 acs. next to Capt. Robert Morris. (This deed made void.)

Let it be remembered that the within mentioned land be made voyd upon the court record - being made over to Ralph Fishbourne by us Dec. the 14th 1668. Samual Winsloe, William Lewis.

The abovesaid land is not here. Seen is a parcel of land sold by "Samual" Winsloe to Wm. Lewis in the S.E. Br. of Chester river called Island ck. named "Mt. Hope." being 300 acs. the former sales being made by the abovesaid writing. (Tal. Co. Land Bk. I. p. 73.)

*Winslow Note: While Wm. Lewis was purchasing the above properties from Samuel Winsloe, a John Winsloe, Gent. was buying and patenting land in the areas of Maj. Wm. Lewis' earlier pats. in New Kent Co., Va.:

*(All of these Winslows appear to be sons of John Winslow of Boston & wife Mary Chilton, - brother of Gov. Winslow of Mass. (See Pedigree in Vol. III *Mayflower Families through Five Generations*, pp. 6-20. 1986.)

1667:   Mar. 27: Mr. Thomas Holmes pats. 575 acs. New Kent Co. S.W. side of Pianketanke Swp to John Roberts land, to Exolls (Axolls) Swp Trans. of 12 persons: John Winsloe 5 times, his wife once.... Berryman Winsloe .... (Nugent, C. & P. II, p. 73.)

1667/8: Feb. 12: Mr. John Winsloe and Richard Awborn pat. 2,000 acs. New Kent Co. S. side of freshes of York River. (Nugent, C. & P. II, p. 54.)

This pat. location is made more precise by the following: Mr. John Page pats. 1900 acs. New Kent Co. S. side York river and the freshes thereof, beginning at the upper bounds of Mr. John Winsloe's land... SAME, same co. and date, (Mr. John Page) pats. 1700 acs. S. side York Riv. bothe sides of Totopotomes Ck. (Mar 14 1672.) (Nugent, C. & P. II, p. 30.) These pats. appear to either be on or adjacent to Maj. Wm. Lewis' Port Holy and Totopotomy Ck. pats.

1667(?) (Undated, but between two 1667 pats): John Winsloe, Gent., 600 acs. New Kent Co. S.E. (*sic*, should be N.E. - see following pats.) side of Mattapony River, 500 acs. to a br. of a swp dividing this and a lower development of Mr. Wm. Wyatt 500 ac. part granted Col. Robert Abrahall 20 Feb. 1654 and assigned to sd. Winsloe. (Nugent, C. & P. II, p. 30.) Note: This is adj. to Maj. Wm. Lewis' three pats. on the Tastine swamp.

1669:   Aug. 7: Mr. John Winsloe pats. 600 acs. New Kent Co. S. side of Peanketank Swp. adj. David Bramm.... (Nugent, C. & P. II, p. 62.) Note: This was one month before the death of Wm. Lewis in Talbot Co. and is in the area of the Maj. Wm. Lewis 2,000 ac. pat. at the head of the Mattapony River. It appears to be John Winsloe's last pat.

1670: Apr. 18: Mr. John Dorwood, 68 acs. N. side of Mattapony, adj. Thos. Hickman Jr.; Maj. Wm. Wyatt and land of Mr. John Winsloe, formerly Col. Robert Abralls. (Nugent, C. & P. II, p. 77.)

1680: Apr. 26: Maj. Wm. Wyatt, 850 acs, New Kent Co. N.E. side of Mattapony, mouth of Matchapungo Ck.... to Mr. John Winsloe's line. 400 acs. by pat. 16 Mar. 1663 and 450 acs. adj.... (Nugent, C. & P. II, p. 208.)

(End of Winslow Note.)

1669: Sept. 5: Death of William Lewis. (Tal. Co. Ct. Proc. In: Md. Arch. Vol. 53, p. 601.)

1669/70: Jan. 9: Henry Willcocks marries Sarah Lewis, widow. (Tal. Co. Ct. Proc. In: Md. Arch. Vol. 53, p. 602.)

1669/70: Mar 12: Will of William Lewis recorded: Abstract as follows: Dated 23 Sept. 1668:
To Wenlock Christison (Quaker minister) and Henry Willcockes, personalty.
To wife Sarah, home plantation,[*] "Sarah's Neck" (50 acs. pat. 1668); and 100 acs "Lewis"(1st Md. pat. 1659)
To dau. Sarah, 680 acs. "Boston Cliffs" on Great Choptank Riv. (Bought fr. Sam Winsloe 1668.) (Sarah married Ralph Fishbourne in 1673.)
To dau. Mary, 450 acs. on Nanticoke Riv. ("Boylton," bought in 1665/6); and 200 acs. on Chester Riv. ("Providence" bought fr. Sam. Winsloe in 1667.) (Mary married Bryan Omealy in 1676.)
To wife Sarah and 2 daus., Sarah and Mary, residue of estate, equally.
Exs.: Henry Willcocks, Henry Southeby, Thos. Taylor of Kent, Thos. Pitt.
Test.: Geo. Collison, Ralph Fishbourne, Geo. Landman, John Burrows.
(Md. Cal. of Wills, Vol. 1., p. 374 - printed version with abstract: Vol. I, p. 51-52.)

Note: On the original will, Box I, Folder 16. Tal. Co. Probate Records, in Md. State Archives, Wm. Lewis has affixed his seal after his signature, of which the left third is still intact: a rose above the first part of a chevron. The entire seal would appear to have been a chevron between three roses, the arms borne by the descendants of Einion ap Geraint, Lord of Pentraeth, Dindaethwy, in Anglesey, Wales, whose arms were: Gules, a chevron between three roses, argent. Some families who claimed descent from Rhodri Mawr, King of Wales, used the same arms..

1678: Feb. 19: (Four men were) chosen to put an end to a difference betw. Bryon Omealia and Ralph Fishbourne about the land Ralph lives upon being in possession thereof in the right of his wife, as also in another tract of land.... "Lewis" lying in (St.) Michaels river (now Miles River), both given.... by Wm. Lewis, dec'd, to Sarah, his wife, now dec'd without issue. (Tred Avon Friends Meeting Minutes 1676-1746, Vol. I, p. 14.)

---

[*] Home Plantation = "Webley" see Md. Hist. Mag. 1954, pp. 41-53.

1690: Nov. 2: Ralph Fishbourne of Talbot, Merchant, to Charles Cartwright, bricklayer, - 100 acs. called "Lewes" on the east side of Chesapeake Bay, S. side of St. Michaels River, adjoining the land of Thos. Emerson. (Tal. Co. Land Bk. VI, p. 29.) Note: By 1700 Ralph Fishbourne had moved to Chester Co. Pa. His son, William Fishbourne, founded one of the "first families" of Philadelphia.

Photo of seal on will of Wm. Lewis (D. 1669) of Talbot Co., MD
(at MD Hall of Records, Annapolis)

2. Col. Matthew Lewis Of Talbot Co. Md (D. 1711)

I. POSSIBLE RELEVANT VA. RECORDS:

1664: 19 July: A Matthew Lewis is apprenticed in Bristol to John Bodenham to serve 5 years in Va. (Coldham, Compl, Bk, of Immigrants, 1661-1669, p. 67.)

1664/5: 23 Mar: A Matthew Lewis is a headright for Col. Gerrard Fowke & Mr. Richard Haiberd for 1680 acs. Stafford Co. Va. (Nugent, C. & P. I, p. 446.)

1671: Inventory of a Mathew Lewis, dec'd presented to the Westmoreland Court by Col. John Washington. (Dorman, Westmoreland Co. Records 1665 to 1677, p. 102.) (orig. rec.)

1671: Sept. 29: A Mathew Lewis a headright for Thomas Rawson for 591 acs. S. side Rappahannock River. (Nugent, C. & P. II, p. 101.)

1672: Oct. 20: A Mathew Lewis a headright of Francis Gower for 714 acs. Rappahannock Co. (Note: his name is one of five that are the same in this pat. and the one above. (Nugent, C. & P. II, p. 120.)

II. MD. RECORDS:

1672: Mathew Lewis a headright for William Morgan for 250 acs. Dorchester Co. Md. (Md. Land Bks. Liber 16, fol. 393.)

1678: Oct/Nov.: The Md. General Assembly approved payment of 400 lbs. tobo. to Corporal Lewis of Dorchester Co. (Md. Archives, Vol. 7, p. 93.)

1678: Mathew Lewis witness to will of Wm. Foorde (Ford), Choptank River, Dorchester Co. Md. dtd. 16 Nov. 1678; rec. 11 Mar. 1679. (Md. Cal of Wills, Vol. I, p. 208-9.)

1689: In a list of complaints by the (Nanticoke) Indians, they mention ten Indians that disappeared between Oxforde Town and Col. Lewes'. (Md. Arch. Vol. 13, p. 231.)
Note: By this time Matthew Lewis apparently owned "Pohickory Ridge Manor" at the ferry point between Talbot and Dorchester Co., where Rt. 50 crosses it today. This was a 1,000 acr. manor that he divided among his grandchildren. The manor was originally granted to Thos. Boylston, who had sold land to Mr. Wm. Lewis of Talbot Co. A Thos. Boylston is mentioned in the 1664 Herald's Visitation of London.

1711: 5 May: The will of Matthew Lewis of this date mentions his son-in-law, Thomas Jenkins, grandsons Matthew, Thomas and Walter Jenkins, granddaughters Margaret and Catherine Jenkins. He leaves an annuity to Margaret Morgan.
Note: The will is sealed with a crest that appears to be a rose. See photo. (Md. Cal, of Wills, Vol. 4, p. 232.)

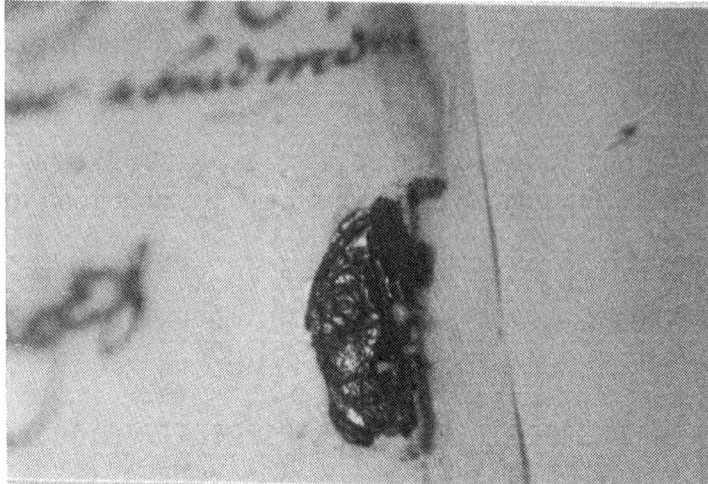

**Photo of seal on will of Matthew Lewis (D. 1711) of Talbot Co., MD.
(at MD Hall of Records, Annapolis)**

3. The Charles Lewis Family Of Talbot Co. Md.

MAIN REF.: *Colonial Families of the Eastern Shore of Maryland*, Vol. 3. By Robert W. Barnes and F. Edward Wright. 1997.

(?) 1675: 23 Jun.: A Charles Lewis apprenticed in Bristol to Robert Finch to serve four years in Virginia. (P. Coldham, Complete Book of Emigrants 1661-1699, p. 245.)

1676: 10 June: John Edmondson of Talbot Co. Md. Lists Charles and Samuel Lewis along with 29 others as servants he has transported into Maryland and sells the 31 headrights to Will. Stevens of Somerset Co., Md. (Md. Land Bks. Liber 14, folio 358-listed in Skorda' Early Settlers of Md. pp. 288-9).

1682: 20 Nov.: Thomas Smithson, John Stanley and wife Judith convey Charles and Samuel Lewis 100 acs. - "Cumberland." (Barnes & Wright, op. cit., p. 255).

1692: 12 Aug.: The will of Dr. Thomas Anderson wit. By Charles Lewis and others. (Barnes & Wright, op. cit., p. 18).

1696: 29th day 8th mo.: Charles Lewis appeared before the Third Haven Meeting (Quakers) and declared that he and his wife had often grieved that they were married by a priest. (Barnes & Wright, op. cit., p. 255).

1709: 1 Nov.: The will of Wm. Troth of Talbot Co. (Proved 6 Nov. 1716), mentioned son-in-law, Charles Lewis; left "Newington" on Choptank River, Queen Anne Co. to his grandson, Wm. Lewis; and also mentions his granddaughters: Fortune, Ann and Elizabeth Lewis. (Barnes & Wright, op. cit., p. 255, 332).

Known children of Charles Lewis:
William Lewis, with wife Elizabeth, sold "Newington" - 240 acs. 24 Mar. 1729 to Wm. Driskill, saddler. (Barnes & Wright, op. cit., p. 256).
Fortune Lewis, on 20th day 3rd mo. 1733, she complained that Saml. Dickenson was indebted to her for part of legacy given her by her grandfather, Wm. Troth - Third Haven Meeting Minutes. (Barnes & Wright, op. cit., p. 332).

Ann Lewis, on 31st day 6th mo. 1709, it was noted in the Third Haven meeting Minutes that a marriage was intended between her and Robert Jones. (Barnes & Wright, op. cit., p. 255).
Elizabeth Lewis, on 10 Feb. 1717, married Jerimiah Neal at Tuckahoe Meeting. (Barnes & Wright, op. cit., p. 255).

4. The Thomas And John Lewis Family Of Talbot Co. Md.
MAIN REF.: *Colonial Families of the Eastern Shore of Md.,* by Robert W. Barnes and F. Edward Wright. 1997.

I. RECORDS OF THOMAS LEWIS (D. 1684-5)
(?) 1668: A Thomas Lewis appears in a list of servants transported into Md. (Listed in Skordas' Early Settlers of Md., p. 289 - Ref. to Md. Land Bk. Liber 12, folio 285.)

(?) 1668: 30 July: In Bristol, Jane Lewis is apprenticed to Ann Hopkins for four years in Va. (P. Coldham, Compl. Bk. Of Emm 1660-1699, p. 128.)

(?) 1669: A Jane Lewis is transported to Md. (In Skordas' Early Settlers of Md., p. 288: Ref. to Md. Land Bks. Liber 12, Folio 243.)

1671: August Court: John Lewis of Talbot Co. ack. Judgement of 440 lbs. tobo. Due Edward Skidmore on behalf of himself and his brother, Thomas Lewis. (Barnes & Wright, op. cit., p. 252).

1673: 2 Apr.: Thomas Lewis of Talbot Co. and wife, Jane, sell their two rights for service to Mathew Warde. (Md. Land Bks. Liber 17, Folio 418: Ref. in Skordas' Early Settlers of Md., p. 289.)

1682: 25 May: Thomas Lewis patents "Lewis' Chance" 50 acs. Talbot Co. (P. Coldham, Settlers of Md. 1679-1700, p. 105.)

1684: 20 Sept.: Will of Thomas Lewis (proved June 1685): Names son, Thomas, left a plantation (unnamed) at age 18; son, John, left 50 acs. "Lewis' Chance" at age 18; dau., Ann, wife of John Davis, to have charge of dau. Ellinor until 16 years of age. Residue of estate between all children equally except Margaret. (Barnes & Wright, op. cit., p. 252).

RECORDS OF THE CHILDREN OF THOMAS LEWIS (D. 1684-5)
  i. Thomas Lewis, Jr. (D. 1719?)
  Note: There was a Thomas Lewis who died intestate in Talbot Co. by 10 Sept 1719 when an Admin. Acct. was filed by John Oldham. He was obviously not the Thomas Lewis, b ca. 1666, who age ca. 57 gave a deposition in Apr. of 1723, and again at age ca. 60 on 6 May 1728. (Barnes & Wright, op. cit., p. 253).

1711: Aug. Court: John Gibbs asked to be bound to Thomas Lewis to learn the trade of a cooper until age 21. Thomas Lewis agrees to look after Gibbs' cattle and stock during the term. (Barnes & Wright, op. cit., p. 253).

1711: Nov. Court: Thos. Lewis appointed constable of Worrell hundred instead of Matthew Mason. (Barnes & Wright, op. cit., p. 253).

1712/13: March Court: Thomas Hollingsworth appointed constable of Worrell hundred in the place of Thomas Lewis. (Barnes & Wright, op. cit., p. 254).

    a. RECORDS OF THOMAS LEWIS JR.'S ELDEST SON, GEORGE:
        1747: 27 Mar: George Lewis and wife, Sarah, convey to Wm. Elbert 50 acs. known as "Lewis' Chance." (Barnes & Wright, op. cit., p. 254).

        1747: 10 Oct.: George Lewis conveys to Thomas Hammond 60 acs., part of "Boaquely" on s. side of Corsica Ck., formerly John Lewis' part and part sold to Richard Tilghman. Originally granted to John Boage for 350 acs. and assigned to Wm. Burgess of A.A. Co., who assigned it to Thomas and John Lewis. Thos. Lewis bequeathed his part to his son, Thomas, who died intestate, and the land became the right of his eldest son, George Lewis. (Barnes & Wright, op. cit., p. 254).

  ii. JOHN LEWIS (B. CA. 1672 - D. CA. 1688 (?), SON OF THOS. LEWIS, SR., RECORDS:
  1686: June Court: Ordered that John Lewis, orphan of Thomas Lewis, abide with his brother-in-law, Henry Everith until next court and then prove that he is fourteen years old. (Barnes & Wright, op. cit., p. 254).

  (?) 1688: Dec. Court: Jeffry Mattershaw was allowed payment for 11 months accommodations of John lewis and his burial. (Barnes & Wright, op. cit., p. 254).

II. Records of John Lewis (D. 1700), Brother of Thomas Lewis, Sr., (D. 1684-5)
1671: Aug. Court: See under Thomas Lewis (D. 1684-5).

1672: John Lewis of Talbot Co. granted one right for service ending in 1664. He sells it to Matthew Ward, Gent. (Md. Land Bks. Liber 16, folio 461.)

1673: 9 Dec.: Sale of "Bouagley" to Thos. And John Lewis - see under Thomas Lewis (D. 1684-5) records.

1677: 15 Oct.: John Lewis conveyed 200 acs. by Daniel Walker, planter, and his wife, Alice, - "Cheshire" on s. side of Chester River adj. Thomas Hinson, "Gray's Inn" (Barnes & Wright, op. cit., p. 253).

1691: John Lewis conveyed 100 acs., "Plaines" on Winchester Ck. By Robert Smith, Gent. (Tal. Co. Land Bk. 5, p. 310.)

1692: 10 Aug.: John Lewis conveys to Matthew Smith and wife Prescilla, 100 acs: "Plaines." (Barnes & Wright, op. cit., p. 253).

1697: June Court: John Lewis charged with threatening the Under-Sheriff, Richard Jones, but was discharged. (Barnes & Wright, op. cit., p. 253).

1698: 10 Mar.: Will of John Lewis (proved 8 June 1700): Extr. And sole legatee of estate, real and personal, was his wife, Elizabeth. Wit. By Henry Everett, Sarah Everett, and Nicholas Marshall. (Barnes & Wright, op. cit., p. 253).

1701: 17 Nov.: Nicholas and Elizabeth Marshall convey Richard Macklin, Gent. "Cheshire" - purchased of Daniel Walker by John Lewis, dec'd., late husband of sd. Elizabeth and to her bequeathed in his will. (Barnes & Wright, op. cit., p. 253).

1703: 10 June: Nicholas Marshall and his wife Elizabeth convey to Robert Smith, 200 acs. "Cheshire" first taken up by Daniel Walker and by him alienated to John Lewis, dec'd., and by his will given to Elizabeth, his wife, and by Elizabeth and Nicholas Marshall sold to Richard Macklin who sold to Nicholas Marshall - at the head of Winchester Ck. (Barnes & Wright, op. cit., p. 253).

5. The Thomas Lewis (D. Ca 1707) Family Of Kent Co., Md.:

MAIN REF.: Colonial Families of the Eastern Shore of Md., Vol. 1, by Robert W. Barnes and
    F. Edward Wright. 1996.

(?) 1675: 30 July: A Thomas Lewis apprenticed in Bristol to Richard Jones, four years in
    Virginia. (P. Coldham, Complete Bk. Of Emigrants 1661-1699, p. 249).

(?) 1675: 1 Dec: A Thomas Lewis appears in a list of 14 servants brought into Md. on this
    date by Thomas Steventon, who swears to this on 19 June 1676 and assigns the
    headrights. (Md. Land Bks.: Liber 15, Folio 353. - Listed in Skordas' Early Settlers of
    Md., p. 289).

1686: 18 Sept: Michael Miller and wife Ann of Kent Co. convey to Thomas Lewis of Kent
    Co., cooper, part of a dividend of 1600 acs. called 'Arcadia' granted to Michael Miller
    (in 1680) (Barnes and Wright, *op cit*. P. 268).

The following children born to Thomas Lewis and his wife, Ester, are listed in the
Kent Co. Records:
    Francis, b. 31 Oct 1686 (d. by 18 July 1729)
    James, b. 1 May 1689. (d. by 9 Sep. 1716)
    Hester (Ester), b 2 Mar. 1692, bp 19 Sep 1697.
        (married Geo. Debruler 20 Oct. 1713)
    Mary, b. 14 Apr. 1694, bp. 19 Sep. 1697
        (married a Tharp)
    Margaret, (twin with Mary) b. 14 Apr. 1694, bp 19 Sep 1697.
        (married Thos. Ricaud [Ringgold?])
    Thomas, (poss. Not by Ester) see his records.
        b. ca. 1705. (d. 1768)
                (Barnes & Wright, op. Cit., p. 233.)

1706: 21 Aug: Date mentioned as that of the last will of Thomas Lewis - not in Md. Calendar
    of Wills.

Records of Francis Lewis (1686-1729):
    Francis Lewis married Martha Pope, a widow.
    Known childred: Frances the elder (dau.)
                 Frances the younger (dau.)
    (One of these Franceses married John Cawlay a mariner of VA.)

1717: 15 June: Ester Lewis of Kent Co., widow, bequeaths to her son Francis all her personal
    estate. (Barnes & Wright, op. cit., p. 232).

1729: 18 July: An inventory of the estate of Francis Lewis was filed by Martha Lewis,
    Admx. Next of kin listed as Mary Tharp and Thomas Lewis.

1739: 10 Dec.: The real estate of Francys Lewis of Chester Town, dec'd., was appraised. It included:

> "The house where Dr. Adair lives"
> The plantation called "Little Grove" and "The Grove"
> The plantation called "Part of Arcadia" or "The Hills"
> > (Barnes & Wright, op. cit., p. 233).

Records of James Lewis (1689 - 1716):

1716: 9 Sep: The estate of James Lewis was admin. by his widow, now the wife of Samuel Clark. (Barnes & Wright, op. cit., p. 233).

1718: 22 Jun.: James Lewis' estate was admin. By Francis Lewis. A payment was made to Thos. 'Ricaud' who married a sister of the deceased. (Barnes & Wright, op. cit., p. 233).

Records of Thomas Lewis Jr. (ca. 1705 - 1768):

1728: 22 Aug.: Thomas Lewis of Kent Co., planter, conveys to Wm. Frisby part of a tract called 'Hitchingham' - 125 acs. Bequeathed him by his father, Thomas Lewis in his last will dtd. 21 Aug. 1706. (Barnes & Wright, op. cit., p. 234).

1757: 20 June: Thomas Lewis, age ca 52, deposed re bounds of the tracts "Arcadia" and "New Forest." (Barnes & Wright, op. cit., p. 233-4).

1758: 22 Aug.: Thomas Lewis of Kent Co. conveys to Mary Bowers, wife of Thos. Bowers, and dau. of the aforesaid Thomas Lewis, part of the tract "Arcadia" released out of the original tract called "Arcadia" by the present Thomas Lewis' father from old Arthur Miller, 50 acs. Where sd. Thomas Lewis' mother dwelled at the time of ther death. (Barnes & Wright, op. cit., p. 234).

1761: 18 Dec.: Thomas Lewis, age ca. 54 deposed re bounds of "Wexford" (Barnes & Wright, op. cit., p. 234).

1768: 4 Jan.: Will of Thomas Lewis of St. Paul's Parish, Kent Co. (Proved 2 Feb. 1768), left estate to grandchild, Thos. Bowers. Exec. Was Thos. Ringgold of Chester Town. (Barnes & Wright, op. cit., p. 234).
Note: It is possible that Thomas Lewis Sr. Married Eliner Stokes on 14 Feb. 1702 (Barnes & Wright, op. cit., p. 235), and that she was the mother of Thomas Lewis, Jr. On 19 March 1718, Arthur Miller and his wife Sarah conveyed to Elinor Goodwing, widow of Samuel Goodwing of the same county, 200 acs. paid for by Thomas Lewis, late husband of the aforesaid Elinor Goodwing, (Barnes & Wright, op. cit., p. 271).

This Lewis family of Kent Co. appears to have been related to the James Lewis family of Anne Arundel Co., since Francis Lewis of Kent Co. (d. 1729) signed as next of kin on the 1726 inventory account of James Lewis (d. 1726).

6. Records Of Glode Lewis (D. 1718) Dorchester Co. Md.

1672: Cload Lewis granted headright for service, Dorchester Co. (Md. Land Bks, Liber 16, fol. 532.)

1679: Claude Lewis of Dorchester Co. granted headrights for service of wife Sarah and dau. Sarah. (Md. Land Bks. Liber WC 2, fol. 71.)

1684: 20 Feb.: Glode and Sarah Lewis pat. "Sarah's Lot" 50 acs. Dor. Co. (P. Coldham, Settlers of Md., 1679-1700, p. 105.)

1705: Glad Lewis of Dorchester Co. owns "Andrew's Desire." (Md Rent Roll: Liber 10 fol. 406.)

1718: Will of Glode Lewis, Sr.: Leaves one shilling to each of his children - Sons: John, Glode, Thomas, Abraham and William. Daus: Sarah Myersby, Elizabeth, Ann Arron, and Jane.
To wife: Ann (second wife) Residue of estate. (Dor. Co. Wills Liber 14, fol. 730.) (Abs. of Md. Cal. of Wills, Vol. 4, p. 187.)

1720: Inventory of Gload Lewis recorded in Dorchester Co. (Dor. Co. Inventories and Accounts, Liber 4, fol. 225.)
Issue: Sons and Daus listed in will above.
Of the five sons, three left wills in Dorchester Co.:
Glode: (D. 1754) left at least one son, Glode (Md. Cal. of Wills, Bk. 29, p. 52.)
Thomas: (D. 1748) No issue? (Md. Cal. of Wills, Bk. 25, p. 461.)
Abraham: (D. 1763) Sons: Abraham, William, Levin, Shadrack, and Elisha; Daus.: Ann Phillips, Hezia Lewis, and Betty Clark. (Md. Cal of Wills, Bk. 31, p. 1032).

7. Richard Lewis Of Somerset Co., Md. Records:

1681: 4 Apr.: William Stephens (Stevens) pats. 150 acs. Pocomoke Hundred: 'Stepney' - Later assigned to Richard Lewis. A later note on the Rent Roll states: No such person or land known. (R.T. Dryden, Somerset Co. Rent Rolls, 1663-1723, p. 104.)

1682: Richard Lewis of Somerset bought 'Stepney' - 150 acs. fr. Wm. Stevens, E. side Chesapeake Bay, N. side of Pocomoke Riv., betw. it and Marumsco Cr. in Somerset Manor. (Hall of Records index no. 54: Ref. to Liber C.B. No. 3, fol. 49.)

1683: Richard Lewis sold 'The Cartwheel' - 150 acs. in Worchester Co., then Somerset Co. to Richard Pepper. (Same land as 'Stepney?') (Hall of Records Index no. 54: Ref. to Liber 22, fol. 89.)

Birth data of Richard Lewis' children fr. Somerset Co. Land Records (Spelled Lewes in Records):

> Samuel Lewis, son of Richard & Margaret Lewis, born 15 July 1680.
> Margaret Lewis, dau. of same, born 4 Jan. 1583.
> Richard Lewis, son of same, born 1 Mar. 1686.
> William Lewis, son of same, born 10 Feb 1688.
> (E. Wright, Eastern Shore Vital Records, Vol. I, p. 129.)

Note: There are no further references to Richard Lewis in the Somerset Co. Records after 1688, but the following Northumberland Co. Va. records may apply to him:

1689: Richard Lewis bought 100 acs. from John Evans in Wicomico Parish, half of 200 acs. Evans bought fr. Ebenezer Sanders whose father, Edward had pat. it. (Note: in 1662, Edw. Sanders pat. 2900 acs. in the forest betw. Lancaster & Northumberland Cos. On br. of Damaron's Cr. W. to head of Coratoman Riv. E. from Machoticke footpath. (Nugent, C. & P. I, p. 429.) (C. Jett, Records of Northumb. Co., Va. p. 54.)

1690: 21 May: Richard Lewis' servant, Joan MacMaghagn, had a bastard child during the time of her service. (W. P. Haynie, Records of Indentured Servants etc. Northumb. Co., Va. 1650-1795, entry no. 893.)

1694: Richard Lewis assigned his 100 acs. of land to Thomas Harding. (C. Jett, *op. cit.,* p. 54, same entry.)

8. Richard Lewis Of Cecil Co. Md. (D. 1720) Family Records

1720: Will of Richard Lewis, Sr., Dtd. 7 Aug. 1719; prob. 4 Aug. 1720: To wife, Anna, dwelling plantation for life; to sons Richard and John entire estate on decease of wife; personalty to son-in-law Thomas Simper and Kesia Clark. Eldest son, Richard to be exec. at death of wife. Wit. by John Numbers (Ombers), John Boyer (Boyeur) & John Robertson. (Md. Cal. of Wills, Liber 16, fol. 152.)

1721: Patrick Murphy of Cecil Co., age about 60, deposes that he brought a lease of ejectment ag. Richard Lewis, John Thomas, & David Evans, who settled on a tract called "Murphy's Forest" taken up by deponent by Md. rights ca. 1694. (Md. Arch., Vol. XXV, p. 373-4.)
Note: In the Cecil Co. Rent Rolls, Richard Lewis was listed with the tracts 'Tryall' and "Concord," and Richard and John Lewis with 'St. John's Manor' (Md. Rent Rolls, Liber 6, rol. 326, 370, 415.)

1727/8: 8 Feb.: Richard and John Lewis wit. the will of Thos. Boyer of Cecil Co. (Abs. of Md. Cal. of Wills, Vol. 8, p. 66.)

1735/6: The will of John Lewis of Cecil Co. dtd. 13 Nov. 1735, prob. 26 Jan. 1735/6: Mentions wife Hester and brother Richard Lewis. (Md. Cal. of Wills, Liber 21, fol. 536.)

1740: 14 Apr.: Richard Lewis of Cecil Co. mentioned as the husband of Amy Van Pool. (Abs. of Md. Cal. of Wills, Vol. 8, p. 85.)

1749: Will of Richard Lewis (Jr.) of Cecil Co. (Md. Cal. of Wills, Liber 27, fol. 45.)
Note: it is possible that this is the same Richard Lewis as the son of John Lewis of Accomac Co., Va., whose last record there was the sale of his land in 1709.

III. LEWIS FAMILIES ON THE
WESTERN SHORE OF
MARYLAND
(ANNE ARUNDEL AND BALTIMORE COUNTIES)

1. Records Of Dr. Henry Lewis (D. 1678), Anne Arundel Co. Md.:

1666: Apr. 3: Court order (Somerset Co.) for Henry Lewis to pay Cuthbert Potter 350 lbs. Tobo for goods delivered. (In Md. Arch. Vol. 54, p. 621)

1670: Henry Lewis wit. will of Geo. Collings, 16 Nov. 1670, Anne Arundel Co. (In: Md. Cal. of Wills, Vol. I, p. 61)

1675: Henry Lewis and Mary Lewis wit will of Wm. Slade, 15 May 1675. Dr. Henry Lewis and John Rix, Executors. (In: Md. Cal. of Wills, Vol. I, p. 172)

1676: Henry Lewis named as one of the Gentlemen Justices of Anne Arundel Co., 13 Sept. 1676. (Md. Arch. Vol. 15, p. 130)
Note: The records of Somerset Co. Md. have references in them during this period to Henry Lewis of Anne Arundel Co. as an Atty and as marrying Elizabeth (Rogerson) Boston, widow Henry Boston of Somerset Co. (C. Torrence, Old Somerset, p. 290, 322.)

1678: Will of Henry Lewis, dtd. 3 Feb. 1678: Body to be buried by former wife, (Mary nee Brown) and children. Wife (Eliz.) to receive Negro, Cow, and "Lewis' Range" 253 acs. S. side of Patapsco River, if no heirs to sons Wm. and Henry. If they die, wife to dispose of. To son William Lewis: "Home plantation"; "Tann Yard", 50 acs. between Severn and Magothy Riv. bought of John Clark. To son Henry Lewis, Horse, silver tobacco box, and 325 acs. called Lewis' Addition. (Md. Cal. of Wills, and A.A. Co. Wills, Liber 10, fol. 27.)

1679: Inventory of Henry Lewis filed 28 Apr. 1679. (A.A. Co. Inv. & Accounts Liber 6, fol. 156 - 165.)

1681: Account of Henry Lewis filed by John Bird and Eliza. his now wife of A. A. Co. Exectrix. (A. A. Co. Inv. & Accts. Liber 7, fol. 8 - 18.)

1683: Petition of the Orphans of Henry Lewis to the Gen. Assembly, (Lower House) that they are being defrauded of their estate by their Father-in-law (Stepfather.) Petition presented and attested to by a member of the House. 1 Nov. 1683. (Md. Arch. Vol. 7, p. 504.)

1683: Upper House concurred in above petition and gave direction to the Judges of Testimentary Causes (To secure what they could of the estate.) (Md. Arch. Vol. 7, p. 587.)

Family Chart of Dr. Henry Lewis (D.1678)
of Somerset and Anne Arundale Cos., Md.

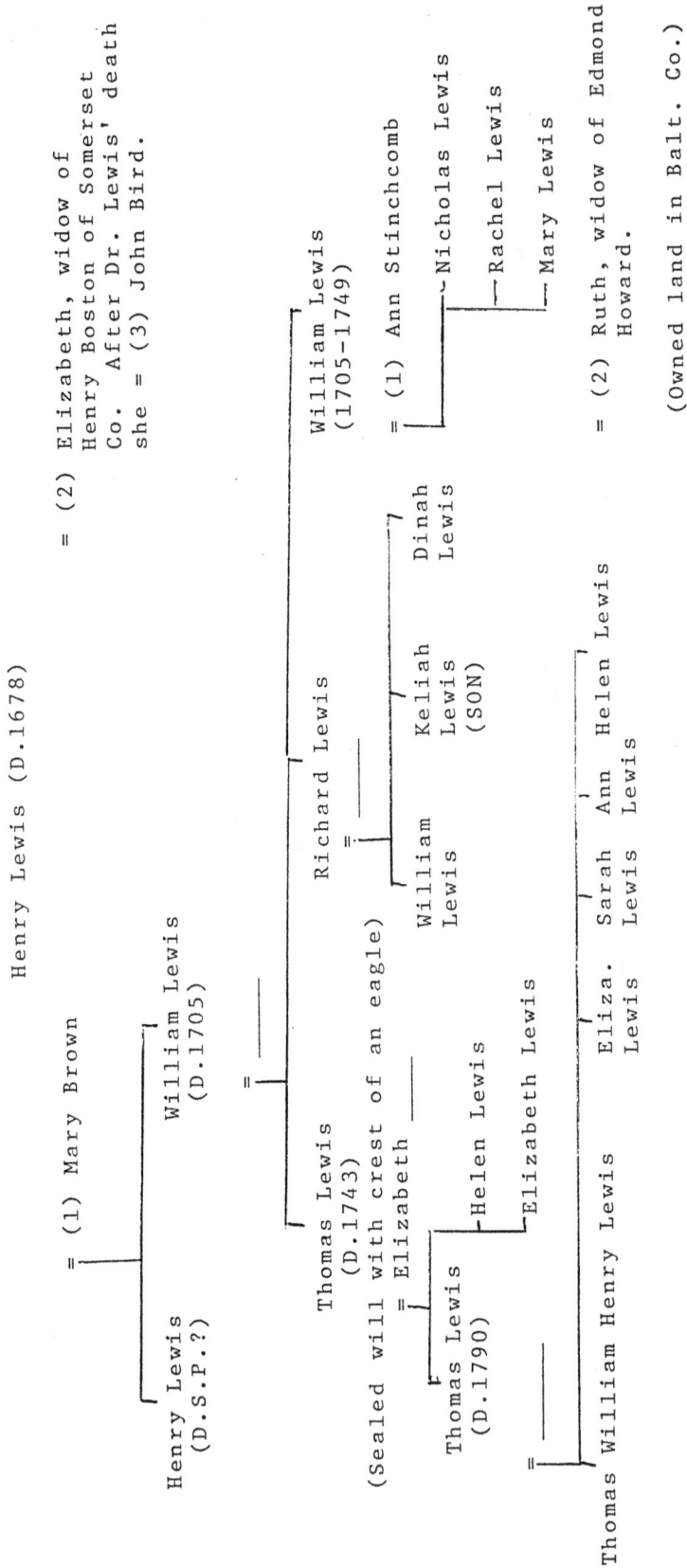

Henry Lewis (D.1678)

= (1) Mary Brown

= (2) Elizabeth, widow of Henry Boston of Somerset Co. After Dr. Lewis' death she = (3) John Bird.

Henry Lewis (D.S.P.?)

William Lewis (D.1705)

Thomas Lewis (D.1743)
(Sealed will with crest of an eagle)
= Elizabeth

Helen Lewis

Elizabeth Lewis

Thomas Lewis (D.1790)

Richard Lewis

William Lewis

Keliah Lewis (SON)

Dinah Lewis

Thomas William Henry Lewis

Eliza. Lewis

Sarah Lewis

Ann Lewis

Helen Lewis

William Lewis (1705-1749)

= (1) Ann Stinchcomb

Nicholas Lewis

Rachel Lewis

Mary Lewis

= (2) Ruth, widow of Edmond Howard.

(Owned land in Balt. Co.)

2. James Lewis Of Anne Arundel Co. Md. (D. 1724):

1673: A James Lewis is a headright of Capt. Wm. Burgess for land in Anne Arundel Co. (Md. Land Records, Liber 17, fol. 424.)

Note: In 1673 and 1676, Capt. Wm. Burgess of Anne Arundel Co. sold land in Talbot Co. to John & Thomas Lewis, see their records.

1705: In the Anne Arundel Co. Rent Roll, ca. 1705, James Lewis is listed with the following parcels of land:

Town Hill, 200 acs.
Mary's Mount, 100 acs.
Arnold Gray, 47 acs.
Diligent Search, 75 acs.

(Md. Rent Roll Records, Liber I, folios 24, 38, 45, 52; also in: R. Barnes, Md. Rent Records, pp. 144, 160, 182.)

1723: Will of James Lewis, dtd. 12 Nov. 1723; Probated 15 June 1726: Mentions wife, Catherine; son Thomas; dau. Catherine Welsh ; and Jane Rakestraw. (Original Will, Box L, Folder 26 - see photo of seal on will; In Md. Cal. of Wills; Liber 18, fol. 544.)

1724: James Lewis buried 4 Apr. 1724. (All Hallows Church Reg.)

1726: Inventory of James Lewis' estate taken 13 Sept. 1726 by Richard More and Thomas Stockett, Jr. Approved by Francis Day and Francis Lewis (son of Thomas of Kent Co.) (A.A. Co. Test. Papers, Box 32, folder 21; Inventories & Accounts, Liber 12, fol. 412 ff.)

Children of James Lewis and Catherine.:

1. James Lewis, Jr. = Katherine: Their children's records fr. All Hallows Church Register:

Grace, b. 21 Dec 1703
Katherine, b. same (Twin)
Elizabeth, d. 9 Oct., 1704
James, b. 10 Apr. 1710; d. 10 Jan. 1710/11
Sarah, b. 8 Oct. 1706; d. 1707

2. Grace Lewis = Edward Mitchell 21 Nov. 1706 (All Hallows Church Reg., p. 72).

3. Katherine Lewis = Robert Welsh 24 Feb. 1706/7. (All Hallows Church Reg., p. 107).

4. Thomas Lewis = Catherine: Had a son, James, b. 21 Dec. 1719 (All Hallows Church Recs.)

5. (?) Jane = a Rakestraw

1728/9   Summons to Sheriff of A.A. Co. to attach body of Wm. Kendall and Katherine his wife, exrs. of James Lewis, late of A.A. Co., dec'd. for Perog. Ct. Tues. March next why they have not passed an acct. of sd. dec'd estate. (Test. papers, Box 32, folder 21). Note James Lewis' widow, Katherine, had married Wm. Kendall (or Randall) Her will, as Catherine Randall, dtd. 8 Nov. 1728, & prob. 14 Mar. 1729/30, names grandsons James Lewis and Robert Welsh, Jr.

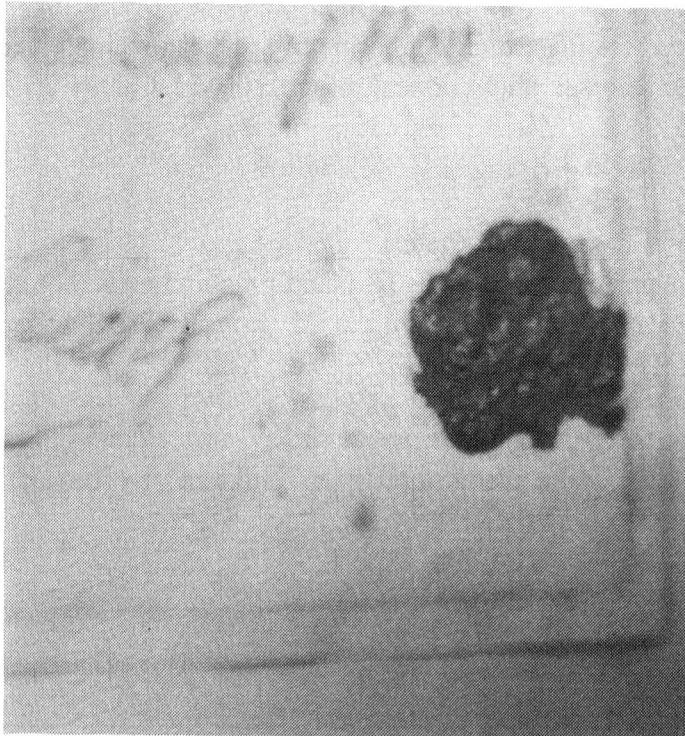

Photo of Seal on will of James Lewis (D. 1724) of Anne Arundel County, Maryland
(at Maryland Hall of Records, Annapolis)

Note: This can be seen as a crest of either (1) Lewis of Llandewi Rhgydderch Monmouthshire: a fleur de lis jessant de lis from the head of a leopard,
or (2) Lewis of Thorndon Hall, Essex: Three plumes issuing from a ducal crown. (Later crests used five plumes to avoid confusion with the crest of the Prince of Wales.)

3. Humphrey Lewis Of Baltimore Co. Md. (D. 1717)

1707: 1 Nov.: Humphrey Lewis pat. 40 acs., "Weaver's Providence" in Baltimore Co. (Coldham, Settlers of Md 1701-1730, p. 98)

1717: 4 June: Admin. Bond posted by Admnx Susan Lewis with John Israel and Christopher Randell. (Also owned 100 acs. of "Brother's Expectation" a 250 ac. tract laid out for Geo Hollingsworth in 1695.)

1717: 21 June: Inventory of Humphrey Lewis by Hector Maclane and Wm. Hamilton.

   Children: Henry, (Poss. Edward)

1730: 21 Nov.: Henry and Keturah Lewis conveyed 250 acs.: "Parker's Palace" to Geo. Buchanan. (Keturah was the dau. of Robert Parker and wife of Henry Lewis.)
   Children:
       Edward, b. 5 Aug. 1730
       Urath, b. 14 Feb. 1732
       Elisha, b. 27 Oct. 1735
       Pleasance, b. 3 Jan. 1737
       Henry, b. 27 Jan. 1739
       (By Comfort: John, b. 8 Dec. 1743)
       Charles, b. 27 Sept. 1746
       Nicholas, b. 5 Aug. 1750

1752: 18 Jan.: Henry Lewis and wife Keturah sold 40 acs. "Weaver's Providence" to Daniel Dulany & Co. (R. Barnes, Balt. Co. Families 1659-1759, p. 402)

1731: EDWARD LEWIS RECORDS:
   Edward Lewis and wife Sarah had the following children:
   John, b. 23 June 1731
   Edward, b. 6 May 1734
   Hezekiah, b. 7 Nov. 1736
   Nathan, b. 4 May 1740 (or 1744)
   Samuel, b. 10 July 1747
   Jacob Hurd, b. 15 Nov. 1748

                            (*Ibid.,* p. 403)

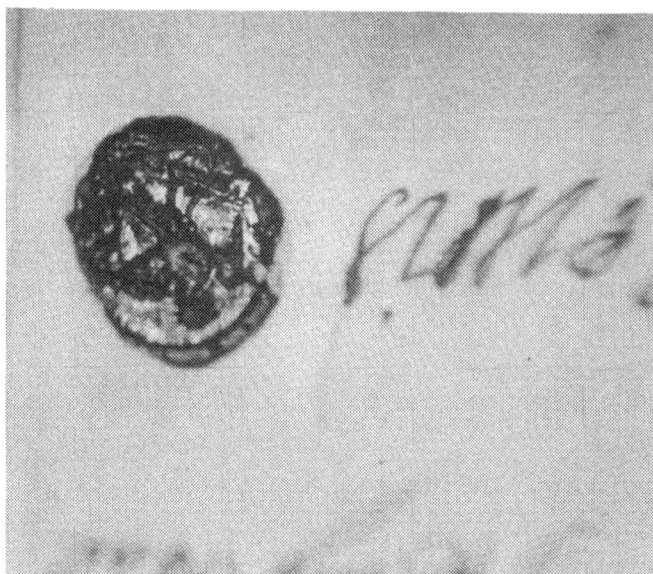

**Photo of seal on will of Thomas Lewis (d. 1743) of Anne Arundel County, Maryland
(at Maryland Hall of Records, Annapolis)**

BIBLIOGRAPHY FOR PART I

PERIODICALS:

Archaeologia Cambrensis. (Old Series: 1846-1900.) Cambrian Archaeological
Association. London, England.

Bulletin of the Board of Celtic Studies. University of Wales Press. Cardiff, Wales.

East Hertfordshire Archeological Society Transactions. East Hertfordshire
Archeological Society. Hertford, England.

National Library of Wales Journal. National Library of Wales. Aberystwyth, Dyfed,
Wales.

New England Historical and Genealogical Register. New England Historic Genealogical
Society. Boston, Mass.

Speculum: A Journal of Mediaeval Studies. Mediaeval Academy of America.
Cambridge, Mass.

Virginia Magazine of History and Biography. Virginia Historical Society. Richmond,
Virginia.

BOOKS:

Bartrum, Peter C., *Welsh Genealogies A.D. 300 - 1400.* 8 vols. Cardiff. University of
Wales Press. 1974.

Bartrum, Peter C., *Welsh Genealogies A.D. 1400 - 1500.* 18 vols. Aberystwyth. National
Library of Wales. 1983.

Bolton, Charles Knowles. *Bolton's American Armory.* Boston. F. W. Faxon. 1927.
(Reprinted by Clearfield Co., Balt. Md. 1989.)

Bradney, Joseph A., *A History of Monmouthshire from the Coming of the Normans into
Wales Down to the Present Time.* 4 vols. in 13 sections. London. Mitchell, Hughes &
Clarke. 1904 - 1933.

Burke, Sir John Bernard, *A Genealogical History of the Dormant, Abeyant, Forfeited and Extinct Peerages of the British Empire*. 1883. (Reprinted by Genealogical Publishing Co., Balt. Md. 1996.)

Burke, Sir John Bernard, *A Genealogical and Heraldic History of the Extinct Dormant Baronetcies of England, Ireland and Scotland*. London. Scott, Webster and Geary. 1841.

Burke, Sir John Bernard, *The General Armory of England, Scotland, Ireland and Wales*. London. Harrison. 1878. (Reprinted by Heritage Books, Inc., Bowie, Md., 1996.)

Burke's American Families with British Ancestry. An off-print of pages 2529 - 3022 from the 16th edition of *Burke's Landed Gentry*. 1939. (Reprinted by Genealogical Publishing Co., Balt. Md. 1996.)

Clark, George T., *Limbus Patrum Morganiae et Glamorganiae*. London. Wyman & Sons. 1886.

Dunn, Lewis, *Heraldic Visitations of Wales (1586 -1613)*. Edited by Sir Samuel Rush Meyrick. 2 vols. Llandovery, Wales. Welsh Manuscript Society. 1846.

Gairdner, John, Editor, *Three 15th Century Chronicles*. The Camden Society. 1880. (Reprinted by the Royal Historical Society. London, 1965.)

Glenn, Thomas Allen, *Welsh Founders of Pennsylvania*. Philadelphia, Oxford, Fox, Jones & Co. 1911 - 1913. (Reprinted Baltimore, Genealogical Publishing Co. 1970.)

Grantees of Arms, Names in Documents and Patents, Alphabetically Arranged by the Late Joseph Foster, to the End of the 17th Century. London. The Harlean Society. Part I (vol. 16) 1915, Part II, (vol. 17) 1916.

Humphrey-Smith, Cecil R., Editor, *General Armory Two: Alfred Morant's Additions and Corrections to Burke's General Armory*. London. Tabard Press. 1973.

Jones, Theophilus, *A History of the County of Brecknock*. 2 vols. London. Philmore & Co. 1898.

Lawrence-Archer, J.H., *Monumental Inscriptions of the British West Indies*. London. Chatto & Wondus. 1975.

Lewis, Robert J.C.K., *Lewis Patriarchs of Early Virginia and Maryland, With Some Arms and Origins.* Bowie, Md., Heritage Books, Inc., 1991.

Lewis, Robert J.C.K, *Welsh Family Coats of Arms.* Bowie, Md., Heritage Books, Inc., 1995.

Lloyd, Sir John Edward, *A History of Wales from the Earliest Times to Edward I.* 2 vols. London. Longmans, Green & Co. 1911.

Morant, Rev. Philip, *The History and Antiquities of the County of Essex.* 2 vols. 1763 - 1768. (Reprinted by E.P. Publishers, East Addsley, England. 1978.)

Morris, John, *The Age of Arthur: A History of the British Isles From 350 to 650.* New York. Scribner. 1973.

Moses, Grace McLean, *The Welsh Lineage of John Lewis (1592-1657) Emigrant to Gloucester, Virginia.* Revised Edition. Baltimore, Clearfield Co. 1992.

Nicholas, Thomas, *Annales and Antiquities of the Counties and County Families of Wales.* 2 vols. London. 1875. (Reprinted by Genealogical Publishing Co., Balt. Md. 1991.

Shaw, William Arthur. *The Knights of England.* 2 vols. London. Sherratt & Hughes. 1906. (Reprinted by the Genealogical Publishing Co., Balt. Md. 1971.

Vermont, F. de V. *America Heraldica.* New York. Brentano Bros. 1886 - 1889.

Visitation of Shropshire. Taken in the Year 1623 by Robt. Trosswell et al. 2 vols. London. The Harlean Society. Vols. 28 and 29. 1889.

Walmisley, Claude A., Editor, *Index of Persons Named in Early Chancery Proceedings: Richard II - Edward IV.* London. The Harlean Society. Vols. 78 and 79. 1928 -1929.

Williams, Johnathan, *A General History of the County of Radnor.* Brecknock. Davies & Co. 1905.

Wright, Thomas, *The History and Topography of the County of Essex.* 2 vols. London. G. Virtue. 1835.

BIBLIOGRAPHY FOR PART II

PERIODICALS:

New England Historical and Genealogical Register. New England Historic Genealogical Society. Boston, Mass.

Tyler's Quarterly: A Journal of American History, Biography and Genealogy. Nashville, Tenn. n.d. (ca 1918 -1935.)

The Virginia Genealogist. Washington, D.C. John Frederick Dorman, Editor and Publisher. (Reprinted by Heritage Books, Inc., Bowie, Md.)

The Virginia Historical Magazine. Richmond, Va. (1891-2, - ?)

The Virginia Magazine of History and Biography. Virginia Historical Society. Richmond, Va.

William and Mary Quarterly. Institute of Early American History and Culture. College of William and Mary. Williamsburg, Va.

BOOKS:

Anderson, Sarah Travers Lewis (Scott), *Lewises, Meriwethers, and their Kin.* Richmond, Va. Dietz Press. 1938. (Reprinted by Genealogical Publishing Co. Balt., Md. 1984+.

Archives of Maryland. Baltimore, Md., Maryland Historical Society. 1883-1947.

Bell, Landon Covington. *Charles Parish, York County, Virginia, History and Registers: Births 1648-1789: Deaths, 1665-1787.* Richmond, Va. Library of Virginia. 1932. Reprinted 1984, 1996.

Boddie, John Bennett. *Colonial Surry.* Richmond, Va. Dietz Press, 1948. (Reprinted: Balt. Md. Genealogical Publishing Co. 1966+.)

Boddie, John Bennett, *Seventeenth Century Isle of Wight County, Virginia.* Chicago, Chicago Law Printing Co., ca. 1938. (Reprinted Baltimore, Md. Genealogical Publishing Co. 1973+.)

Boddie, Jonn Bennett, *Southside Virginia Families*. Redwood City, Calif., Pacific Coast Publishers, 1955. (Reprinted, Balt. Md. Genealogical Publishing Co. 1966+.)

Boyd, J. W., *A Family History: Wright - Lewis - Moore and Connected Families*. J. W. Boyd. Atlanta, Ga. 1968.

Calendar of Virginia State Papers..., New York, Kraus Reprint Corp. 1968. 11 Vols.

Chapman, Blanch Adams, *Wills and Administrations of Isle of Wight Co., Virginia, 1647 - 1800*. Smithfield, Va. 1938. (Reprinted with Index, Balt. Md. Genealogical Publishing Co. 1975+.)

Coldham, Peter W. *The Complete Book of Emigrants. Vol. I: 1607-1660; Vol. II: 1661 - 1699*. (4 Vols.) Balt. Md. Genealogical Publishing Co 1987 - 1993+.

Cook, Michael Lewis, *Pioneer Lewis Families*. 5 Vols. Evansville, Ind. 1978 - 1986.

Davis, Eliza Timberlake, *Surry County Records, Surry Co. Virginia, 1652 - 1684: Books I and II*. E.T. Davis 195_. (Reprinted Balt. Md., Genealogical Publishing Co. 1980+.)

Davis, Eliza Timberlake, *Wills and Administrations of Surry County, Virginia, 1671 - 1750*. Smithfield, Va. E.T. Davis. 1955. (Reprinted Balt. Md. Genealogical Publishing Co., 1980+.)

Des Cognets, Louis. *English Duplicates of Lost Virginia Records*. Princeton, N.J., 1958. (Reprinted Balt. Md. Genealogical Publishing Co. 1981+.)

Dorman, John Frederick. *Adventures of Purse and Person, Virginia, 1607 - 1624*. 3rd Revised Edition. Alexandria, Va. Order of the First Families of Virginia, 1607 - 1625. 1987.

Dorman, John Frederick. *York County, Virginia Deeds, Orders, Wills Etc*. No. 9, Pt. 1, 1976; Pt. 2, 1977. Washington, D.C. Dorman. 1977.

Dorman, John Frederick, *Westmoreland County, Virginia Records 1658- 1661*. Washington, D.C. Dorman. 1970.

Duvall, Lindsay O. *Virginia Colonial Abstracts*. Series 2. 6 Vols. Easley, S.C. Southern Historical Press ca. 1978-1979.

Duvall, Lindsay O. *York County, Virginia, Wills, Deeds, Orders, Etc. 1657 - 1659*. See above Reference. (Vol. 5.)

Executive Journals of the Council of Colonial Virginia. Richmond, Va. D. Bottom, Superintendent of Public Printing. 1925 - 1966. 6 Vols.

Fleet, Beverley, *Virginia Colonial Abstracts*. Originally published in 34 soft cover vols. 1937 - 1949. (Reprinted Balt. Md. Genealogical Publishing Co., 1988+ in 3 Vols.)

Gray, Gertrude E. *Virginia Northern Neck Land Grants*. Balt. Genealogical Publishing Co. 1987 - 1993+. 4 Vols.

Great Britain Public Record Office. *Calendar of State Papers*. London, Eng. 1860 - 1969. 44 Vols. See Colonial Series 1677-1686: America and the West Indies.

Hawkins, Alfred Raymond, *Cwrt-y-Gollen and its Families*. Brecon, Wales. Brecknock Museum. 1967.

Hayden, Horace Edwin, *Virginia Genealogies*. Wilkes-Barre, Pa. E.B.Yordy, 1891. (Reprinted by Genealogical Publishing Co., Balt. Md. 1966+.)

Hopkins, William Lindsay, *Middlesex County, Virginia: Wills and Inventories, 1673 - 1812 and Other Court Papers*. Richmond, Va. W.L. Hopkins, ca. 1989.

Hotten, John Camden. *The Original Lists of Persons of Quality...and Others Who Went From Great Britain to the American Plantations 1600 - 1700....* New York. J. W. Bouton. 1874. (Reprinted by Balt. Md., Genealogical Publishing Co. 1962+.)

Jett, Caroline, *Records of Northumberland County, Virginia: Abstracts from the Earliest Extant Records: 1647-1652; Index and Will Abstracts from Record Book 1706-1713; and selected records from Order Book 1737-1743*. Bowie, Md. Heritage Books, Inc. 1994.

King, George Harrison Sanford. *The Registers of North Farnham Parish, 1663-1814, and Lunenburg Parish, 1783-1800, Richmond County, Virginia*. Fredericksburg, Va.: G.H.S. King, 1966; Easley, S.C.: Southern Historical Press, 1986.

King, George Harrison Sanford. *Marriages of Richmond County, Virginia, 1668-1853*. Easley, S.C.: Southern Historical Press, 1986.

Lewis, George Robert, *History of the Lewis Family, 1619-1972*. Washington, D.C. G.R. Lewis, 1972.

Lewis, James F. and Booker, James Motley, *Northumberland County Virginia Wills and Administrations, 1713-1749*. Kilmarnock, Va. J.F. Lewis and J. M. Booker, 1964.

Lewis, Robert J.C.K., *Welsh Family Coats of Arms*. Bowie, Md. Heritage Books, Inc. 1995.

Long, Daniel Reid, *John Lewis, "The Lost Pioneer;" His Ancestors and Descendants, 1670-1970*. Baltimore, Md. D.R. Long, 1971.

Minutes of the Council and General Court of Virginia, 1622-1632, 1670-1676. Richmond, Va. The Colonial Press, 1924. 2nd Ed. Richmond, Va.: Virginia State Library, 1979.

Moses, Grace McLean. *The Welsh Lineage of John Lewis (1592-1657) Emigrant to Gloucester, Virginia*. Rev. Ed. Balt. Md. Clearfield Co. 1992.

National Society of Colonial Dames of America in the State of Virginia. *Parish Register- of Christ Church, Middlesex County, Virginia, 1653-1812*. Richmond, Va.: W.E. Jones, 1897. New Edition with a new index, 1988.

Neal, Rosemary Corley. *Elizabeth City County, Virginia (Now the City of Hampton): Deeds, Wills, Court Orders, etc.* Bowie, Md. Heritage Books, Inc. 1986.

Nugent, Nell Marion, *Cavaliers and Pioneers: Abstracts of Virginia Land Patents and Grants. Vol. I: 1623-1666; Vol. II: 1666-1695; Vol. III: 1695-1732;* Supplement, *Northern Neck Grants No. 1. 1690-1692.* Vol. I Reprinted by Genealogical Publishing Co., Balt., Md. 1963+. Vol. II, III and Supplement Reprinted by the Virginia State Library 1980+.

Saint-George, Sir Henry, *The Visitation of London, Anno Domini 1633-1634 and 1635*. London, Eng. The Harlean Society. 2 Vols. 1880-1883.

Sorley, Merrow Egerton. *Lewis of Warner Hall*. Columbia, Mo., E.W. Stephens Co., ca. 1937. (Reprinted Baltimore, Md., Genealogical Publishing Co., 1979+.)

Sparacio, Ruth and Sam, *King William Co., Va. Records 1702-1705*. 1996; *Lancaster Co., Va. Records 1652-1710*. 1992-1995; *Middlesex Co., Va. Records 1673-1720*. 1989-1995; *Northumberland Co., Va. Records 1650-1711*. 1992-1995; *(Old) Rappahannock Co., Va. Records 1656-1692*. 1989-1990; *Richmond Co., Va. Records 1692-1733*. 1991-1997. McLean, Va.: The Antient Press, 1320 Mayflower Drive. 1989-1997.

Vermont, F. de V., *America Heraldica*. New York: Brentano Bros., 1886-1889.

The Vestry Book of Petsworth Parish, Gloucester County, Virginia 1677 - 1793. Transcribed, annotated and indexed by Churchill Gibson Chamberlayne. Richmond, Va.: Virginia State Library, 1979. (Reprint.) (Also did *Vestry Bk. of St. Paul's Parish, Hanover Co., Va., 1706-1786*. Richmond Va., Library Board. 1940.)

Weisiger, Benjamin B., *York County, Virginia Records, 1659-1662*. 1989. *York County, Virginia Records, 1665-1672*. 1990; *York County Virginia Records, 1672-1676*. 1991. Richmond, Va. B.B. Weisiger, 8921 Ginger Way Dr., 1989-1991.

Whitelaw, Ralph T., *Virginia's Eastern Shore: A History of Northampton and Accomac Counties*. Gloucester, Mass., P. Smith, 1968. (Reprinted Camden, Me.: Picton Press. 1989+) 2 Vols.

BIBLIOGRAPHY FOR PART III

Archives of Maryland., Balt. Md., Maryland Historical Society. 1883-1947. Vols.: 5, 7, 13, 15, 17, 25, 49, 53, 65, 66, 69.

Barnes, Robert W., *Baltimore County Families, 1659 - 1759*. Balt., Md., Genealogical Publishing Co. 1989.

Barnes, Robert W. *Maryland Rent Rolls: Baltimore and Anne Arundel Counties, 1700 - 1707, 1705 - 1724*. Balt. Md. Genealogical Publishing Co. 1976.

Barnes, Robert W. and Wright, F. Edward, *Colonial Families of the Eastern Shore of Maryland*. Vol. I and III. Westminster, Md. Family Line Publications. 1996, 1997.

Bates, Marlene Strawser and Wright, E. Edward, *Early Charles County, Maryland, Settlers, 1658 - 1745*. Westminster, Md. Family Line Publications. 1995.

Coldham, Peter W., *Complete Book of Emigrants, 1607 - 1660. Vol. II: 1661 -1699*. Balt. Md. Genealogical Publishing Co. 1987 and 1990.

Coldham, Peter W., *Settlers of Maryland 1679 - 1700; Vol. II: 1701 -1730*. Balt. Md. Genealogical Publishing Co. 1995 and 1996.

Cotton, Jane Baldwin, *The Maryland Calendar of Wills*. 8 vols. 1635-1743. Westminster, Md. Family Line Publications. 1988. (Reprint)

Dryden, Ruth, *Calvert Papers: Somerset County Rent Rolls, 1663 - 1723*. Westminster, Md. Family Line Publications. n.d. (1992?)

Haynie, W. Preston, *Records of Indentured Servants and Certificates for Land, Northumberland Co. Virginia 1650 - 1795*. Bowie, Md. Heritage Books Inc. 1996.

Jett, Caroline, Records of Northumberland Co. *Virginia: Abstracts from the Earliest Extant Records, 1647 -1652; Index and Will Abstracts from Record Book 1710 - 1713; and Selected Records from Order Book 1737 - 1743*. Bowie, Md. Heritage Books Inc. 1994.

Jourdan, Elise Greenup, *Abstracts of Charles Co. Maryland Court and Land Records, 1665 - 1695, Vol. II*. Westminster, Md. Family Line Publications. 1993.

Mickley, Minnie Fogel, L.C. Sue, *Registers of Births-Charles County, Maryland; Charles Co. Maryland Baptismal Records*. No Publisher or Date.

Nottingham, S., *Certificates and Rights, Accomac Co. Virginia, 1663 - 1709*. Onancock, Va. 1929.

Nugent, Nell Marion, *Cavaliers and Pioneers: Abstracts of Virginia Land Patents and Grants*. Vol. I: 1623 - 1666; Vol. II: 1666- 1695; Vol. III: 1695 -1732. Supplement: Northern Neck Grants No. 1, 1690-1692. Vol. I: Richmond, Va. Dietz Pr. 1934. (Reprinted by Genealogical Publishing Co., Balt., Md. 1963 on.) Vols. II, III, and Supplement. Richmond, Va. Virginia State Library. 1980 on.

Torrence, Clayton, *Old Somerset on the Eastern Shore of Maryland: A Study in Foundations and Founders*. Richmond, Va. Whittet and Shepperson. 1935. (Reprinted by Family Line Publications, Westminster, Md. 1992.

Wright, F. Edward, *Maryland Eastern Shore Vital Records, 1648-1725*. Silver Spring, Md. Family Line Publications. 1982.

www.ingramcontent.com/pod-product-compliance
Lightning Source LLC
Chambersburg PA
CBHW080613270326
41928CB00016B/3041